HOMEFRONT
911

HOMEFRONT 911

HOW FAMILIES OF VETERANS ARE WOUNDED BY OUR WARS

STACY BANNERMAN

Arcade Publishing • New York

Arcade Publishing books may be purchased in bulk at special discounts for sales promotion, corporate gifts, fund-raising, or educational purposes. Special editions can also be created to specifications. For details, contact the Special Sales Department, Arcade Publishing, 307 West 36th Street, 11th Floor, New York, NY 10018 or arcade @skyhorsepublishing.com.

Arcade Publishing® is a registered trademark of Skyhorse Publishing, Inc.®, a Delaware corporation.

Visit our website at www.arcadepub.com.

10 9 8 7 6 5 4 3 2 1

Library of Congress Cataloging-in-Publication Data

Bannerman, Stacy.
Homefront 911 : how families of veterans are wounded by our wars / Stacy Bannerman.
pages cm
Includes bibliographical references.
ISBN 978-1-62872-569-8 (hardcover : alkaline paper) —
ISBN 978-1-62872-634-3 (ebook) 1. Families of military personnel—United States. 2. Veterans—Family relationships—United States. 3. Families of military personnel—Mental health—United States. 4. Veterans—Mental health—United States. 5. Families of military personnel—Services for—United States. 6. Veterans—Services for—United States. 7. Afghan War, 2001—Veterans—United States. 8. Iraq War, 2003-2011—Veterans—United States. 9. Civil-military relations—United States. I. Title.
UB403.B36 2015
362.86'30973—dc23

2015019123

Jacket design by Georgia Morrissey
Cover art: Shutterstock

Printed in the United States of America

To the cast and contributing writers of *Homefront 911: Military Family Monologues* (Christina Piper, Karen Santiano Francis, Judy Linehan, Michael McPhearson, Tricia Sparks Radenz, Sara Rich, Ambra Roberts, Tammara Rosenleaf, Melissa Seligman, and Wife During Wartime). This book also belongs to the invisible ranks: the military family members and veterans' caregivers who have served so nobly, suffered so silently, and sacrificed so much.

CONTENTS

INTRODUCTION

EVERY MORNING I FLIP A COIN: heads, I stay, tails, I go. I'm trying to decide whether or not to leave Lorin, my husband of nearly fifteen years, a two-time Iraq war veteran who just completed six weeks of treatment for a crystal meth addiction. I also go to counseling, and pray, and meditate; I get acupuncture to relieve the chronic stress and anxiety that seem to have taken up residence in the nucleus of my cells. I have chiropractic adjustments regularly, and have altered my diet in an attempt to boost my immune system, which faltered badly in 2013, landing me in the hospital with a periorbital cellulitis infection so severe I was asked for my advance directive.

I get a massage once a week; Lorin hasn't touched me with love or lust since 2010 and I am so starved for the feel of human hands on my skin that I will pay someone to provide it. I talk to other family members of veterans and attempt to have some sort of social life, which is complicated by being married but effectively single, since he is unable, or unwilling, or some combination of both, to accompany me anywhere.

I do all of the crap that I, as the spouse and caregiver of an 80 percent service-connected disabled veteran with severe post-traumatic stress disorder (PTSD) and a mild traumatic brain injury (TBI), am encouraged to do to take care of myself, to "put on your oxygen mask first." That's what the people at the Veterans Administration (VA) down here in White City, Oregon, (the people who don't live with what I live with) tell me to do. None of it seems to help. So I flip a coin. This morning it was heads, buying me—or sentencing me to—another twenty-four hours, depending on how the day unfolds. I love my husband, but I just don't know when he's coming home, and it feels like I've been waiting far too long already.

I learned how to wait during two deployments that lasted twelve and thirteen months each, and then another year apart while he was at Fort Lewis, Washington, with the Warrior Training Unit. Being the one left behind, without children or family or military spouse friends nearby, requires a shoring up and pulling in of emotional energy. With no one in physical proximity to open your heart to, you endure by keeping it closed.

I got so good at waiting that when I came home from work one day to find a glass vase containing a dozen American Beauties by the front door, tucked out of sight from the street, I wondered, *Who the fuck are those from?*

The swearing problem started during my husband's first deployment, when I was learning military culture, and the acronyms, and how to deal with the part of his employment contract requiring that, every day at work, there were people whose job it was to kill him and it was his job to kill them back. I wanted to kill the women who told me they understood how hard it was to have your husband gone, because their husband traveled for work, too, and once he was in Dallas for, like, three weeks!

I tried a few times to gently explain the differences between a three-week business trip to Texas and a thirteen-month combat deployment to Iraq, but was so quickly tuned out or met with such blank stares that I quit. Being unable to evoke my husband with words, to keep him alive in conversation, made it feel a little bit like he had already died.

I grieved for him; I grieved for *us* almost every single day. At forty-three and forty-eight, we were middle-aged and getting older fast—this war was aging us in dog years. The Army kept preaching resilience. How I came to hate that word, as if the problem and the cure were both wholly within my domain if only I were a little more flexible. If only I were Army Strong. If only I got on board with being an Army of One, a short-lived messaging campaign the Army abruptly discontinued when it determined it wasn't necessarily the message they wanted to send. Or perhaps it was a tad too close for comfort.

If there is an Army of One, it's not deploying to Iraq. I wasn't prepared at all for this life, and I still cannot quite fathom how it became mine.

*   *   *

One week after Seal Team Six killed Osama bin Laden, the *New York Times* ran an article by military spouse Rebekah Sanderlin in their *At War* blog.[1] Sanderlin pulled few punches as she described

---

1. Sanderlin, "At War: Notes from the Front Lines," *New York Times*.

dealing with her husband's three deployments, her two bouts with depression, and how she nearly lost her marriage to war. Sanderlin also laid out what a lot of military family members were saying to themselves and one another as we watched the news feeds of elated young Americans congregating at Ground Zero and the White House, chanting, "We got him."

For America's troops and their families, who carried 100 percent of the weight of two wars for too long, the only "we" has been us.

During World War II and the wars in Korea and Vietnam, the last three major wars of the twentieth century, taxes and the draft ensured that all Americans served or sacrificed something. In contrast, less than 1 percent of this nation has been directly affected by the wars in Iraq and Afghanistan. The unprecedented imbalance of the burden of service and simultaneous abdication of civilian sacrifice has created an epidemic of disconnection between the civilian and military communities. According to Air Force researchers and other reports, that divide seems to be contributing to skyrocketing rates of post-combat mental health problems in returning veterans. The divide is also deeply felt by the families who are struggling with the stress and strain of the churn cycle, their loved one's service-related injuries and post-combat changes, and homefront war wounds of their own.

I am one of those family members. I met and married Lorin Bannerman when he was a civilian, several years before the wars began. Lorin retired from the Army National Guard in 2010, after serving two tours in Iraq, earning the Bronze Star and a Combat Infantry Badge (CIB). For a long time, I thought our post-war marital struggles and my mental health issues were unique and the result of some personal failing. I thought there was something fundamentally flawed within me because, after all, I hadn't been deployed, so what was my problem? As a military spouse, I was supposed to be resilient, cheerful, patriotic, and uncomplaining. My job was to stand behind the Blue Star flag with a smile on my face and keep my suffering to myself. The stigma surrounding mental illness in the military extends also to the family, particularly the spouse.

Ask any military spouse how she's doing on any given day, and I promise you, the answer will be "fine." Even if her five-year-old girl is on antianxiety medication, and her seven-year-old boy has started hitting his classmates and wetting the bed again because their father is gone on his third tour in six years, her reply will be "fine."

She may take a prescription medication—or three—just to get out of bed, and it may take a box of wine every night to get her back into it, but still she will tell you she's "fine."

If her familiar stranger of a veteran with PTSD or a traumatic brain injury sustained during multiple tours is now home, vibrating with combat-infused adrenalin, recklessness, and rage that once (well, okay, twice) manifested with his hands wrapped around her neck, choking her into unconsciousness, she. Will. Still. Be. Fine.

There are, of course, many spouses who are fine, just as there are many returning veterans who are fine, albeit changed, frequently for the better. But many of us are not. We are expected, and often told, to shut up and suck it up by Family Readiness Group volunteers, veterans, and, all too often, other military spouses. We are silenced by the reminder that it was our soldier, sailor, airman, or Marine in harm's way, not us.

This has been echoed by civilians, along with the disclaimer: "You knew what you were getting into."

Or, better still, "You signed up."

But I didn't, and the more I talked, the more I heard from other military spouses who were going through the same things.

They spoke of vivid nightmares when their husband or wife was overseas, of anxiety attacks so intense they could barely breathe, and crushing depression that rendered them unable to get out of bed. They told me about their kids, growing up sad, scared, and sometimes suicidal in the shadow of war, and failing to bond with their mom or dad because multiple tours meant the military parent was gone more than they were home. They talked about how it felt to be fighting the war at home, alone, and the challenges they encountered in trying to get the care, support, and services they—and their children—so desperately needed. They told me what was really going on behind closed doors, when the Welcome Home ceremony was over, and the Yellow Ribbons were back in the box.

America's War on Terror, hallmarked by lengthy, multiple deployments and a stupendously high percentage of psychological problems among returning troops, has deeply affected millions of military family members, who have suffered an escalation in mental health problems effectively identical to those experienced by the troops themselves.

According to a comparison of data from the Veterans Administration, the Army Reserve Family Programs website, and other sources, by early 2009, 35 percent of Iraq and Afghanistan veterans had been diagnosed with a mental health issue, as had 35 percent of children of recently returned veterans. Both populations also showed a 50 percent increase in mental health problems from 2003 to 2008. Further evidence suggesting a direct, causal relationship between parental deployment and children's mental health is that when the United States "surged" in Iraq, sending more than twenty thousand soldiers and Marines to stabilize the country, mental health hospitalizations of military kids "surged" as well. The first and largest study of the readjustment needs of returning troops and their loved ones found that "according to both broad and strict screening criteria, spouses and service members reported similar levels of major depression and generalized anxiety disorder."[2]

Over the course of the wars, the Departments of Defense and Veterans Affairs tracked the relentless rise of service member and veteran suicides, but it was left to the military family community to keep watch over our own. After two years of receiving a growing number of eyewitness and anecdotal accounts of family members who had killed themselves, or tried to, including a seven-year-old boy, I testified about it before a House Veterans Affairs Committee in 2009. The following year, reports of suicides and suicide attempts by military family members had become so frequent that Deborah Mullen, whose husband is retired Admiral Mike Mullen, former chairman of the Joint Chiefs of Staff, became the first senior military spouse to break the code of silence surrounding self-harming behaviors in military families and began publicly pushing the Pentagon to pay attention.

After nearly five years of advocacy and lobbying alongside Kristina Kaufmann, Karen Francis, and other military spouses, as well

---

2. Committee on the Initial Assessment of Readjustment Needs of Military Personnel, Veterans, and Their Families; Board on the Health of Select Populations, "Preliminary Assessment," Institute of Medicine of the National Academies.

as the National Military Family Association, in January 2013 we finally witnessed the Pentagon's Defense Suicide Prevention Office send a report to Congress outlining the first-ever proposal to track those deaths. But the general public is largely unaware of the massive toll of multiple deployments on military families, 92 percent of whom feel Americans "do not understand or appreciate their sacrifices," according to a survey conducted by Blue Star Families in 2010.

This epidemic of disconnection between military and civilian communities contributes to the profound isolation that exacerbates behavioral health issues for military families, particularly Guard and Reserve, who lack the formal and informal supports and services available to active-duty families residing on or near post. Coupled with the warrior culture's stigma toward psychological problems, which extends to the families, the separation between service members and the rest of society is an effective, if unintended, barrier to receiving care.

When the service member is physically or psychologically injured, the whole family is hurt. In fact, emerging research suggests that the emotional wounds of war carry biological consequences for the veteran parent, the civilian spouse, and the military child that may well be intergenerational, possibly heritable.

There is no way to write about today's military families without including the troops and veterans; we are inextricably intertwined. But this book spotlights the largely hidden issues, challenges, and realities that are exclusive to the spouses, kids, and family caregivers of veterans. The ratio of severely wounded service members surviving potentially fatal injuries is more than five times higher in the wars in Iraq and Afghanistan than in any previous war, as is the proportion—roughly 50 percent, according to the Veterans

Administration—of post-9/11 veterans with post-traumatic stress disorder, traumatic brain injury, or both who are being treated by the VA. It has been well chronicled that these invisible injuries can profoundly alter the personality of the warrior. But they also have significant, life-altering, and potentially life-limiting effects on the veteran's children and spouse, who is often the veteran's caregiver, which have been largely ignored and untreated.

Shortly after President Obama took office, the White House announced a government-wide approach to strengthening services for military families. Enhancing "the well-being and psychological health of the military family" was priority one. Goals for getting there included promoting psychological fitness, improving financial readiness, providing substance abuse treatment, and making the court system more sensitive to veterans and their families.

All good things. But the refusal to acknowledge, much less address, the fact that on some days there are more military family members killed by veterans than troops killed by terrorists, is to fatally fail military families.

Rates of child neglect, domestic abuse, and veteran intimate partner violence in active-duty, reserve, and retired military households have exploded, increasing by 177–300 percent between 2004 and 2010, according to the Pentagon, the Department of Veterans Affairs, and the National Domestic Violence Hotline. At the same time, the psychological, physical, and financial health of family caregivers of injured Iraq and Afghanistan veterans is imploding. Military families have always borne the burden of the war at home, but never before have we been quite so alone for so long. The post-9/11 wars have required repeat deployments of married troops, parents, and citizen soldiers. In previous wars, these populations were far less likely to be deployed multiple times, and generally exempt from the draft, because of overwhelming concerns it would be too much of a hardship on the families.

It appears those concerns were justified.

When the soldier signs up, the family gets drafted. The wounds of war that have been inflicted on the homefront are, in some ways, no less devastating than those incurred on the war front. America has embraced its promise to care for our veterans. It is my hope that we will also recognize our responsibility to tend to the families that are wounded by our wars. And it is my prayer that we will come to understand there is no such thing as an acceptable loss.

CHAPTER ONE

The End of the American Homefront

I WAS FIVE OR six when I first saw the inside of a VA hospital. My parents didn't elaborate much about why we were going to see Grandpa as they loaded me and my two siblings into the wood-paneled station wagon in Bismarck, North Dakota.

I spent the better part of a day sticking to the vinyl bench seat, looking out the rear window, watching the heat shimmer off the interstate as I-94 unfurled into an endless ribbon of tar.

I was hot, cranky, and itching to play beneath the shady trees dotting the cool, lush carpet of grass at the VA campus in Miles City, Montana. But first I had to go see my grandpa, a World War I vet. My grandparents divorced before I was born, so I'd only seen Grandpa Charles a couple of times. But this frail and furious old man lying in a hospital bed with awful dark lesions on his skin wasn't merely a stranger, he was alien, and I retreated to the corner of the room. Grandpa died within a few months of our visit, and I never wanted to set foot in another VA hospital.

I would be well into adulthood before my mother shared how her gentle, beloved bear of a father had returned from war with a field pack full of thunder, transforming her childhood home and memories into drinking, swearing, and ruinous rages and fights— literal, physical fights. There was before and there was after, and in the after, the last time, the final skirmish before the divorce, a bread knife and a frying pan were weaponized, with screaming and blood spilled, while my mother, a child of perhaps eight, cowered on the ratty linoleum floor.

A few years after the visit to the VA hospital, my mother had a knife and a pan in her hands when she turned on me. I stood, terrorized and dumbstruck with pain, bleeding heavily from a head wound, watching, disconnected from the fact that the spreading pond of blood on the crappy linoleum floor was mine, until my father whisked me to the ER to get sewn up. The crazy continued for nine more years, until my mother walked out a few weeks after I graduated high school. Decades later, when things went from bad to worse to shit with Lorin, it didn't feel so much wrong as familiar.

*   *   *

The VA Southern Oregon Rehabilitation Center & Clinics (SORCC) was on the left at the last of three stoplights that move traffic along through White City on Crater Lake Highway 62, heading from Medford, Oregon, to Shady Cove. White City began as Camp White, established in 1941 as an Army training facility for the 91st Infantry Division during World War II.

The military commandeered over seventy-seven square miles for the base, which briefly served as a German POW camp, and provided training for more than 110,000 troops. Dozens of bunkers were built to stage exercises for machine gun crews, and the gray cement pillboxes squatting in the pastures provided a stark structural backdrop for the cattle grazing peacefully around them. When the war ended, the military hospital and barracks were turned over to the Veterans Administration and reopened as the only free-standing domiciliary in the country. We lived about eleven miles away, as the crow flies, on what was once the old artillery training field, and the hardpan pasture and old white oak trees still spit out the occasional casing or bullet.

We were at the SORCC to meet with Chris Petrone, the OIF/OEF/OND[3] program coordinator, and have him make a referral that would place Lorin on a waiting list for an inpatient PTSD treatment program. After vowing never to set foot in a VA hospital again, I was a little pissed off and somewhat mystified to be doing so nearly every week for the past several years. I would tell Lorin that, too, about every fourth time we went, but this was not that day.

Four years earlier, we had walked down these same hallways to meet Dr. Tiffany, a VA psychiatrist who had prescribed PTSD meds for Lorin. We got to Tiffany's small, clean but cluttered office, with sunlight seeping through barely open blinds. We took seats in opposing corners and I scanned the medical journals and degrees hanging in cheap frames on the wall.

---

3. Operations Iraqi Freedom, Enduring Freedom, and New Dawn.

Dr. Tiffany handed Lorin the PTSD symptom card, a brief questionnaire designed to provide a snapshot of the patient's state of mind that week. While Lorin was completing that, the doctor pecked away for a few more minutes on his keyboard, and then turned toward us.

"How are you doing?" he asked Lorin, glancing at me, as tears slowly leaked out of my eyes.

"Okay," replied Lorin.

"Okay?"

"Yeah, okay. Nothing's changed."

"Well, are you taking the medication?" the doctor asked.

"No."

"Why not?"

"Because I don't like taking pills. Especially not the horse pills you prescribed."

"Have you tried cutting them in half? Maybe that would help."

"Maybe, but there's so many of them that I feel like I'm going to choke," said Lorin sullenly.

"Then don't take them all at once. But they aren't going to work if you don't take them," replied the doctor, glancing at the paperwork Lorin had handed him. "It looks like you're still having difficulty concentrating, is that right?"

"Yeah. I think I must have ADD or something, because I just can't focus on anything. I get totally distracted every time I see a shiny new object."

"For some guys, wearing sunglasses helps with that, you might want to try it."

Then he went through the checklist, asking Lorin how he was sleeping (not much, not well), if he was having trouble managing his anger (yes), if he was doing things he enjoyed (no), until he got to the bottom of the list of classic PTSD symptoms. Then he put the card aside and asked how I was doing.

Nobody ever asked how I was doing.

Tell the truth or don't? This was Lorin's show, not mine. I didn't want to say something that would inadvertently get him in trouble—I had no idea what that could possibly be, but still. I was also worried about saying something that would get me a shitty long ride home with Lorin at the wheel, spewing on me as he drifted across the center line of the narrow old two-lane HWY 234, going about seventy-three miles an hour while I stomped on the nonexistent passenger-side brake. In the future, I would drive my own car to VA appointments. Since this was the first time I'd been asked, there was a chance it would be the last time, too, and so I tightened my resolve and spoke:

"Not great. Sometimes I don't even know who he is anymore. I don't know who, or what, I'm married to. He's angry all the time, it seems like, and when I try to help him, he gets even angrier. I got one of those little day-of-the-week pill boxes and put his meds in that, but he won't take them."

I glanced at Lorin, who was sitting in his chair like he was waiting for his number to be called at the DMV. I wanted to get up and walk away, but I swallowed back tears and went on.

"I found him a counselor that he won't go to. I want to do things with him, have fun, go places, but he won't. He doesn't want to spend any time with me at all. He won't have sex with me, and I am tired of begging him to touch me."

Humiliated, I dropped my head. Dark spots appeared as tears fell on my shirt. Clearing my throat, I continued. "I can only try so many times and get rejected before I'm going to quit. Even the things he says he wants to do, like yoga, or acupuncture, I've found those things for him, for free, and still he won't go."

I was embarrassed to be saying this to a stranger, and a little dismayed it sounded like I was pleading, or whining, probably both, but I lacked the energy to keep pretending everything was fine.

"He said he would see a Native American shaman if they were also a veteran, because he's part American Indian, and I spent weeks scouring the Internet, doing research, sending emails, and getting referrals, but I finally found him. I met with the guy, and paid him to come out to our place. So he drove all the way up from California, and Lorin refused to meet with him. I find everything he asks for, everything he says he wants, and then he doesn't do it. And I've wasted my time, and my energy, and I still have to deal with the fallout."

"What do you mean fallout?" asked the doctor.

"He yells, he just yells all the time, for the stupidest things. The other night, I was going to pick up Chinese food in town, but when I called, he never answered his phone, so I just gave up and came home. I got home, and he's in the kitchen, and he asked me where dinner was. I told him I didn't get it, because I didn't know what he wanted, and he went off on me. Bad. I mean, *really* bad," I said. "He was shouting, and swearing, and calling me names. Just really, really angry, to the point I was starting to get scared. And for what? Because he didn't get General Tso's chicken?"

Dr. Tiffany took a slow, measured breath, shifting in his chair to more fully face Lorin, who appeared to be on the verge of nodding off.

"I'm going to tell you what I see here. I've been at this for a long time, and I've probably seen thousands of veterans and their wives come through that door, and it usually goes one of two ways," he said. "At some point, and I've seen this especially with the older veteran's wives, the wife basically accepts that this is as good as it's going to get, and she decides to stay. Those women get tired, and they get worn out, but they stay, kind of agreeing to half a life."

The good doctor's projection of a future hell sent a spear of apprehension through me. It was a vision so goddamn painful, and such a fear, and so taboo, that even within the military spouse community, where we talk about almost anything, we rarely speak of it. I got a call, though, one night, from a friend of mine, married with children to an Army vet with severe PTSD and a TBI. All I could do for the first few minutes was listen to her softly weeping, and when she was finally able to string together some words, she told me she'd been to the VA that day with her husband, and had seen her future in the defeated faces and slumped shoulders of the wives of Vietnam War veterans.

"The worst of it," she had said, "was that those women weren't even married when their husband deployed. I talked to them. They have only had to deal with the aftermath. Most of them didn't even know him before."

She paused, and then whispered, "Sometimes I wish I didn't, either."

"I know. I feel the same way. I know he's gone," I had replied, voice cracking. "But I will miss him for the rest of my life. The man I married died over there, and my family doesn't begin to understand what that's like. Nobody does."

"My family? Hah! My parents are divorced, and frankly couldn't give a fuck about what I'm dealing with," she had snapped. "I don't even bother going to family events—he won't go with me anyway—because for them, it's like the war never happened. They don't want to hear what's going on. I've been carrying our whole household through four tours, and taking care of our three kids, and working part-time, and I am already tired. But those women today, they seemed so hopeless, like they were just waiting to die. I don't want that to be my life."

I didn't either, but I didn't have a single word to give her to make it better.

I was hoping Dr. Tiffany did have something to say to make me feel better. What he said, though, was, "Or, the other thing that happens is that after several years of this, if the vet refuses to get treatment, the wife decides that she's had enough, and she leaves."

Tiffany glanced at Lorin, sitting stoically, and went on,

"Lorin, you've got a good woman here, and she loves you, but let's say that your life is a car. You're heading down a particular road right now, and if you keep going in that direction, if you don't change course, what's going to happen one of these days, and it could be a year from now, a few years from now, maybe ten years from now, I don't know, but the wheels are going to start coming off. And the most important wheel that you've got is sitting in the chair over there."

Tiffany paused, and then said, "If you lose her, if you lose that wheel, you're going to crash, and crash hard. So, what I'd recommend is that you get into an inpatient PTSD treatment program right now, and you need to plan on being there for at least six weeks."

Turning toward me, he said, "I know that you're trying to help him, but he's got to figure it out, so you need to back off a little."

"There's no way I can go to treatment for six weeks. No way. Not going to happen," Lorin said.

"Why don't you at least think about it?" asked Dr. Tiffany as he opened the office door. "Let me know what you decide."

I never saw Tiffany again, and neither did Lorin. But I did, finally, back off.

NOW HE'S IN THE ditch, and I got dragged down there with him. If we were going to have any chance of getting out of it, Lorin had to get treatment for his PTSD, and for that, he needed a referral.

Chris Petrone's office was pretty much like Dr. Tiffany's, minus the clutter that accumulates after decades on the job. Chris, a social worker, had been the program coordinator for post-9/11 veterans coming to the White City VA SORCC since about 2008. Lorin rarely dealt with Chris, since he wasn't a vet, and Lorin didn't trust him. As Lorin's caregiver, I'd tried to run interference between them for years, but only Lorin could choose when, where, or if he wanted to go to treatment.

Right before we got to Chris's door, I whispered, "Please, Lorin, be nice."

"What the fuck do I have to be nice for?"

Oh my god. It's 8:30 in the morning, and I just wanted to go home and crawl into bed.

"You be nice because Chris is still a human being. And granted, he's made mistakes, but in case you haven't noticed, he ain't the one who just finished treatment for meth. So it's possible that he might, just might, know a little more about some things than you do. And how you treat VA staff makes a difference in how you get treated."

Lorin had applied for the PTSD program at the Walla Walla, Washington, VA, hoping he could stay there after the substance abuse portion was completed. It would have meant optimal continuity of care, but they wouldn't take him because they said he was "too irritable" and needed a much more intensive treatment program than they could offer. Irritability is a classic PTSD symptom, and maybe he wouldn't be so irritable if he could get treatment (or take his meds), but when I tried to point out that clearly there's a problem if you're too cantankerous for the professionals trained to treat cantankerousness, Lorin got mad.

We took seats next to each other, and Chris introduced us to the social work intern we'd agreed to let sit in on the meeting. Within minutes, Lorin was off to the races, going around and around with Chris about travel reimbursement. The VA policy is to reimburse travel costs, but only for the nearest facility, if that was provided as a first option to the patient. The Roseburg, Oregon, VA had a substance abuse program and was just ninety miles from where we lived, but I had told Chris I didn't think Lorin would be interested.

Without consulting Lorin, Chris had put in the referral for Walla Walla, claiming Lorin had refused Roseburg. Lorin hadn't ever actually been asked, and Chris copped to that and said he would correct the notes so Lorin could get his travel reimbursed.

But Lorin wouldn't let it go and kept badgering Chris about it, saying, "Look, you're costing me money here. You don't even know the policy, and you're putting things into the system that aren't true."

Chris said, "Well, Lorin, I told you I made a mistake, I misunderstood. I also said I would correct it. Can we move on?"

"I never said I wouldn't go to Roseburg, because I was never asked!" he yelled. "Now I have to spend my time going around trying to fix your mistakes."

Lorin continued ranting as Chris looked at me, raising his eyebrows as if to ask, "Really? This is what you deal with?"

Finally, Chris broke in and said, "Look, Lorin, I got it. I got it. I think we've all had a taste of your anger."

"Come to my house for the buffet," I said under my breath, before turning to the intern and asking, "So, what other majors were you looking at?"

She burst into laughter and the rest of us followed, and I sank back into the chair.

*   *   *

Lorin wasn't in the Guard when we met in 1999. I didn't know he had been until they called the next year and asked him to reenlist. He was about four years short of the twenty required for retirement benefits, so it made sense to get back in. He loved that uniform.

The first time I saw him in it, I was sitting in our driveway in south Spokane, Washington, waiting for the remote garage door opener to do its job. I'd glanced over my shoulder to look at something, and when I turned back, the garage door was up, and Lorin was standing there in his forest green camos, the strap to his gas mask under his chin and the face plate resting on his head, looking like he'd been busted. I rarely saw him in uniform after that.

I'd once asked Lorin what it was about the uniform, why he'd signed up.

"My grandpa was a soldier, and my dad was in the Air Force. I wanted to serve, too," he replied. "I like what the Guard's about, I liked helping out during the floods and the fires when I was in the Guard during the nineties. And if I'm called, I will go to war. I may not agree with all of the things this nation does, and all of the things that the people of this nation say, but I will defend their right to say them."

But it wasn't until he'd been to Iraq and back that I got what that uniform meant to him.

In the early fall of 2003, a massive bird had landed on the roof of our neighbor's house. Lorin saw it first and pulled me out to the backyard, but by the time I got there, it was gone. I had a feeling then, though, that something was coming and heard a voice whisper in my head, "Get ready, it will be here soon."

A few weeks later, we learned that he'd be going to war.

STATIONED AT LSA Anaconda from March of 2004 through early April of 2005—the most-attacked base in Iraq at the time—Lorin was in charge of a mortar platoon. He was going on patrols outside the wire, driving convoys, and blowing things up, getting the boots-on-the-ground combat experience that an 11 Bravo Infantryman signs up for. Infantry is the primary land combat force of the Army, Army Guard, and the Marine Corps, the branches of service that sustained roughly 96 percent of the casualties in Iraq. 11 Bravo is the military occupation specialty (MOS) tasked with finding and fighting the enemy on the ground.

Lorin's progression from civilian to combat veteran is captured in the few photos I have of him from that year. The first is at our home, right before he deployed with the Washington Army National Guard 81st Brigade, and he's in his desert combat uniform and body armor, squatting in the living room hugging his dog, his face open, eyes shining, a boy excited about his big adventure. The next, he's in Kuwait prior to movement into Iraq, gazing into the camera. His spirit seems further back behind his eyes, but it's in there, I can still see it.

In the last photo, the only one I have of him actually in Iraq, he's in the same desert uniform and body armor, sitting in the driver's seat of a Beverly Hillbilly Humvee—the nickname for the vehicles Guard troops uparmored with scrap metal to make them safer in Iraq—his sunburned head shaved bald. He's turned toward the camera with a look that says, "Go ahead, make my day," and it's evident in his eyes that something has left his soul.

He came back from that tour with a Combat Infantry Badge and a Bronze Star, neither of which he was willing to tell me how he had earned. Most veterans don't talk about war much with their spouses. They don't talk about it at all, unless they're with their battle buddies or other vets, and there's beer involved. So we talked about sports and TV shows, mundane, trivial things, which was fine; I just wanted to hear the sound of his voice.

We went to movies and out for dinner at ClaimJumpers and other restaurants he'd missed in Iraq. He'd gotten in the best shape of his life while he was over there and started going to the gym with me. He quit after a few workouts because they wouldn't put a butt can in the weight room, and he had no interest in exercising if he couldn't smoke.

We'd get together with my friends or family, but not often. I was still smarting from how they'd pretty much abandoned me during Lorin's deployment and how, just because their lives hadn't been changed one iota by the war, they seemed to assume that mine hadn't, either. Or that everything would go back to normal, now that Lorin was home. They seldom asked how I was, or what they might do to help. I didn't want to need their help, anyway. I was going to suck it up and soldier on, and force our lives forward.

Lorin and I were trying to move forward, but the six free couples-counseling sessions made available by Military OneSource had been a waste of time. It took the first few sessions just to get the civilian counselor up to speed about military culture. We had to tell her that he drove like a maniac because you have to in a war zone trying to dodge improvised explosive devices (IEDs) and rocket-propelled grenades (RPGs). I also had to explain that I had spent a year living in the dark, with the front drapes closed, afraid of seeing a black sedan with government plates parked curbside, because that's what the Casualty Notification Officers arrive in.

Lorin heard about one vet who had just started talking about his battle buddy getting hit by an RPG when his civilian counselor interrupted to ask, "RPG? Is that a Volkswagen?"

Said vet walked out and hasn't been back to counseling since.

The only advice our counselor had was "give it time," which was basically the same thing it said on the Yellow Ribbon reintegration brochure I was given by the Guard. I had given it time, but time wasn't going to cure what ailed him: post-traumatic stress disorder.

Lorin completed a mental health assessment about seven months post-deployment, but it took us a full year after that to get the results. While we waited, our marriage was falling apart. I knew something was wrong, but I was just the wife and needed to relax. Because the problem wasn't him, it was me, and "It was [my] job to take care of him," according to the VA staffer working for the Washington State Department of Veterans Affairs. The help he needed was light years beyond my capacity to provide, and he absolutely refused to get counseling or treatment. I hadn't the first clue what to do for my husband, but maybe if I read enough books, and got enough information I could figure it out. Maybe I could figure Lorin out. Maybe I could heal him.

So I signed up for a two-day seminar about war and the soul conducted by Ed Tick, author of the book by the same name. I asked

Lorin to go, but he had no need, nor use, for a workshop about healing the trauma of war. It was drill weekend anyway, so he couldn't
have been there even if he'd wanted to, but he agreed to swing by
after he was finished at the armory.

When he strode into the sanctuary of the small church in Seattle that Sunday afternoon, all six feet, one inch of him calmly composed, dignified, radiating a quiet strength, I saw that when he was
in uniform, he became the most of who he was. And who he had
become was an Army non-commissioned officer (NCO), a warrior
for the United States of America.

That was the first day that I loved him in uniform.

But he couldn't let it go, couldn't let go of what he'd done and
seen over there. And treatment wasn't an option. What they don't
tell you about PTSD is that it's a progressive disease. Without an
intervention, it gets worse. In early 2007, I moved out, and eventually filed for divorce. But he kept calling, and I kept answering, and
over the next nine months, we began to find our way back together.

We started dating, and found a different therapist who had years
of experience working with vets and their wives. After Lorin promised
to seek treatment for his PTSD, I went to the courthouse in Kent,
Washington, and had the judge dismiss the divorce filing. A few
months later, we were driving around, scouting out possible locations
for my start-up nonprofit, the Sanctuary for Veterans & Families,
when Lorin glanced out the window and exclaimed, "Look, there's a
great blue heron! Remember the last time we saw one of those?"

When we saw the bird this time, we laughed, because lightning doesn't strike in the same place twice, and the Pentagon policy
was clear that Guard units weren't eligible for redeployment until
they'd been home for five years. It hadn't even been three years, so
I ignored the shadow that swept through the car.

His mobilization orders arrived shortly afterward.

*　　*　　*

When America got the war it wanted in 2001, and again in 2003, I presumed the nation would go along. After the September 11 attacks, the country was about as united as fifty states could be through the desire for retribution. Galvanized by the first strike on American soil since Pearl Harbor, Congress authorized President George W. Bush to use "all necessary force against those nations, organizations, or persons he determines planned, authorized, committed, or aided the terrorist attacks."

Operation Enduring Freedom was launched on October 7, 2001, and the war in Afghanistan began with the support of roughly 90 percent of Americans. Operation Iraqi Freedom commenced on March 19, 2003, with the "Shock and Awe" campaign that targeted the Iraqi capital of Baghdad and the northern cities of Mosul and Kirkuk. This overwhelming use of force was matched by overwhelming support at home. The day after hostilities began, a CNN/ *USA Today*/Gallup poll found that 76 percent of Americans were in favor of having America's Armed Forces fighting on a second front. But the efforts on the war fronts were not matched with any effort whatsoever to secure a homefront.

A strong homefront is created by harnessing civilian participation in events and activities in direct support of a war waged overseas. Now, for the first time in modern history, the United States had embarked on protracted wars on two fronts without mobilizing the nation by way of a war tax, draft, war bonds, rationing, or other means.

All that President George W. Bush asked was for "continued participation and confidence in the American economy. . . . Go down to Disney World in Florida. Take your families and enjoy life the way we want it to be enjoyed."

Rather than implement a surtax tied to the war, Congress approved a $1.35 trillion tax cut in 2001, with particularly generous reductions for the rich.

Bush administration budget director Mitch Daniels justified the cuts by saying, "Americans are being taxed at the highest peacetime rates in history."

Peacetime? For whom?

The administration went on to raise the debt ceiling seven times while waging war in Iraq and Afghanistan, painting the abandonment of the longstanding tradition of wartime taxation as patriotic. A few years later, Congress passed legislation to repeal the excise tax on phone service. Imposed in 1898 to help pay for the Spanish-American War, the 3 percent telephone tax had been increased, sometimes up to 10 percent, during World War II and again for the Vietnam War, to help pay for military operations. In 2007, over 70 percent of eligible Americans who filed a 2006 federal income tax return got a telephone excise tax refund while an additional twenty thousand troops were surging into Iraq.

Over the course of the wars, Congress repeatedly approved massive "emergency" appropriations to foot the bill, expenditures that were rarely questioned by the public. But the public hadn't been seeing the cost of the wars at home.

In keeping with the ban against press coverage of returning war dead that was implemented during the first Gulf War—a.k.a. Operation Desert Storm—President George W. Bush prohibited pictures of troops killed in Iraq and Afghanistan from appearing in the media. When a photo of twenty flag-draped coffins being loaded into an aircraft carrier was published on the front page of the *Seattle Times* in 2004, the photographer, Tami Sicilio, a government contractor, was swiftly fired. As had happened during Vietnam, the picture of war dead provided a spark for the antiwar movement, but it didn't catch fire until a year later, when Gold Star mother Cindy Sheehan began her Camp Casey vigil outside of President Bush's ranch in Crawford, Texas. Then the nation began to pay attention.

I had met Cindy and her husband, Pat, about six months earlier, outside of Fort Bragg, an Army post in North Carolina. It was a little less than a year after their son, Casey, had been killed in Iraq. When I saw them for the first time in the hallway of a hotel, Cindy was leaning against the wall for support. Pat had a shell-shocked look on his face common to the civilian men who had never worn the uniform but had raised boys who joined the military and died as a result. After a while, I also began to comprehend that the caul of grief that clung to Cindy was wrapped around every Gold Star mother. There are no politics in mourning.

When Cindy sat down in August of 2005, the movement stood up. The nearly month-long protest in Crawford drew hundreds of supporters to Texas and kicked off a rolling antiwar protest against the Iraq War. The Bring Them Home Now campaign was built around three buses filled with military family members and veterans following three different cross-country routes.

I rode the northern tour bus, which we referred to as the Bi-Polar Express, and spent several weeks travelling from city to city, giving speeches and participating in rallies. The buses converged in Washington, DC, in September 2005, culminating with a march that drew over a quarter of a million demonstrators to the National Mall. By putting a human face on the war, military families drew it back into the news and back into the hearts and minds of the American people. But with so few Americans having skin in the game, public interest inevitably began to wane, and then media attention plummeted.

Civilian America was, however, watching reality TV, with a few friendly commercial reminders that the troops were coming home. Budweiser and several other companies began airing spots depicting returning veterans, with no mention of the wars themselves. Big business's unwillingness to hitch its wagon to the war persisted even as reality TV figured out how to make a profit by profiling troops reuniting with their loved ones. TLC's *Surprise Homecoming* and Lifetime's *Coming Home* provided a snapshot of the emotionally fraught moment when service members see their family for the first time after a deployment lasting anywhere from three months to a year and a half or longer.

America binged on the immensely popular shows, which may also have helped purge some of the feelings of guilt a number of concerned civilians expressed to me, moved by courage or compassion to speak through their discomfort and lay bare the shame they felt, knowing these wars were costing them nothing. The TV programs, however, may have come at a price for the military kids captured by the cameras.

In previous wars, married men with children were exempt from the draft, and soldiers serving in a war zone were generally single males in their late teens or early twenties. So there's still a whole lot we don't know about how children emotionally process a parent's deployment, or the impact of multiple tours. What we do know is that military kids are in a heightened state of anxiety when a parent is in a combat zone, and while military spouses' anxiety typically returns to normal after a deployment, the anxiety levels of the kids tend to remain elevated for long after their soldier-parent has come home.[4]

"Reunion porn," which is what some in the military community call it, offered a dramatic payoff for the viewing public, with none of the inconvenient reality of the deploy-rinse-repeat churn cycle that had made the Guard into what was—for all intents and purposes—an active-duty force, and ratcheted regular service branches into hyperactive-duty status. The frenetic tempo of operations (OPTEMPO) of troops being rotated in and out of Iraq and Afghanistan meant some soldiers and Marines had already served an unprecedented six or more tours in the sandbox. So Lorin serving a second one maybe shouldn't have been that big of a deal, and I suppose I should have seen it coming. But I had believed the Pentagon would stick to its policy, and I thought we were done with war. The mobilization update arrived on March 19, 2008, five years to the day after the initial invasion of Iraq.

Lorin couldn't wait to go back.

He quit his day job as a food broker shortly after he got his orders for a second tour. He'd been struggling with civilian work since his return, and he missed being in charge of a platoon. He chafed at the tediousness, and was infuriated almost daily by "the sheer amount of stupid" because, he said, "stupid kills."

---

4. Lester et al., "The Long War," *Journal of the American Academy of Child Adolescent Psychiatry.*

He also quit PTSD counseling, which I was fine with. He'd only been to a few sessions, but getting him to begin processing what happened during his first tour wasn't a good idea while he was preparing for his second. And the angry outbursts, avoidance, and hypervigilance and arousal that were so hard to live with here could keep him alive over there. He could deal with the PTSD when he got back, but I wasn't going to stay in Washington State and wait for him.

While scouting around online for possible sites for my sanctuary project, I'd come across an animal shelter in southern Oregon that was just getting going. According to the website, they had plans to provide ecotherapy, animal-assisted activities, and other programs for veterans, at-risk youth, and the elderly. Sanctuary One was situated on fifty-five acres of rolling hills embraced by National Forest Service land and the Siskiyou Mountains in the gorgeous Applegate Valley. With a historic barn, irrigation rights, and several pastures, it was an ideal haven for abused and neglected farm and domestic animals, with enough space for people to have some room to move and get their hands dirty.

During the hiring process, the board committed to supporting the programs and services I envisioned for veterans and their families, and I moved to Medford, Oregon, and began work in May. Lorin stayed behind for training at Camp Murray, the Army Guard post adjacent to Fort Lewis, and drove down a few times a month. By August, he was at Fort McCoy, Wisconsin, and then he was gone.

Some of the soldiers with children got to go back to Washington State to spend a last few days with their families before shipping out, but Lorin left straight from Fort McCoy. This time, there would be no mobilization ceremony at the Tacoma Dome; there would be no tearful hugs, no kisses good-bye in the dawn's early light. One day, he was in Wisconsin and the next, he was at Ar Ramadi, Iraq, and I was once again holding the space for him to come home.

*   *   *

For the people left behind, war changes every facet of how we live. When our soldiers are in harm's way, we hold the psycho-spiritual weight of the single most important decision a nation can make: to wage war. The men and women in the military raise their hands and take an oath to protect this nation from enemies, foreign and domestic. Our oath is that we hold them in our hearts and minds, that we ground the weight of war in the soil of our lives, and that we too sacrifice and serve in some fashion. The emotional tether that ties civilian America to war entails a giving over, a relinquishment, of some dimension of our lives. The homefront is the outward manifestation of that place within us where patriotism resides. It is our practical and psychological investment in the nation's battle with a common enemy.

If we do not agree with that battle or with that identification of other as enemy, then we speak to that. And if we champion the battle, as the vast majority of Americans did, naming Bin Laden, al-Qaeda, and terrorism writ large as the enemy, then democracy demands we bear the burden of the consciousness of war.

War is about so much more than the logistics of standing up a brigade, providing body armor, and getting boots on the ground. The people of America have a moral responsibility to take mindful collective ownership of the ethical and spiritual implications of war, of the fact that our sons and daughters have been sent half a world away in our name, at our urging, and with our consent.

Speaking just a few days after his son had been killed in Afghanistan, Lieutenant General Robert Kelly, Secretary Gates's senior military aide, remarked, "As a democracy—'We the People'—and that by definition is every one of us, sent them away from home and hearth to fight our enemies. We are all responsible."

The failure of the Bush administration to leverage American patriotism and tie it to the tradition of collective wartime sacrifice that would bind the people to the war effort was a critical mistake. The disparity between the wars America wanted and the burdens Americans were asked and were willing to bear to fight them ushered in the end of the American homefront as we'd known it.

We placed the terrible, awesome power of life and death in the hands of our military, and then refused to accept the terrible, awesome responsibility for the consequences of that choice. In so doing, we failed our troops. We failed their families. We failed ourselves.

Political leaders put the last nail in the notion of war as a shared venture when, rather than reinstate the draft, they put the burden of wartime service on the back of a small, all-volunteer force, supplemented with a heavy reliance on civilian contractors. When the draft was operational during World War II, one out of every five American families had one or more members serving overseas at some point.

During Vietnam, it was roughly one in ten.

During the wars in Iraq and Afghanistan, America's longest war, it has been fewer than one in one hundred.

Less than one-third of Americans supported the return of the draft, but almost everyone claimed to support the troops. Throughout the first years of the war, it seemed like every other car on the road had a magnetized yellow ribbon slapped on the back. Asserting that "Freedom Isn't Free," even as they paid nothing, scores of Americans cheered the troops who had signed up to serve their country. People waved the flag and bought "Support the Troops" bumper stickers, but for many of us with loved ones overseas, that slogan had been stripped of meaning.

In the words of retired Army Lieutenant Colonel Andrew Bacevich, whose son was killed in Iraq:

> [W]hat exactly does it mean to support the troops? It ought to mean more than putting a bumper sticker on the back of your car. I don't think we actually do support the troops. What we the people do is we contract out the business of national security to approximately 0.5 percent of the population, about a million and a half people who are on active duty. And then we really turn away. We don't want to look when our soldiers go back for two or three or four or five combat tours. That's not supporting the troops. That's an abdication of civic responsibility. And I do think there's something fundamentally immoral about that.[5]

Fundamentally, morality is about knowing the difference between right and wrong, and being accountable to that knowledge. Maybe it was harder for Lorin to hold himself to moral behavior when suffering a PTSD-related moral injury, the result of an incident in Iraq that so grotesquely violated his core ethical and moral beliefs

---

5. Bill Moyers Journal, "The Conversation Continues," *TruthOut*.

he has been at war with himself ever since. Moral injury is characterized as "perpetrating, failing to prevent, bearing witness to, or learning about acts that transgress deeply held moral beliefs and expectations."[6] And maybe this nation was suffering a moral injury we hadn't even named in the execution and prosecution of these wars.

According to the just war theory, there are basic standards that must be met prior to a formal declaration of war. Those standards include waging war as a last resort, after all nonviolent attempts at resolution have been exhausted. Just war theory mandates the war must be proportional to the wrong suffered, and civilian casualties must be minimized. To that end, just war theory requires the weapons used in war must differentiate between combatants and noncombatants, which is extremely difficult in a war with no front lines. When drones are deployed, discrimination between armed forces and unarmed civilians becomes virtually impossible. Perhaps the single most critical determinant of whether a war may be defined as just is that war is declared only as a response to a specific, direct attack. Al-Qaeda was found to be responsible for the attacks on America, and although al-Qaeda had a strong presence in Afghanistan, it is a terrorist network, not a nation. This left some Americans to wonder about the lack of a formal declaration of war, to question why we invaded Iraq, and to ask whether the invasion met the standard of a just war. Because the bottom line is that, as a rule, we can tell if something is morally wrong or right. We know it, we can feel it, and hopefully, we hold ourselves accountable to what we know.

---

6. Litz et al., "Moral Injury and Moral Repair," *Clinical Psychology Review*.

Lorin's accountability began when he started the substance abuse program at the Walla Walla VA on March 19, 2014, exactly eleven years to the day after the invasion of Iraq. Any lingering doubt I may have had about whether or not Lorin's combat service was the causal factor in his crystal meth addiction was erased when his admission ticket for treatment was stamped on the anniversary of the war. Lorin is accountable for his behavior, but what about the administration and politicians who sent him to war?

Where's their accountability?

What about the people who wanted the war, but refused to fund it, fight it, end it, or draft their own children to wage it? How about them? And how will I be able to hold myself accountable to my marriage vows when so many others failed to be accountable to the vows that they made, failures that have culminated in a soul-sucking decision for me?

So I flip a coin.

Today it was tails.

CHAPTER TWO

Unintended Casualties

"THEY TOLD ME THERE'D be casualties, enemy combatants, they said. They didn't tell me there would be a whole family shot dead in their car on the way to a wedding," said Lorin, sitting on the high-backed patio chair, head down, scanning the pavement for something that wasn't there.

"They didn't fucking tell me there'd be kids."

But of course, there were. There always are, especially in a war with no clear enemy and no front lines. A war like Iraq, where more than three-quarters of casualties were civilians, according to the Iraq Body Count project. Could he really not have known?

I never asked, dropping that question on the thousands of others I would never raise. Less because I was afraid he would get angry than because I feared I would hurt him by the asking. I would ask something clumsily, not knowing what to say or how to say it, and so would say it wrong. I'd say it so badly that it would further tear the gaping wound in his soul. Still deeper, far below that, I wasn't sure I wanted the answer. Because either he understood that kids would be part of the collateral damage and was lying to me, or he was in such denial about an unavoidable consequence of modern war that he was lying to himself. I didn't want to carry the weight of knowing his response. I didn't want to carry another thing. I didn't want him to bring me one more grain of Iraqi sand. I already had the phantoms of the two children who were killed on April 5, 2004, less than one month into his first deployment.

I WAS STILL GETTING used to him being gone and hadn't gotten the hang of carrying my cell phone with me. I'd been out running errands and the phone rang shortly after I came home.

"It's me, I've been trying to call you," he grumbled.

"I just got home. What's going on? Are you all right?" I asked.

"Yeah, I'm fine, well, I mean, I'm not hurt or anything."

"Tell me what happened," I said, struggling to keep calm.

"You can't say anything about this right now, because they're still wrapping up the investigation. But they told me that we didn't do anything wrong, it was just an accident."

He blew out a long, deep breath, and went on. "We were firing a couple of practice rounds. The forward observers (FO) were out there, and they didn't see anybody. Nobody was supposed to be there. The area was empty. They said it was empty. So we fired a couple of rounds, just like we were supposed to, and the next thing I know the FO's are yelling, 'Check fire! *Check fire!*'"

I flinched, awaiting his next words.

"I'm not sure what happened next, because I wasn't right out there, so I didn't actually see it, thank God. Somehow two people had gotten out into the practice area."

Stupefied, I asked, "What?"

"Apparently, between the time when the observers were out there and we gave the order to fire, some Iraqis wandered into the firing area," he said, sounding like he was reading the After Action Report.

"Were they soldiers?"

"No. They were civilians. They were on their way to school and work."

I fumbled the phone, inadvertently buying a few seconds to figure out what I was going to say, knowing my next words were critical.

"I am so sorry; I wish I could be with you right now. How are you doing with this?"

"The first couple of days were awful, and I still struggle with it, but they said I didn't—that none of us—did anything wrong. They said those kids came out of nowhere, and it just couldn't be helped. I've prayed about it a lot, and I feel really bad about it, but at least I didn't see the bodies. It's harder for the guys who did."

Before I could say, "I suspect that it is," Lorin said that his calling card was almost out of time. "I love you."

"I love you, too," I responded quickly.

"I really, really love you."

"I know, honey, I really, really"—*click*—"love you, too."

He was gone.

I sat back in my chair and glanced around the room, staggered that it looked like nothing had changed. Lorin told me later he wished he could have gone to the kids' funeral, wished he could have found their parents and apologized. I wish he could have, too. Maybe then he would have left them there. He says that sometimes he thinks he sees them out of the corner of his eye, but can never turn fast enough to be sure. The VA would probably call it a delusion. But they're real to him, and sometimes I think I sense them, too.

*   *   *

"They just brought a fifteen-year-old kid into the ER! He shot himself. He was screaming, and they tried to make everybody clear out. Oh Christ, oh Jesus," wailed Tammara.

I first met Tammara on the Bring Them Home Now bus tour. She was driving the bus, which was actually a motor home with a satellite dish bolted to the roof so we could track media and get email. A native of Montana, Tammara had been living in Killeen, Texas, with her husband, Sean, ever since he'd been stationed at nearby Fort Hood a few years earlier. When I climbed into the shotgun seat of the rental RV to read maps and navigate, I took a look at her ink, assorted piercings, blazing red waist-length hair, tie-dyed Zubaz pants, and the fanny pack strapped around her middle, and thought, *Fuck. Perfect.* This, I learned later, was pretty much what she thought when she saw me, with my cropped hair, polo shirt, baseball cap, and Dooney & Bourke handbag. By the end of the tour, we'd become friends, and by the end of the year, we were battle buddies.

We'd call each other whenever there was some domestic shit-storm with our soldier, a new political clusterfuck, or a service-connected tragedy, over there or over here. So, basically, several times a month, and more during the 2007 surge in Iraq. Because when our troops surged over there, the demand for mental health services and hospitalizations surged in military families over here, particularly for children.

"He shot himself! Oh my god, oh my god!"

I could almost see her hugging herself tightly, babbling into her Bluetooth, rocking back and forth, trying to make whatever just happened stop and go away.

"Whoa, shit, slow down. What?" I closed the document I was working on, got up from my desk, and walked outside, watching the kids in the cul-de-sac jump the curb on their skateboards.

"I'm at Darnall. I came here to see Marissa. She's an inpatient; I think she just had a total breakdown. I went to her place last week, and the house was a disaster and the kids were filthy. There wasn't any food there, and all she was worried about was showing me the spice rack. She was very proud of that. This place is lousy with military spouses. They told me that about half the beds here are wives who had to be hospitalized for mental health reasons. I was on my way out when a teenage boy was brought in to the ER by his mom."

"What happened?" I asked.

"I overheard a lot of what they were saying, and near as I can piece it together, it sounds like they had just cleared security and driven onto post when he pulled a handgun out of the glove box and shot himself in the gut. I guess his dad is on his third tour, maybe it's fourth, and his mom had been telling the boy it was going to be okay. And he grabbed the gun and shot himself, screaming, 'It will never be okay again.' He was bleeding so much . . ."

"Oh my God, that poor kid. They cannot keep sending these soldiers on so many fucking tours. Keep me posted on how he's doing, if you can. Marissa, too. You gonna be all right?"

"Yeah," she hiccuped, "I think so."

31

"Okay, buddy, call me if you need to."

I'd gotten another call, some months back, about a second-grader who attempted suicide while his father was serving yet another tour in Iraq. He was seven years old.

When I was seven, it was 1972, and there were sixty-nine thousand US troops in Vietnam. Men were still being drafted and deployed, but not my dad. So I was spared the same circumstances that led a seven-year-old to try to kill himself. Four-plus decades ago, parents were exempt from conscription because of overwhelming concern about the harmful effects of deployment on children. Only 15 percent of Vietnam-era active-duty troops were parents, most of them officers, many of whom deployed only once if at all. Roughly half of the troops who have served several tours in Iraq and Afghanistan are parents, and their kids were at least two and a half times more likely than civilian children to develop psychological problems.[7] If we were a nation at war, rather than a military at war, this would be an American problem. We are not, so it's a Pentagon problem. Colonel Kris Peterson, a pediatrician at the Military Child and Adolescent Center of Excellence at Fort Lewis, Washington, admitted that there is a "very large gap" in providing care.

Mental health-care resources are spread so thin that soldiers' kids wait months for psychiatric care, but there's no Department of Military Children's Affairs, no powerful lobbyists or highly paid advocates for military kids. They lack the social cachet and political currency of combat veterans, and there's just no way to spin a suicidal second-grader into a poster child for patriotism. Since there's not a Walter Reed to tend the invisible war wounds of Army kids,

---

7. Flake et al., "The Psychosocial Effects of Deployment on Military Children," *The Journal of Developmental & Behavioral Pediatrics.*

there is no potential political lightning rod that could galvanize the people or embarrass the administration.

According to Kimberly Hefling of the Associated Press, between 2003 and 2008, inpatient visits among military children increased 50 percent, and children of US troops sought outpatient mental health care two million times, double the number at the start of the Iraq war.[8] During that same time frame, Veterans Administration research showed that the prevalence of new mental health diagnoses in troops who served in Iraq and Afghanistan had also nearly doubled, as reported in *Stars and Stripes* in July 2009. The same study revealed that approximately 35 percent of Iraq and Afghanistan veterans who accessed the Veterans Affairs health-care system were diagnosed with a mental health problem.[9] That figure dovetails perfectly with the results of a suicide prevention project in San Antonio, Texas, which was posted on the Army Reserve Family Programs website in July of 2009. The research found that "nearly 35 percent of more than 200 children from local military families needed to be treated for mental health conditions."

Eleven-year-old Daniel Radenz was one of them.

Daniel was a gregarious honor roll student who loved his pet rabbits, Steve, Alvin, and Gilligan, and liked to play tricks on his two teenaged brothers, James and Zach. His dad, Lieutenant Colonel (LTC) Blaine Radenz, had been stationed at Fort Hood since 2004, and the family lived about fifteen miles away in Kempner, Texas, where his mom, Tricia, worked as an ER nurse at a civilian

---

8. Hefling, "More Military Children," Associated Press.

9. McCloskey, "Study Reveals Sharp Rise," *Stars & Stripes*.

hospital. LTC Radenz left in June of 2008 for his second tour in Iraq. The first had been twelve months; this one would be fifteen. Shortly after school started in August, Tricia began getting calls from Daniel's teachers, expressing concern that his grades were "slipping, he's withdrawn, and lost interest in everything."

Already worried about his insomnia and loss of appetite, Tricia called the Darnall Army Medical Center at Fort Hood and was told they couldn't fit Daniel in for several weeks. Tricia took the time slot, but as the calls from the school escalated, so did her unease. When one of the teachers asked Tricia if Daniel was getting help, she told her he had an appointment the following week.

"I don't think he can wait," the teacher replied.

Tricia drove Daniel to Darnall's Department of Child Psychiatry that day and refused to leave until he was seen. He was diagnosed with major depression and a sleep disorder and prescribed 10 mg of Celexa, which is an antidepressant, and Restoril, a sleep medication recommended for brief treatment periods of two weeks or less. More than half of military kids suffer sleep disorders during a parent's deployment, and there is an incontrovertible link between deployment and mental health diagnoses in school-age children.[10] In addition to medication, Daniel also began weekly sessions with the school counselor and seeing the psychologist and psychiatrist on post. Terrified his dad would die in Iraq, Daniel would wake up bawling in the middle of the night until Tricia brought him into her bedroom to sleep. This went on for months, and then Blaine returned for his two-week R & R in March of 2009.

---

10. Siegel and Davis, "Health and Mental Health Needs of Children," *Pediatrics*.

"It seemed like Daniel was back to himself, he was doing so well," said Tricia. "But when Blaine left again, he took a nosedive."

His doctors doubled the dosage of Celexa and added Strattera and Wellbutrin to his list of medications. Daniel began to talk about running away from home and withdrew even further. He started having hallucinations at school, yelling and jabbering, which scared the other kids and his teachers. During band practice one day, he ran out of rehearsal and was found crouched in the hallway, hitting himself and clawing his face. The behaviors became so disruptive that he was repeatedly pulled from the classroom and off the playground. Strattera has been linked to hallucinations, and Wellbutrin side effects include suicidal thoughts, suicidal gestures (characteristically cutting of the body), suicide attempts, and actual death by suicide. In March of 2004, the FDA issued a warning for Wellbutrin, stating that the drug can bring about suicide and violence in children and teenagers. This FDA public health advisory cautioned doctors, patients, and families to be exceptionally vigilant for signs of worsening depression or suicidal ideation at the commencement of antidepressant therapy or whenever the dosage is altered.

Between 2005 and 2009 the under-eighteen military child population grew by less than one percent. Antipsychotic drug use in that same group went up about 50 percent, and antianxiety drug use jumped by nearly 40 percent. That reflected a similar trend in the active-duty force, which saw a 76 percent increase in prescriptions for psychiatric medications since 2001.[11]

---

11. Jowers and Tilghman, "Military Kids," *Army Times*.

Troops have historically been barred from using such drugs in combat, but by 2009, when so many were serving a third, fourth, or fifth deployment, an anonymous survey found that roughly 12 percent of combat troops in Iraq and 17 percent in Afghanistan were taking prescription antidepressants or sleeping pills, according to the Army's fifth Mental Health Advisory Team report. Dr. Peter R. Breggin, author of *Medication Madness: The Role of Psychiatric Drugs in Violence, Suicide, and Murder*, claims that during Vietnam, "A mere one percent of our troops were taking prescribed psychiatric drugs. By contrast, in the past year one-third of marines in combat zones were taking psychiatric drugs." Two of the more commonly prescribed drugs were Celexa and Wellbutrin, which have been linked to an increased risk of violence or suicide.

Neither is recommended for children. A few weeks into his treatment with Celexa and Wellbutrin, Daniel began secretly cutting himself. He managed to hide his wounds from everyone until the day he found a piece of jagged metal on the playground during recess. Slipping away to the boy's bathroom, the fifth-grader slashed his arm deeply enough to create what staff later described as "a blood bath." Using his own blood as paint, he wrote THE END in large block letters on the bathroom wall.

Tricia was called while the school nurse tended to his wounds, and after he was bandaged up, Tricia bundled her boy into the car and took him home. Keeping an eye on Daniel, Tricia made frantic phone calls to the Psychiatric Department at Darnall, leaving meticulously detailed messages about Daniel's deterioration. But the calls were never returned. Desperately afraid for her son's life, Tricia finally got her husband on the phone and told him the full extent of what was happening with Daniel.

During a deployment, the spouse who stays behind is directed by the Family Readiness Group (FRG), command, and other military spouses to keep communications with their soldier upbeat. We are instructed to avoid or minimize sharing information that might distract the soldier from the mission. The deal made between the military and the spouse is that the former will provide the training and gear to shield the soldier from war, as much as possible; it is the job of the spouse to shield that soldier from home. Just as there are things that happen downrange that the family will never know, there are also things that happen at home the veteran will never be told.

When Blaine heard about Daniel, he told his wife, "I'm on the first smoking bird out of here." Four days later, he was home on emergency leave.

During a lengthy meeting with the psychiatrist and psychologist at Darnall, Blaine asked why they hadn't returned his wife's calls or voice mail messages; they apologized, explaining that they were understaffed due to budget cuts, so no one was checking the machine. The couple showed them Daniel's notebook sketches of mutilated bodies and hanging corpses. They pleaded to get Daniel admitted, stating that they "thought he needed an environment where he was closely monitored."

The doctors disagreed, dismissing the sketches and self-mutilation as a phase that would pass. They noted that Tricia and Blaine seemed "on edge," and made a date the next week to conduct another review of the case. Daniel was not deemed appropriate for admission to the psychiatric ward at the follow-up appointment since his dad was back, and the family was making sure that Daniel was never by himself. So once again, they took their youngest child home.

"We were afraid to let him go to the bathroom alone," said Tricia, who saw to it that there was someone stationed outside when he did.

About a week after their appointment, shortly before LTC Radenz was scheduled to return to Iraq, the family was working in the yard on a clear, sunny morning in early June. Daniel had woken up in good spirits, chattering about his plans for the summer during breakfast. He helped sweep grass cuttings from around the pool, laying the broom aside a few times to catch dragonflies for his bug collection. When Blaine went inside to start making sandwiches for lunch, he took Daniel along, and Tricia went into the shed searching for trimmer line for the weed eater.

When she returned, she told James, "Go get Daniel, so we can finish the yard before lunch."

Thirteen-year-old James walked into the room they shared and saw Daniel's lifeless body suspended from the top rail of the bunk bed.

"Mom, help, Daniel hung himself!" James screamed, running into the backyard.

James was still screaming when Blaine sprinted into the room and unwound the camcorder strap from Daniel's neck. Blaine began CPR immediately. He was hunched over Daniel's lifeless body when Tricia flew through the doorway. For the next endless minutes, Tricia and Blaine struggled to bring Daniel back.

"I kept thinking, *this can't be real. This can't be real.* We performed CPR until EMS arrived and the helicopter landed to fly him to Scott & White Hospital. I rode with him, wishing we would never stop. I worked in an ER; I knew what they were going to say," Tricia recalled.

"But until we got to the hospital, he didn't have to be dead."

Daniel Radenz died by suicide on June 9, 2009. His funeral was held four days later at the largest Baptist Church in town, packed to the rafters with students, teachers, and coaches from area schools, as well as school board members and administrators and local business owners. The nurses, doctors, and EMS workers from the hospital were there, along with firefighters, law enforcement officers, and dozens upon dozens of friends. His eulogy was given by a Texas Ranger who had been James and Daniel's football coach for two years and spent time with Daniel when Blaine was deployed.

"Fort Hood was represented by three military personnel. My husband later told me he was totally devastated," said Tricia. "Darnall sent some ugly ten-dollar flowers. They didn't send anyone to represent them. Had I relied on the military to give my family support, you can see how much my family would have received."

Tricia obtained all of Daniel's medical records shortly after his death and sought out advice from several lawyers, each of whom stated that Daniel's treatment was "clearly a case of malpractice, a failure to diagnose, and a failure to inform."

"His providers killed him as sure as if they held a gun to his head and pulled the trigger," Tricia said. That trigger may well have been Celexa, which has never been approved for pediatric use.

In 2003, the US government sued Forest Pharmaceuticals, the manufacturer of Celexa, citing that Forest had illegally and actively marketed the drug for use in children when the FDA had only approved it for use in adults. The US Department of Justice also penalized Forest for withholding the negative results of a Celexa study in adolescents and promoting only positive study outcomes to physicians. The company pled guilty to several crimes, including paying kickbacks to doctors to persuade them to prescribe the drugs. Forest paid over $313 million in 2010 to settle criminal complaints.

Tricia sent several emails to Fort Hood personnel asking why federal employees at Darnall were prescribing Celexa to children when the federal government was suing the drug's manufacturer, but they were never answered.[12] I spoke with Judy Tyler, the records manager at Darnall who also processes Freedom of Information Act requests on the phone, in the fall of 2014. She said that the post has no local policy, but "uses FDA guidance" when prescribing black box medications to military children—"black box" referring to the FDA warning required for prescription drugs that can cause serious injury or death. But the antidepressants they prescribed have been found to increase the risk of suicidal thinking and behavior in children, adolescents, and young adults in short-term studies of major depressive disorders when compared to placebo.

The warnings were explicit and Daniel's symptoms were well documented, so why wasn't he more closely monitored, and then pulled off the drug when the suicidal ideation began? Why was he prescribed two more medications, Strattera and Wellbutrin, which also had black box warnings linked to worsening depression and suicidal thinking in children and adolescents? Apart from criminal negligence, what would explain a scenario where doctors prescribe Celexa to an eleven-year-old child, combine it with Wellbutrin, Restoril, and Strattera, and then ignore the clear clinical worsening of the child's symptoms, the suicidality and changes in behavior?

---

12. The Fort Hood PAO did not respond to my multiple requests for information about policies pertaining to prescribing black box medications to children of service members.

Issues of criminal liability and malpractice would have been addressed in court had Daniel's father been a civilian. Because Daniel's health care was provided by his father's employer, the United States Army, the Radenz family was never able to find an attorney willing to take his medical providers to court. Members of the Armed Forces and their families are prohibited from filing claims against the federal government for death or injury arising from military service. The Feres Doctrine shields military medical providers from malpractice suits, and typically overrides the Federal Torts Claims Act that allows civilians and other government employees to sue the government for injuries cause by intent or neglect. The United States Supreme Court passed the Feres Doctrine in 1950 as a failsafe against the buyer's remorse that could happen when the inherent hazards of wearing the uniform were realized.

Daniel's case was clearly outside of the intent of that law, but challenging it would be an uphill battle. However much they wanted justice for Daniel, dealing with his death took all of the Radenz family's resources in those first few years after he was gone.

"Our surviving sons both have symptoms of PTSD," Tricia reported in an email. "James still cannot sleep with the lights off. I have lost my career as an emergency room nurse due to the PTSD I experience and the need to be available to my children. We will all require counseling for the remainder of our days. Now we experience financial hardship and I am selling anything of value to remain in our home and provide stability for my children. The blanket of protection freely given to providers affiliated with the government only encourages incompetence."

LTC Radenz was contractually bound to continue working for the government, but Tricia began speaking out about suicide in military children. In November of 2011, she joined me and a handful of other military family members at the US Capitol to perform *Homefront 911: Military Family Monologues*. The thirteen narratives are based on actual accounts compiled from hundreds of interviews with military family members, stories that document how more than a decade of war is coming home for the families left behind.

Tricia was adamant she read the monologue depicting her son's suicide. We had a back-up plan in case she couldn't finish. When she got to the end, she stood on stage, with then Secretary of the Army John McHugh and several senators in the audience, surrounded by other military family members ready to catch her if she fell. She was trembling with grief and rage and who knows what else, but she read those last three lines:

Now he sits in the room where he last held his boy.
And waits for the pain to subside.
On Father's Day, the Colonel remembers cutting down his boy,
    howling with grief, and unwrapping the rope from his neck.

I asked her afterward how she did it.

"People need to understand that it can happen to anyone," she replied. "No one is immune from suicide. I wish I had known more. I wish I had known to ask him. There were so many times I could have had that dialogue and didn't, out of ignorance, and fear, and the misconception that I would give him ideas if I asked him. He already *had* ideas."

After a brief silence, Tricia continued: "That day when he killed himself? We figured out that when he and Blaine went into the house to start making lunch, Blaine went to the bathroom first. When he came out, he thought one of us had come in and gotten Daniel and taken him back out into the yard with us. And that's when it happened. Daniel must have marched right in there and did it so fast. It's a lot easier to have that talk than to wish you'd had that talk. And if me doing this means that even one person has that talk, then it's worth it. That's how, that's how I did it. Daniel was an unintended casualty of war."

*   *   *

As operations chief in Baghdad, Major Jodi Smith was familiar with war casualties. Her duties included collecting critical information about unit fatalities and relaying it to the company commander, according to an essay Smith wrote in 2011 for the *Washington Post*. When her phone rang during a lunch break in Iraq, she didn't recognize the number. The voice at the other end was an ER physician calling from Newport News, Virginia, to tell her that her oldest son, Nick, twenty-one, had a self-inflicted gunshot wound to the head and was in a coma. The major departed immediately, and had been stateside for about twenty-four hours when he died. Nick was an active member of Kappa Delta Rho fraternity at Christopher Newport University and a student leader in the Catholic Campus Ministry. His classmates and campus officials were stunned to learn that he'd taken his own life.

"Based on the circumstances and evidence, the police think Nick intended a suicide gesture," wrote Jodi. "He succeeded, and now I am the ghost."

Adolescent boys and very young men seem to struggle more with a parent's deployment than do their female counterparts.[13] At the very least, their difficulties manifest differently, and they display a marked tendency toward increased binge drinking, drug use, and suicidal gestures and ideation. The University of Washington's School of Public Health found that holds true even when compared to boys in civilian families, with 14 percent of civilian adolescents reporting suicidal thoughts, as compared to 26 percent of tenth- and twelfth-grade boys with a currently deployed parent.[14] The tendency toward suicide and suicidal ideation, including depression and feelings of hopelessness, in military youth appears to escalate with each deployment. Data collected in 2012 and 2013 as part of a study of secondary school students in California found that 21 percent of the military kids reported having a suicide plan and nearly 18 percent had attempted suicide. By comparison, slightly more than 7 percent of civilian youth disclosed a suicide attempt during the same time frame.[15,16] The findings did not include the actual number of completed suicides. Researchers also discovered that 35 percent of military kids reported periods of feeling sad or hopeless and 24 percent claimed symptoms of depression if a parent had had a single deployment during the past decade. More than one deployment pushed the percentages to 38 and 28, respectively.

Grade school children weren't included in the study, but even the youngest kids are turning out to be more vulnerable to deployment-

13. Fauntleroy, "Parents' Military Deployments," Center for Advancing Health.
14. Guiden, "Adolescent Boys," *UW Today.*
15. Zarembo, "Multiple Military Deployments," *Los Angeles Times.*
16. Zarembo, "Military Children," *Los Angeles Times.*

related stresses than once thought. Mental health visits for children under the age of five soared 73 percent between 2005 and 2009, according to data made available by TRICARE, the military's health insurance system.

"When Amber's dad left for his second yearlong tour in Iraq with the Army National Guard, she threw up every single morning for nearly three months," said her mother, a trim, educated, professional woman in her early thirties.

"She cried almost every day, barely slept at night, and screamed so bad when I went to drop her off at kindergarten that I just quit taking her. I don't care if she's behind a year. There aren't any other kids in her class whose dads are gone, anyway, so the teachers had no idea what to do."

Like a lot of other military spouses, she cut back her work hours to take care of Amber, who was diagnosed with anxiety and separation issues and given an antianxiety medication. Amber was five. A 2011 study of more than half a million military children found that when a parent was deployed, behavioral disorders such as attention deficit disorder and stress disorders, including PTSD, increased 18 and 19 percent, respectively.[17] By 2010, the Department of Defense (DoD) had admitted that "ongoing studies highlight the primarily negative impact of deployments on children."[18] And in 2011, military children—children who had access to TRICARE, which bills itself as "the world's greatest health care for the world's greatest military," children who had at least one parent with a

---

17. Mansfield et al., "Deployment and Mental Health," *Archives of Pediatrics and Adolescent Medicine.*

18. Department of Defense, "Plans."

regular paycheck, children who had a parent in the home, and a bed to sleep in at night—were considered an at-risk population. As of 2014, an estimated 1.5 million military kids, or roughly one-third of the population to date, had developed a mental health issue during or after the deployment of a parent or sibling. The Code of Support Foundation, which helps connect civilian Americans with opportunities to support the troops and military families, suggested on their website that the percentage of distressed military kids may be closer to two-thirds. For the first time in US history, there were more military children struggling with the behavioral consequences of war than the warriors themselves.

Fewer than one hundred thousand school-age military kids attend classes on or near a military base that provides a learning environment with staff connected to the military, aware of the strains of deployment and how to access resources.

When school staff are knowledgeable about the military, "the teacher, the principal, and the community get what they're going through, understand what they need, and provide all the supports," said Ron Astor in an interview with Liz Dwyer published by TakePart.com on March 25, 2014. Astor is a professor at the University of Southern California's School of Social Work, and expressed concern for the million-plus military kids enrolled in public schools whose parents are active-duty military, reserve, or post-9/11 veterans. "The civilian principal and teachers don't know that they're even there," he said. "The isolation and invisibility they experience has a profound negative effect. . . . It could be their parent's seventh deployment, and it could be their [family's] tenth move, and the teacher or principal will just see academic or behavioral problems."

Ingrid Herrera-Yee lived on post with her boys, ages two and seven, when her husband, Ian Yee, was deployed to Afghanistan in 2008. Staff Sergeant Yee was already a veteran of two tours in Iraq when they married in 2006. Ingrid and I were introduced by Karen Francis, a mutual military spouse friend, who had endured her husband's multiple deployments, first as a Guard spouse and then an active-duty wife after her husband transferred from the Guard to the Army. Ingrid's husband had done the reverse, joining the Massachusetts National Guard after four years with Big Army. Ingrid was recognized as Spouse of the Year for the National Guard in 2014, and in early 2015, I asked her what was different about the Army compared to the Guard.

"I can't imagine having to experience the first tour without [on-post support]. There was an amazing sense of community." Ingrid said that when her boys "were acting out," what made the critical difference for her school-age son was "being able to go to support groups for kids in school. And at lunch time, they sit at a table with other kids with a parent deployed."

"Now that we no longer live on base," she said, "we have to explain everything a lot more, especially at their schools."

Schools near Fort Bragg, the largest Army base in the nation, have a program called "Living in the New Normal" to assist military kids dealing with trauma and loss. Army wife Rebekah Sanderlin's husband was stationed at Fort Bragg, but he'd been gone nearly sixty of the past eighty months. Sanderlin is the blogger for *Operation Marriage* for the *Fayetteville Observer*, and she said on the program:

"[M]ost young military children don't know that their lives are unusual now. They can't remember life before mommies and daddies went off to war. As awful as it sounds, this is normal for them, the old normal. It's not even new anymore."[19]

Since her husband's return from his third deployment in Afghanistan, the family has begun to find "familiar routines. Still, our four-year-old son asks me almost every day if Daddy has gone to work for the day or for longer. His little mind can't figure out if he'll see Daddy at dinnertime or not again until another Christmas has passed. He panics when he thinks that he didn't get to say good-bye. How can I explain the difference between a deployment and a work day to a kid who can't even tell time?"

Children that young also struggle to find the words for what's behind their feelings. Sanderlin's son "says things like, 'I'm sad,' but he can't articulate why." Sanderlin's daughter was born during the most recent deployment. "For the first months of her life, she knew her father as an eight-by-ten picture taped to the backseat of the car. She had almost no contact with men, so every time she heard a male voice, she would become startled, and her eyes would widen. She has grown familiar with my husband's voice now, but she still stares at him like he's a rare, precious specimen."

The post-9/11 generation of military kids doesn't know life without war. "They will remember the bitter pain of hugging their father good-bye, knowing that they'll be three inches taller when they see him again," said Sanderlin. "They will remember that some of their friends never got to see their fathers again."

"The Army is not really grasping what's going on with the kids," said Beth Pyritz, a twenty-seven-year-old mother of five

---

19. NPR, "Military Families," *All Things Considered.*

whose husband, an Army specialist, was serving a fifteen-month tour in Iraq, his third in six years. During a deployment, the practical realities of military kids are similar to, and in some cases better than, those of children of divorced or single parents. But after the initial shock and loss of the separation, children of divorce tend not to present with mental health issues requiring clinical intervention.

In every study conducted, the mental health of the mother predicted the mental health of the military child. "Nearly 50 percent of spouses reported depression as well as significant anxiety symptoms during a soldier's deployment."[20] "According to the 2008 Health Care Survey of DoD Beneficiaries, "more than 60 percent of deployed Guard and Reserve spouses reported increased stress." So it's no wonder that the kids were struggling, too. But skyrocketing stress in the civilian parent during combat-related deployments wasn't only tied to mental health problems in the kids; it was also driving a staggering rise in the rates of child abuse and neglect.

"War has a profound emotional impact on military personnel and their families. The rate of occurrence of substantiated maltreatment in military families was twice as high [during] deployment."[21] Most victims were four years old or younger and the perpetrator was usually the civilian parent who remained at home while a spouse was deployed. During a deployment, children of enlisted soldiers were also more than three times as likely to

---

20. McFarlane, "Military Deployment," *Current Opinion in Psychiatry*.
21. Rentz et al., "Effect of Deployment," *American Journal of Epidemiology*.

be maltreated.[22] Of the incidents that occurred, more than two-thirds were "moderate or severe." Another study published in the *Journal of the American Medical Association* found that the incidence of child neglect was almost four times greater in military families. The primary offenders were non-Hispanic white civilian females, who, according to other informal surveys and anecdotal reports, were also reporting higher rates of secondary PTSD. War-related "secondary trauma" shares some of the same symptoms as a full-blown diagnosis, including emotional withdrawal, increased anxiety, and poor anger management, which could be deadly.

The number of military kids killed by their parents, the spouse, and/or the service member, has more than doubled since 2001. A decade after the war in Afghanistan began, children who live near Fort Bragg and Camp LeJeune, North Carolina's largest military bases, were twice as likely to be murdered by a parent as children living in other parts of the state, according to the North Carolina Child Advocacy Institute. In many cases of child deaths, military officials had already received reports of child or domestic abuse in the home. Six of the fourteen Army kids who died from neglect or abuse in 2007 were the subjects of previous reports filed with the Army's Family Advocacy Program (FAP). Five of the other cases involving child fatalities were on the Army's radar, but the family's involvement with other military or civilian assistance offices never made it into the FAP files. Roughly 80 percent of the Army kids who died that year were already known to the system. In comparison, 10 to 15 percent of civilian child deaths occur in families that have

---

22. Gibbs et al., "Child Maltreatment," *Journal of the American Medical Association*.

received services or intervention from a social service agency in the preceding five years, according to the Department of Health and Human Services.[23]

Pentagon officials cannot say for sure how many military child deaths there are, and the discrepancy between records from the FAP and the individual service branches can vary by 50 percent or more. For example, the FAP office recorded twenty-four child deaths from abuse or neglect in 2006, but service records indicated at least thirty-eight. The military child abuse death rate in 2006 was about 2.7 per 100,000 children, while the civilian rate averaged 2.2 per 100,000. The Pentagon's Family Violence Policy Office was closed the following year. It wasn't until some six years later, in the midst of major media coverage about what the *Army Times* called the "Army's Hidden Child Abuse Epidemic" that the DoD organized a child abuse working group to conduct a rapid review of child and domestic abuse.

In the interim, there were 12,881 registered cases of child neglect, abuse, sexual assault, and murder in the Army, Navy, Air Force, and Marine Corps in 2012, a 40 percent increase from 2009.[24] An *Army Times* investigation discovered there were 29,552 cases of child abuse and neglect in active-duty Army families from 2003 through 2012, according to Army Central Registry data. Of those, 15,557 were committed by soldiers, the rest by civilians—primarily spouses. Sometimes it was both.

As noted by the *Military Times* in 2013, "Eight-year-old RJ will probably have to be fed through a tube for the rest of his life because

---

23. Tilghman, "Deployments," *AirForce Times*.
24. Sandza, "Pentagon," *Army Times*.

his mother's boyfriend, Sergeant Rocky Donadio, beat him so badly that doctors had to remove part of his pancreas and intestines."[25]

Donadio thrashed the boy after he mistakenly erased Donadio's Xbox *Grand Theft Auto* profile. Donadio was deployed for a year in Iraq from November 2005 to November 2006. He was awarded three Army Achievement Medals, three Good Conduct Medals, and an Army Commendation Medal. Now, he is serving a seventy-five-year sentence for the 2009 assault at Fort Sill, Oklahoma. RJ's mother, Misty Stobaugh, was also charged and convicted of abuse and served her sentence with the Oklahoma Department of Corrections.

Keegan Metz's wounds were "beyond repair" on February 7, 2009, when emergency medical workers arrived at the toddler's home, according to court testimony. An article by Tavia D. Green in the *Leaf-Chronicle* reported that Dr. Adele Lewis, medical examiner, performed Keegan's autopsy, and ruled his death a homicide. "He had injuries to his brain, swelling to his brain, and bleeding behind his eyes," Lewis said. "It takes a significant amount of force. Maybe a major car wreck or a two- or three-story fall [to cause an injury like that]."[26] Twenty-three-month-old Keegan's injuries included multiple hemorrhages in his eyeballs, neck trauma consistent with being strangled or choked, facial bruises, damage to his genitals, and evidence of sodomy. His stepfather, twenty-six-year-old Joshua Starner, and mother, twenty-seven-year-old Caitlyn Metz, were found guilty of felony murder, aggravated child abuse, and aggravated child neglect. Starner, a former soldier at Fort Campbell who served in Iraq from September 2007 to October

---

25. "The Human Toll of Child Abuse in the Army," *Military Times*.
26. Green, "Clarksville Murder Trial," *Leaf-Chronicle*.

2008, was also convicted of aggravated sexual battery. Metz was convicted of facilitation of aggravated sexual battery.

The beatings and torture that killed five-year-old Talia Williams were so severe that the case against Naeem Williams became the first death penalty trial in the state of Hawaii, which abolished capital punishment in 1957. The allegations of abuse included the child being forced to eat her own feces, being whipped with a belt while tied to her bedpost, and being kicked with such force that a boot print was found on her chest. The boot print purportedly belonging to Williams, an Army specialist who was stationed at Schofield Barracks, Hawaii, who had obtained custody of his daughter, Talia, just seven months before she was killed. They lived in base housing along with Williams's wife, Delilah Williams, who was also charged with, and pled guilty to, murder. Delilah testified against her husband in the March 2014 trial, and the former soldier was found guilty and sentenced to life without parole in February 2015. After seven full days of deliberation, the emotionally exhausted jurors voted 8–4 in favor of the death penalty, but failed to reach the required unanimous verdict.

US District Judge J. Michael Seabright said that the trial testimony continues to haunt those who heard it, comparing the treatment of the girl to a "house of horrors." Talia's biological mother, Tarshia Williams, was among those who testified against her former husband. When the criminal trial was over, the civil suit filed by Tarshia in 2005 against the US Army for failing to protect her daughter proceeded. In the six months leading up to Talia's death, social workers, military day care providers, and military police were alerted to potential abuse in the Williams' home on four separate occasions. Civilian child protective services received a hotline complaint accusing the father and stepmother of abuse, but it was not investigated or communicated to the Army, which typically handles reports of child abuse through the military police and the Family Advocacy Program. Even after the child was examined by a doctor and obvious signs of cruelty were found by military providers on post, there was no intervention on her behalf.

Court documents showed that an Army major general observed that there was "a series of missed opportunities to potentially prevent the death of the child." The Army's defense to the federal judge's ruling that granted Talia's mother permission to sue is that it is neither the duty nor legal responsibility of the FAP office and other military officials to keep Talia—or any child—safe from abuse. The US Government seemed to disagree, awarding Tarshia a two-million-dollar settlement over the death of her daughter.

CHAPTER THREE

An Army of One

I GOT MY FIRST service-connected prescription shortly after my husband got the call for his second tour. He came home one night and handed me a Memorandum for Soldiers of the 81st Heavy Combat Brigade Team, Subject: Mobilization Update. Colonel Kapral continued for a whole page, but I never read further than that fourth line: "We have received the mobilization order." I should have known that second tour was on the way, because we'd seen that goddamn bird again a month earlier. But I ignored it.

Just like I'd been ignoring how, for the past few months, Lorin had been leaving for work at Camp Murray, where the Washington National Guard is headquartered, at zero dark hundred, and often returning after I was asleep. I ignored it like I ignored how he'd been incrementally pulling away, shutting down emotionally, after he had finally started to open up. Just when I'd found his heartbeat again, I lost it. I ignored all of that. I put it out of my mind. But even after I saw his orders, even after I told him and myself that it would be fine, I could do this, that it would be easier because I had already done it before, the lie refused to hold.

A few weeks after seeing the mobilization memo, I was jogging on a treadmill at the gym near our home in Kent, Washington. In those weeks I'd already freaked out a few times—racing heart, feeling of panic—and called Military and Family Life Counseling (MFLC), a program for military dependents that provides short-term, nonmedical guidance. The licensed clinical professional suggested I exercise more and practice calming breath techniques. She said it would help reduce stress and anxiety and provide positive self-care skills. Maybe I shouldn't have been working out and deep breathing at the same time. She hadn't said, and I hadn't asked. I did ask if she had ever been through a deployment herself. Nope. She had no family in the military, had no idea what it was like. "But I'm sure it must be challenging."

The GRE is challenging. Spending a year or more waiting outside the emergency room that is a combat deployment, knowing your infantry soldier is in there, but not knowing how they're doing, or when they're coming out, or how many body parts they might be missing when they do, or if they're even going to make it, and preparing a small part of your psyche for them to be dead already and packing that pain every single day? That's not challenging. That's terrifying. That's anticipatory grief.

So I ran and I breathed, increasing the speed and incline, until I was bawling on the treadmill. And I couldn't stop it, any of it. I couldn't stop running, or sobbing, or him from being gone again. I couldn't stop another endless year of isolation from people who didn't have a loved one at war, because I no longer knew how to have a conversation that didn't include the one fact around which my life revolved. I couldn't prevent another year of triple-checking doors I was certain I locked, of being so consumed with worry I might have left the stove on, or a candle burning—even when I knew I hadn't, because I could clearly recall turning it off or blowing it out—that I had to drive back home to make sure. I checked, and checked, and checked again (three seemed to be the magic number), and then performed the same compulsive routine when I locked the door and left for work for the second time.

I hadn't ever done that before, and never did it when he wasn't at war. But he was going again, and I couldn't halt the coming thirteen months, maybe longer—what if they, like the Minnesota Guard, ended up spending a miserable twenty-two months in the suck? Twenty-two months of night recon for strange cars on my street, and twenty-two months of my heart skipping a beat when any dark, unfamiliar vehicle cruised toward the house. I hated myself for this, all of it: the anxiety, weakness, and fear. Mostly I hated that I couldn't keep it contained, that I cried at the slightest thing, at nothing, and even the tiniest note of compassion from any-one, anywhere, about anything at all, triggered tears.

"How have you been? Is there anything bothering you?" asked the nurse at my annual physical exam.

"No, I'm fine." For a few seconds, I was, and then I was not. Sobbing, I gasped for air, trying to pull all of the aching sadness back inside me. I cleared my throat several times and shut it down, and hoped we could pretend it never happened.

"Huh. *Hrrrm*. Okay. Sorry about that. Everything's fine."

The nurse tilted her head slightly and raised an eyebrow.

"I just," I was sobbing again, "I just, I just . . ." panting, fighting to push it down.

"It's okay, take your time. I'm not going anywhere."

She wasn't, but he was, and I was such a fucking baby. The anger was good. Self-loathing was even better, because it was guaranteed to stop the tears.

"Okay, again, *ahem*, sorry. I don't know what happened there."

"That's all right. Do you want to talk about it?"

"Not really, no."

"Are you in danger? Do you feel like you're safe at home?"

"No, no, it's nothing like that." I sighed and said, "My husband is getting deployed again to Iraq. We just found out a few weeks ago. I've been through this before, so I don't know what my problem is, but I can't seem to stop crying. Sometimes, for no reason whatsoever, I get so scared that my heart starts beating really fast, and I think I'm going to die. I have no idea what that's about. What is that?"

"It sounds like a panic attack. Have you ever had them before?"

"No."

"Are you talking to anybody about this?" she asked. "Have you seen a counselor?"

"No. I called the Military Family people, and they just said I should work out. And meditate, which hasn't helped at all."

"I'm going to write you a prescription for Klonopin, but it's just for a month. The next time you feel an attack coming on, take one. And see if you can find a counselor."

I called Military OneSource, a twenty-four-hour hotline that offers information and referrals for TRICARE members and their dependents. They directed me to their website, where I could get a listing of providers in my area, and recommended I find a primary care physician and ask for a mental health referral once I'm settled in southern Oregon. Lorin promised that, after this tour, he was getting out for real this time, but he couldn't let his men go to war without him. After two and a half decades, his retirement was finally on the horizon and neither of us was particularly interested in sticking around Seattle. So I moved to Medford before he went to training at Fort McCoy, Wisconsin. He would be in Iraq regardless of where I lived, so I figured I might as well live somewhere I liked.

I loved the Rogue Valley, which gets nearly two hundred days of sunshine a year, and where camping, hiking, skiing (water or snow), kayaking, and horseback riding are all just a twenty-minute drive away. It's home to the world-famous Shakespeare Festival in Ashland, a wealthier town than Medford or the cluster of outlying rural communities where families struggling to stay afloat during the foreclosure crisis were as likely to raffle off a handgun as hold a yard sale. There are a lot of working poor, and migrant and seasonal farm workers come through Jackson County to harvest grapes, pears, and other produce. La Clinica was set up with a sliding scale fee structure for the poor and uninsured and regularly receives grants from the federal government to provide medical and dental care for low-income residents and people in need. Between my salary and Lorin's tax-exempt combat pay, we are way above the typical financial profile of La Clinica's clientele, but it was the only place I could find that would take TRICARE insurance. I was in the cramped, cluttered lobby, perched on the edge of a tired old chair in a random arrangement of furniture, waiting for the harried-looking receptionist to call my name.

I'd been to Madigan Medical Center at Fort Lewis—the US Army's second largest medical treatment facility—a few times during Lorin's first tour. It was a state-of-the-art complex that featured an immaculate, glass-ceilinged atrium bordered by massive planters. The cool, clean expansiveness of the space was matched by the cool, clean military precision with which my appointments were handled; all of that was absent here.

It became evident I was the first military spouse this primary care physician had seen when, as I tried to explain what's going on, the expression on her face became one of increasing puzzlement. She looked at her watch, and then told me I could come back and talk to a nurse again in six weeks. Would I like a prescription for Xanax?

"Sure," I said. "Whatever."

I stomped out, grumbling, not for the first time, about TRICARE and the paltry government reimbursement rates that make it hard for Guard and Reserve families to get even basic health care, especially in rural areas. For the nearly 25 percent of Guard/Reserve spouses who need counseling during a spouse's deployment,[27] finding behavioral health care is even more difficult, sometimes impossible. What happened to me is the standard process: spouses are told to go to a primary care provider (PCP), who is then supposed to refer us to a mental health specialist. But we wait for that appointment forever, get a few minutes, and leave with medication more often than a referral. Civilian TRICARE providers are few, far between, and overwhelmed.

The DoD offers mental health programs for spouses and other military family members, but the need so far surpasses availability that it's almost impossible to get professional help. The on-post mental health providers are so flooded with uniforms that

---

27. Department of Defense, "Health Care Survey."

the adult mental health facility at Fort Campbell and other posts have stopped serving spouses altogether. As reported by the *Army News Service* in October 2009, there is "a severe shortage of mental health-care facilities for families, both on-post and off, especially as post-behavioral health centers are already filled to capacity with soldiers," said Army psychiatrist Colonel Kris Peterson.[28] Spouses with serious anxiety or depression are either handed off to nonmedical resources like chaplains, who are so busy seeing soldiers that spouses' calls are rarely returned, or MFLCs, who don't keep case notes or track clients and are prohibited from providing medical treatment. Nonetheless, that's where they're sent, according to numerous military providers and Army public-affairs officers. Military OneSource also offers online nonmedical counseling, with the disclaimer that it's "not suitable for mental health conditions such as depression and anxiety, [or] for those who have been prescribed psychoactive medication."

Many of the wives have prescriptions for antianxiety and antidepressives, and when we get together we talk about who's taking what and which meds work best. Xanax gets a lot of love, and, based on anecdotal reports, it's being passed out to the spouses like candy at Halloween by physicians on-post and off. The military spouse grapevine has been telling the boots-on-the-ground-truth about what's really happening on the homefront years before the topic becomes a blip on the radar of the DoD or the variety of congressional committees that purportedly oversee the armed services. By the time there's a congressional hearing or a DoD task force, what started out as a concern in the spouse community has metastasized into a

---

28. Collins, "Army Psychiatrist," *Army News Service.*

significant problem, whether it's mental illness, a lack of family support programs, or problems finding daycare or health providers. But the Pentagon doesn't track spouses like they do the troops and military kids. Instead, the DoD and VA have been rolling out all manner of telehealth and Internet counseling programs for treating behavioral health issues. But like many military wives, I was already isolated enough. Skyping a stranger somewhere on the East Coast or pounding out on my keyboard how I felt to the mental health equivalent of the Psychic Friends Network was not that appealing.

A near majority of Guard spouses live in rural areas where Internet service is unreliable and sometimes goes down for days. However, the Guard, like the Army, seems to operate on the assumption that all spouses have their own computers and high bandwidth Internet providers, and relies on technology as the primary portal for resources and communication. Had the Pentagon paid any attention to us at all, they would have known that Guard spouses are less likely than active-duty spouses to use online counseling or resources, including military wives' websites and blogs. We're often not even aware they exist. The vast majority of Reserve spouses are thirty years of age or older, whereas slightly more than half of active component spouses are younger than thirty. Seventy-eight percent of Guard/Reserve spouses work outside of the home, as compared to 53 percent of active-duty spouses, and two-thirds of us never anticipated that our loved ones would be deployed.[29]

"I raised my right hand and took an oath to go wherever this country would send me," said Colonel Kevin Gerdes of the Minnesota

---

29. Booth, "What We Know," Caliber.

Army National Guard. "Micki and my boys did not. They were drafted."

No one expected Army Guard troops would complete the longest tour in Iraq of any branch of service. And if Secretary of Defense Robert Gates can admit that they "pulled a bait-and-switch" on the Guard by repeatedly deploying our citizen soldiers, then certainly the folks at the National Guard Bureau had to have known we never thought we'd ever have a Blue Star flag flying at our homes. The Blue Star flag, or service flag, is displayed by the immediate family of a service member when the country is at war. The banner is composed of a white field bordered by red, and a blue star for each family member in uniform.

The mobilization of the soldier demands a significant shift in the spouse's personal and social identity. Guard spouses, who do not have access to the formal and informal supports and health services available to active-duty spouses living on or near post, consistently report higher levels of stress (68 percent), and poorer levels of coping and support, than active-duty Army and Marine Corps spouses (60 percent). Roughly 40 percent of active-duty military spouses indicated that they felt their mental health had suffered during their service member's deployment, and if the deployment was extended, nearly half reported depression as well as significant anxiety symptoms.[30] A study assessing the effect of deployment on spouses of service members by the Walter Reed Army Institute of Research found that 20 percent of the active-duty Army spouses met the criteria for PTSD, akin to the roughly

---

30. McFarlane, "Military Deployment," *Current Opinion in Psychiatry*.

17 percent of soldiers who screened positive for PTSD after an OIF/
OEF combat deployment.

A handful of other studies have suggested that spouses "appear
to develop mental anxiety or trauma as a result of experiences prior
to, during, and after the service member's deployment. . . . According to both broad and strict screening criteria, spouses and service
members reported similar levels of major depression and generalized anxiety disorder."[31]

Rates of disordered alcohol and drug use among Army wives
with a deployed spouse were almost 50 percent higher than in wives
whose husbands remained at home, particularly among the lower
ranking enlisted.[32] "Clinically significant" parenting stress was
reported by nearly half of parents with a spouse in harm's way.[33]
But the stigma that prevents troops from seeking mental health
help also affects military spouses, many of whom believe that a wife
who asks for help is weak, and "not cut out to be an Army wife."
Even when clinical care is available, 66 percent of the military
spouses who participated in a 2008 American Psychiatric Association survey "worried that looking for assistance for their own issues
would harm their loved one's chances of promotion."

Deborah Mullen spent a lot of time talking to the spouses of
active-duty personnel during her husband's term as chairman of
the Joint Chiefs of Staff. Some of them had sought help, others had
not. But consistently, they would tell her that they were "literally

---

31. Committee on the Initial Assessment, "Preliminary Assessment," Institute
of Medicine.

32. Mansfield et al., "Deployment," *New England Journal of Medicine*.

33. Flake et al., "The Psychosocial Effects," *Journal of Developmental and
Behavioral Pediatrics*.

unable to get up in the morning and get their children to school, [and suffered] depression, anxiety, sleeplessness, and anger."

In fact, "commanders at all levels [are] reporting that Army families are becoming increasingly anxious, even angry, about current and future deployments."[34] We were angry because we were being betrayed by the institution that we depended on for almost everything, and that held the contract for our loved one's lives. The deploy-rinse-repeat churn cycle of multiple and extended deployments, including stop-loss orders, was breaking every policy the military had in place pertaining to dwell time, the required period between tours for units to rest, recuperate, and retrain. For Big Army, the minimum is one year, for Guard it was four years. The troops, and by extension their dependent family members, literally live and die by rules and regulations. To have them repeatedly broken by the very entity that created them was infuriating. But when Lorin got redeployed more than a year before his brigade was supposed to be eligible, there wasn't a single thing I could do about it, and I just wasn't prepared.

"WE'RE LEAVING IN four days," said Lorin, calling from Fort McCoy. It was mid-August 2008, and although I knew it was coming, I still had to pull the cell phone away from my ear so he didn't hear me cry. The twenty-something-year-old soldier sitting behind the desk processing my paperwork for a military ID card glanced up and then quickly away. He knew the drill. I was at the National Guard Armory in Medford, listening to Lorin ramble for a few more minutes before he said good-bye. I tipped my head back to try to stop

---

34. US House of Representatives Committee on Appropriations, "United States Army Military Readiness report."

the tears. Failing at that, I got up and told the soldier I'd be back in a few.

"That's fine, ma'am, take your time," he said.

Now that it had begun, all I could think of was time. Time lost, gone; the time we didn't have any more, wouldn't have for the next year, and all of the time we'd sacrificed to this war in the years before that. But he'd been active-duty Guard for almost a year, ever since he quit his civilian job when, after learning that the 81st could be deployed again at some point in the future, they started making veiled threats about firing him. So I was a soldier's wife in a way I hadn't been before, and I sucked it up and dried my eyes and went back to sit for the picture ID.

"Sorry about that," I said. "He's leaving in a few days."

"No worries, ma'am, it happens a lot. It's hard for the families."

For as much as the military measures readiness, it's been mission failure for National Guard families. The drastic, often unplanned, changes that a Guard member's deployment causes for the spouse and children may be thought of as an acute stressor, which can be particularly harmful to the family unit.[35] We're supposed to be able to go to the Family Readiness Group (FRG) for help, but oftentimes our soldier is gone before that group ever gets started, or we live too many hundreds of miles away to attend.

Most of the meetings are focused on us getting whatever information command wants us to have, fund-raising for supplies, potlucks, making posters and videos to send to our soldiers, and planning a welcome home event. The FRG hasn't changed all that much from

---

35. Wheeler, "Coping Strategies" (conference, American Sociological Association, Montreal, Quebec, August 11, 2006).

the time that forty military wives cobbled together a club, called the Association, during the Revolutionary War.[36] It became known as the "waiting wives club" during WWII and was formalized after the first Gulf War into the FRG. But it's still more about supporting the troops than supporting the families.

The Guard FRG basically disappears between deployments. It's only operational during a mobilization, and it's pretty sketchy even then. The volunteer FRG coordinator for southern Oregon families of the 41st Brigade quit her paid job to focus on supporting Guard families. She received no training, and it was her first deployment but the brigade's second. She left after less than three months. Shortly after her husband deployed, she moved to a different state and filed for divorce, which was a punch in the gut for the families as well as the soldiers overseas. I can only imagine what it was like for the soldier himself. Two volunteers later, about halfway through the deployment, regular monthly meetings began.

I sat in on some of the FRG meetings for the Oregon Army National Guard 41st Brigade during their second tour. Nearly half of the kids and the wives were in counseling, but I found this out after the meetings, not during. The things we really needed to talk about were seldom mentioned, because we'd all heard about, or had already experienced, the negative pushback this could create for our soldier. Some spouses don't trust the military to help them, or they've learned the hard way that it won't. When the wife of a Guard soldier serving his second tour in Iraq was medevaced out and put into MEDHOLD at Fort Lewis, she requested assistance from the FRG to increase the basic allowance for housing. They

36. Dinola, "Stressors," *Military Medicine*.

had relocated shortly prior to the tour, and their housing allowance should have been raised in keeping with the more expensive zip code. Their home was nearly in foreclosure, the wife had two small kids to take care of and a third on the way. When her injured husband was told to shut her up, she asked me to help. She wouldn't go to the FRG anymore because "they don't know what they're doing, and I don't want to get my husband in trouble."

I have lost count of the times my husband has been reprimanded because of me. Silencing the spouses may be an effective strategy in the near-term, but command really needs to stand down on this. Guard spouses are not active-duty wives. We don't know the acronyms and did not get the PowerPoint Ranger tab. We don't receive the deployment binder, peer support, and weekend orientation sessions given to active-duty spouses. There are no officers' spouses' clubs, and we're never going to have a few minutes of kvetching with another spouse from our soldier's unit at the post exchange, because we don't go there.

The gap between formal and informal family support services available to active duty and Guard is comparable to the difference between living in Trump Tower and living in a trailer park, which is exactly what I said to Trooper Sanders, the White House Military Family attaché. He recoiled slightly when I said it, but he didn't correct me. It's clear that while our citizen soldiers have been fully operationalized, the programs and services for their families have not. Fort McCoy's Army Community Services mailed my family support letter in late January of 2009, five months after my husband had shipped out, letting me know that my "Soldier has been mobilized," and directing me to the nearest military installation in Washington State, some four hundred miles away, for assistance.

I needed help *here*, because even though he left months ago, I still could not wrap my mind around him being back at war.

Shortly after the letter arrived, I finally found a psychologist and a psychiatrist, who diagnosed me with an adjustment disorder or "situational depression," a temporary condition triggered by an outside stressor. Situational depression occurs when someone can't adapt to a significant loss or major life change, and it presents with feelings of hopelessness, frequent crying, and a lack of interest in work, activities, and life in general. Between the weekly counseling sessions and Lexapro, I was functional, but just barely. The best I could do was marginally enough to keep me from getting fired, and I was the executive director of Sanctuary One. It was the first year of operation for the fledgling nonprofit that would eventually serve as a care farm offering service learning and therapeutic programs for at-risk, under-served populations, including women veterans and military families. The first order of business was developing policies, programs, and procedures for animal intake, care, and adoption and getting the property in shape to serve as a shelter for abused and abandoned animals. I knew nothing about irrigation, pasture management, or animal rescue. Normally, I'd have buckled down and learned everything I could, as quickly as possible. But my life *wasn't* normal, *I* wasn't normal, and I probably phoned it in more days than not. And that *was* normal for the nearly 22 percent of spouses who confessed that deployment-related stress or psychological issues negatively impacted their job performance.[37]

---

37. Hoge, Castro, and Eaton, "Impact of Combat Duty" (symposium, RTO Human Factors and Medicine Panel, Brussels, Belgium, April 24–26, 2006).

Monique Rizer was a family readiness group leader during much of her husband's fifteen-month mobilization, which included a yearlong tour in Iraq as an Army Reservist. She's been the deputy director of Spouse Programs at the Military Officers of America Association since 2010, and testified to the Senate Veterans Affairs Committee on June 13, 2007, about how her husband's deployment "resulted in a gap in my employment history and changed my future career course. . . . After his two-week leave in January of 2006, I was overwhelmed and sought counseling." Another wife wrote to Monique, "after [my] Reserve spouse's second deployment in four years, with a total of two years away, [I] was compelled to close [my] business." She's looking for a more stable, less challenging job, but is consumed "with worries that he will be called back again."

I couldn't explain what was going on to Sanctuary One's board of directors, which was pretty removed from the wars. I didn't have to explain anything to the four staff members, who were all post-9/11 veterans, Guard soldiers, or family members. I'd implemented a veteran/military family preference hiring policy that had earned me two awards from the National Guard Commission for the Employer Support of the Guard & Reserve. By accident and design, my job provided me an ad hoc family and my only tangible support.

Finding support can be particularly difficult for Guard families, who aren't really part of the greater military family and aren't really civilian, so we never quite feel like we belong. We are embedded in civilian communities who seem to have forgotten there is still a war going on. When I disclosed that my husband was deployed, and some people expressed surprise because they "thought that was over," I didn't know whether to laugh or cry.

The joke among Guard families is, if you want to know who's got a soldier deployed, look at their lawn. When ours got tall, my neighbor called my landlord to complain. Once word got out about it in the local Guard community, Rick McReynolds, a retired Army National Guard colonel, started showing up every week with a mower loaded in the bed of his red Ford pickup. I was so grateful I plied him with baked goods until he asked me to please, stop, he'd taken up running and the cookies were slowing him down; I ignored my neighbor for the rest of the year. My husband could deal with him when he got home.

Guard spouses are very aware of America's apathy about the wars. This matters because it directly influences how well they, and their kids, fare during all phases of deployment. Sabena Vaughan, a former Marine and Iraq war vet and a mother of five, was facing eviction in the winter of 2009 while her Guard husband was deployed. This was illegal under the Soldiers' and Sailors' Civil Relief Act of 1940, which provides protections to reserve components called to active duty, including reduced interest on mortgage payments and credit cards, a delay of all civil court proceedings, and immunity from eviction if the rent was $1,200 per month or less. But many family and service members aren't aware of the law, or lack the legal support and wherewithal to enforce it.

Sabena was able to keep a roof over their heads with the help of the local United Way, but having an established entity to advocate on her behalf might have prevented the whole situation in the first place. I had written a bill to create the Oregon State Military Family Task Force, which could conceivably assist with those types of situations, and asked Sabena to testify. She said:

I wish I could tell you that having been in my husband's shoes as a deployed Marine made my personal experience with Stephan's first deployment easier in some way . . . but I can't. Being the family member of a deployed service member is far, far, more difficult than being the one deployed.

House Bill 3391, championed by State Representative Sal Esquivel (R-Medford), sailed through the legislature, creating the nation's first statewide, state-sponsored task force comprised exclusively of military family members, with support from the Department of Veterans Affairs and the Oregon Military Department. The Military Family Task Force leverages the expertise of military families in assisting policymakers to identify and develop policies to better serve the needs of twenty-first-century military families.

Sal and I had met in 2008 when he spoke at a town hall meeting in Medford and I learned that he had served in Vietnam. I approached him then about sponsoring legislation for military family leave in Oregon. A few other states had already passed legislation that permitted military family members to take up to two weeks of unpaid time off to spend with their service member before or after a deployment, or during the two weeks of R & R.

"Send it to me. I'll take a look and we'll get it drafted," said Sal, without hesitation. He sponsored Oregon HB 2744, which passed unanimously. Sal sat on the Veterans Committee, and he understood what the deployments were doing to the families left behind better than any other politician I had ever met. As the wars had dragged on, the stresses upon all military families, especially those with members in the ground forces, had become both cumulative and exponential. Earlier studies conducted on wives of deployed troops discovered a spectrum of symptoms and diagnoses, including depression, anxiety, insomnia, adjustment disorder, nervousness, headaches, dysphoria, and changes in eating habits. By 2010, some of those diagnoses had spiked 300 percent among wives of active-duty soldiers with long deployments, and were expected to be even higher among Guard and Reserve spouses, who weren't included in the study.[38]

The behavioral health issues on the homefront had become acute and chronic. In the words of Secretary of the Army John McHugh, "If Army leadership doesn't take care of the Army family, then the leadership has failed."

Roger that, Sir. Because as the military spouse goes, so goes the soldier, the marriage, and the kids. We are the heart of the Army, and that heart is breaking.

"I will not break. I cannot break."

Those are the words Tabatha Renz repeated while lying "in bed at night alone during [her husband's] current deployment to Afghanistan." According to an article she wrote for the *PolicyMatters Journal*, they are the same words she said to herself as they fought to find their way back together after his last tour in Iraq. They are:

> [t]he same words uttered by countless other military spouses who are expected to hold everything together despite their lives having been flipped upside down. The Army told me I must be strong, I am the backbone. The uniformed men, one after another, said that if I break, my husband would break. It is my

---

38. Mansfield et al., "Deployment," *New England Journal of Medicine.*

responsibility to make sure that does not happen. Not on this deployment or the next one or anytime in between.[39]

We are not the property of the United States military. We did not sign up, and the only oath we took was likely our wedding vows. But the pressure put on the wives by the DoD and its enforcers to keep the soldier, and the family, together is pervasive and overwhelming.

"At some point, everybody hits the wall," said Kristi Kaufmann in an interview with Richard Sisk for the now-defunct blog *War Report Online*. Kaufmann is the executive director of the Code of Support Foundation supporting the troops and families. Divorced at present, she was married to her soldier, an Army colonel, for the first decade of the wars.

"I've walked the line. I've wanted to fall completely off the grid. . . . I just had to admit to myself that I had to talk to somebody," Kaufmann said.

Talk therapy and medication gave me a much-needed basement, but I had to build my own steps out. I couldn't find them in any of the booklets, brochures, or PowerPoint presentations the military provided. Those things told me what to expect from, and how to care for, my soldier, but they offered nothing for dealing with my own service-related injuries. I had to research and learn through trial and error what I needed to live with and through the war. Because what I didn't need was to be running harder and faster all by myself on a treadmill that was taking me nowhere. So I went to the Flying L Ranch.

---

39. Renz, "Military Spouses," *PolicyMatters Journal*.

TUCKED UP AGAINST I-5 on the outskirts of Ashland, the Flying L is a haven for horses and humans alike, which is exactly what Leslie Hunter had in mind when she purchased the eleven-acre spread. It's got a few rental units for tourists seeking a rustic ranch vacation, as well as several pastures, about a dozen stalls, a round pen, and an arena, and there's almost always something happening. On any given day, it could be a riding camp for kids, or the field castration of a stallion on the front lawn of the big red farm house (much to the chagrin of passersby), which makes the Flying L simultaneously serene and mildly chaotic. Leslie has over three decades of hands-on experience working with horses and has taken thousands of people—from novice to expert riders—on trail rides, horseback riding retreats, and equestrian adventures.

I called and booked a short ride, letting Leslie know I hadn't been on a horse in years. I met her and four other riders at the trailhead on a blustery spring day. Leslie gave me her "down-and-dirty" riding lesson (heels down, toes up, hold the reins like an ice cream cone), and then we mounted up and headed for the hills. The other riders all knew each other and chattered constantly, and while I had nothing to say, between the sound of their voices and the back and forth, up and down movement of the sassy little Arabian mare, the clamp around my soul began to loosen.

I started volunteering at the ranch a few days a week, cleaning stalls, scrubbing greenish-black algae rings from water troughs, and grooming horses. When my work contract with Sanctuary One ended—much to everyone's relief—in May of 2009, I went almost daily, shoveling horse shit for hours on end. I rarely spoke, just kept showing up, hauling wheelbarrows full of manure to the pile, sometimes helping Leslie catch horses, and then tacking them up and going on rides. That little ranch was my Zen garden; I raked patterns in the decomposed granite for hours at a time.

After a while, Leslie gave me my own horse: a handsome, dark bay, half-quarter, half-Morgan, sixteen-year-old gelding named Hickory. It was love at first sight, and most days, when I got to the ranch, I'd call for Hickory at the fence and he'd come galloping up. But not that day, the day I learned my husband wouldn't be coming home for at least six more weeks.

I hadn't seen Lorin for over a year (he'd donated his two-week R & R to a soldier with children), and was desperately lonely for the feel of something solid and alive. So I opened the gate to the pasture, inhaling the soothing scent of timothy and rye grass baking in the sun, and walked out to find Hickory. Tears trickled down my face, but I kept walking until I was standing in the field with a herd of forty horses slowly circling around me, weeping from sheer loneliness, breaking from the weight and ache and exhaustion of this war.

I was so tired, tired of building the wall that would protect me during deployment. I was tired of taking it down brick by brick when he came home, but only halfway, because he might not be home for good. Tired and afraid that maybe this time would be the time I couldn't take it down anymore. I ran out of tears and looked up to see Hickory patiently waiting, the rest of the herd gone back to grazing. I draped myself over Hickory's back, pressed my nose into his mahogany withers, and breathed in the sweaty smell of horse until my heart matched his. I couldn't stand another day with my husband in Iraq.

"Nothing is really what I expected it to be when I married Caynan," wrote Carissa Picard, founder and president of Military

Spouses for Change, in an article for Truthout.org in early 2009. She's a feisty little scrapper with two young boys from a previous marriage. Her husband (now ex), Chief Warrant Officer Caynan Picard, is an active-duty helicopter pilot who served a year in Central America and is now deployed to Iraq. I met Carissa in Washington, DC, when a group of military spouses were lobbying on the Hill for better behavioral health care for military families and legislation to allow portability of professional licensures between states so that military spouses weren't forced to retake exams every time their spouse got reassigned to a new post.

"I never expected to feel so lonely," she said in *Truthout*, "so isolated, so out-of-place and out of sorts all the time, always in that in-between place of neither here nor there, neither this nor that. As an Army wife (excuse me, as six percent are male, Army 'spouse'), you are no longer a civilian, but you are not a soldier either. I don't know what military life was like before 9/11, but I can tell you what it is like now: and it isn't quirky and wacky and 'just like civilian life but different.'"

In advance of Caynan's Iraq deployment, Carissa relocated to Fort Hood, her fifth move during the eight-year marriage, abdicating her license to practice law in another state in the process. She's one of thousands of active-duty military spouses who lose professional licensures and certifications, legal, clinical, educational, etc., when the military issues orders for a new Permanent Change of Station, which forces the family to pick up and move every two to three years on average.

Carissa wrote, "There is no star for a lifetime of sacrificing one's own career and/or educational aspirations to support a service member. In times of peace, as well as war, the military demands that family comes second to the military. ('Army needs come first!') The inability of the service member-parent to participate in parenting brings tremendous challenges to working in an era where two-income households are the norm for maintaining a decent standard of living. The lack of family, friends, and community makes loneliness an expectation, not just a fear."

Yet, everything relating to the service member's spouse and children is unofficial. We're supposed to fall in line with the military lifestyle "without being seen, heard, prepared, paid, or recognized for our service. We are called 'the silent ranks,' but really, we are invisible too." One of the slogans of the post-9/11, all-volunteer Army is "We recruit the soldier but retain the family." But the older saying that "if the Army wanted you to have a family it would have issued you one" remains true. The impact of war on the Household Six (military slang for the civilian spouse who's in charge at home, typically the wife) is "second only to [that] of the service member," said Carissa.

"There are many things that I may not be able to tell you about actual combat, but this much I know is true: by the time this deployment is over, my husband will not be the only veteran in this marriage."

When my husband's deployment finally ended, I found out only because I happened to check the 81st Brigade's website that day. I left multiple messages on Lorin's cell phone and started calling around to the Guard family POCs, pushing it up the chain of command until I got a response and got ahold of Lorin. Per Guard protocol, I should have been informed via the phone tree notification procedure for alerting family members to their soldier's return. With the exception of one phone call about halfway through his deployment, "just to see how you are doing," I received nothing from the Guard FRG for the sixteen months-plus he was engaged in some phase of deployment with the 81st.

Karen Francis's husband, Steve, was a chief warrant officer with the Minnesota National Guard unit that had their one-year tour in Iraq extended several times. Steve's Guard unit stayed in Iraq for nearly two years. In fact, it was the length of that tour that helped convince Steve to go Big Army, figuring if he was going to be gone that long, he might as well go full-time and get full benefits. Since Steve went active duty, she has weathered two more of her husband's deployments. In the process, Karen has become something of a mentor to the younger wives and parents of single soldiers who depended on her thirty-three years of experience as an Army wife, as well as Army mom.

"I became the wailing wall everybody cried on," Francis said. "It seemed like there was always another injury, another death. You can only go to so many funerals. If we're sensible, we get counseling."

But she didn't, even during her toughest time, that hellishly long twenty-two months when Steve was in Iraq.

"I was in Minnesota," said Francis in a phone interview. "Jesus, they don't know the military in Minnesota. There's no base, there's no post, no military presence. I never got a single phone call from anybody, I got no support. I was trying to cobble together my own mental health, but most civilian providers don't know the difference between a colonel and a corporal. I wasn't going to go to someone like the MFLC counselor, a civilian marriage therapist who said that I needed to talk with my husband. No shit! He was in a combat zone half a world away and I got a phone call from him once a week, if I was lucky. The emails just don't cut it." Francis muttered, "Tells me I just need to talk to my husband . . ."

What she ended up doing instead, once she realized she had not been touched in more than a year (Minnesotans, many of them Scandinavian, are not a particularly expressive people; they are not huggers), was begin weekly massage therapy sessions and "talk on the table. I swear, without her, I would've really lost my mind. Looking back on it, I should have gotten counseling, but I couldn't find a counselor who got it. But it's not just any old mental health, but do you speak my language, do you understand me? I think that is so crucial."

As noted by Richard Sisk, blogging about military wives and suicide for the *War Report*, Francis recognizes the counselors "are up to their asses with PTSD and the uniform takes priority" over the wives and other family members. "You're on an emotional roller coaster and things start to fall off the roller coaster. Spouses start to realize they can only do this for so long, and they begin to look for a way out, even suicide."

Since we're not soldiers, there are no official military spouse–specific crisis hotlines, no twenty-four-hour mental health clinics, no pre- or post-deployment mental health questionnaires. The invisible injuries of the silent ranks are unnamed, unnoticed, and unofficial. But if this country is committed to keeping an all-volunteer force, it has to commit to their families. Keeping military families safe and sound and strong pays off by making service members safer, sounder, and stronger, too. It keeps them in uniform longer, too, as family dissatisfaction is one of the primary reasons that troops don't reenlist. What fortifies the families fortifies the forces, which ostensibly was the purpose for the Senate

Armed Services Subcommittee on Personnel Hearing in the summer of 2009.

There was a long line of folks waiting to get seated, but my husband's dog tags were dangling from my neck, and the aides pulled
me from the line and escorted me to a chair directly behind Sheila
Casey, wife of General George Casey, the commanding officer in
Iraq from 2003 to 2006. The hearing had just begun, and already
the twenty-something staffer sitting to my left was nodding off. She
was paid to be here, but you can't pay someone to care. My written
testimony was included in the record, but the families of citizen soldiers don't have a seat at the table for this and most other hearings,
conferences, or town hall meetings on military families.

If there was an A-Team of active-duty officer's wives, the women
at the Senate hearing were on it. Spouses aren't supposed to "wear
the rank" of their service member, but the higher up the soldier
is on the chain of command, the greater the responsibilities and
expectations of the spouse. To a person, they were wearing pearls
and twinsets, or some close cousin thereof. When signaled by the
chair, Sheila Casey, whose husband, George, was then Chief of
Staff of the United States Army; Jennifer A. Mancini, wife of Chief
Petty Officer Steven F. Mancini, United States Navy; and Mrs.
Colleen Smith, married to Colonel Andrew H. Smith, commanding
officer, Marine Barracks, Washington, DC, United States Marine
Corps, took their seats at the table with an economy of time and
movement.

Officers' wives have latitude not available to their loved ones,
but I almost fell off my chair when Mrs. Casey said, "Army families
are sacrificing too much . . . we can no longer expect them to just
make the best of it. This is not a snapshot in time . . . families are

stretched and stressed. Military families are the most brittle part of the force—*everything* is becoming an issue."

She talked about the intolerable pace of deployments, and said that the only reason the uptick in Army divorces wasn't significantly higher is because "our soldiers don't have time to get divorced." Mrs. Casey predicted that "the worst is yet to come," a prediction repeated by every other panelist. In the meantime, "military families are barely hanging on."

Every wife testified that the OPTEMPO was unsustainable. One of the women talked about the day their Marine got back from an overseas mission that'd lasted longer than six months. They were so excited to see him again they'd just left all his gear—rucksack, combat boots, foot locker, and all of the other detritus of deployment—in the front hall of their home, figuring they'd have plenty of time to deal with it later. But that very same day, he got orders for his next deployment. He never unpacked. One after another, the senior spouses and flag wives talked about children growing up without fathers; fathers so emotionally disconnected they would never bond with their kids; military families falling apart.

They testified, and my heart broke for the hundreds of thousands of military spouses who have been virtual widows for the past half a decade and more; for the tens of thousands of military wives and husbands who are embarking on journeys that will not have happy endings, and there's not a single thing they can do about it. I ached for the lives and years we will never get back. The effects of this war will reverberate for generations, and I fear that America, like the slumbering staffer, will sleep through that, too. Military spouses are the hub of the military family; we support our soldiers during deployment, take care of the kids, and are the primary advocates and caregivers of our wounded warriors. Nearly 70 percent of us also hold down jobs. I am tired of hearing about the uncanny resilience of the military spouse, as if I, somehow, have failed by not emerging unscathed from too many years of war, and well more than two years without my husband. Rubber bands are resilient, too, but with time and use, they lose their ability to hold what they once did. When they are stretched beyond their limits, they snap. And so it has been for the military spouses who have committed or attempted suicide since these wars began.

The military has all manner of metrics on the wave of suicides among active-duty troops, but the numbers on suicides and suicide attempts by military family members usually appear only in police records. A 2008 report published by *Military Medicine* found that military spouses presented with mental health concerns, including suicide, at the same rate as service members.[40] In 2009, the Army partnered with the National Institute of Mental Health to conduct the largest study ever of mental health and suicide in the military. But military family members weren't included in the research, which was announced the same summer that several spouses of multiply-deployed husbands were reported dead of self-inflicted injuries.

One of the women was a pregnant forty-year-old Army wife in Fayetteville, North Carolina, who called 911 threatening to harm herself. When the police arrived, she was dead of an apparent self-inflicted gunshot wound. I recall hearing about another, younger Army wife whose husband was deployed and she was alone. The first time she attempted suicide, someone found her. She was put in

---

40. Dinola, "Stressors Afflicting Military Families," *Military Medicine.*

the hospital on post and kept for a few days. Then she was released. Her husband was still deployed, and she went back, alone, to the house where she tried to die.

And she finished what she started.

Another Fort Bragg wife committed suicide by carbon monoxide poisoning, locking herself and her young children in the family car parked in the garage with the engine running. Two months earlier, her husband, a lieutenant colonel in the Army, had been deployed to Iraq, just after the birth of the couple's daughter.

Shortly after PFC Carla Santisteban came back from Afghanistan with the 15th Brigade Support Battalion, 2nd Brigade Combat Team, 1st Cavalry Division, based at Fort Hood, her husband, Rihad Ezzeddine, killed their two girls, ages nine and four, and then killed himself.

During her ex-husband's most recent deployment, Carissa Picard sent an email on May 8, 2009, that revealed:

> Here at Fort Hood, Texas . . . they cannot give me figures on spouse suicides but they . . . see so many attempted suicides in the emergency room that the medical staff have become quite adept at handling them. My theory is that these spouses may have reached the point of needing emergency mental health care and this is the only way to receive it.

When a friend of mine living at Fort Hood learned of her husband's second deployment, she had to be hospitalized due to concerns she might harm herself. Sheena Griffin's marriage was already hurting when her husband, also a soldier at Fort Hood, began training for a deployment to Afghanistan. She called to tell him she was thinking about killing herself and the children. By the time the sheriff's deputies arrived, the house was in flames. When they were finally able to gain entry to the home, they found the two boys, aged eight and nine, and their thirty-six-year-old mother lying in the boys' room, dead from gunshot wounds to the head.

Cassy Walton, wife of Iraq veteran Nils Andersson, also shot herself while living in Texas. Her husband had committed suicide several days earlier, and Cassy followed suit while wearing his dog tags and fatigues.

Forty-year-old Monique Lingenfelter was married to Sergeant Fred Lingenfelter, who was assigned to the 95th Civil Affairs Brigade (Airborne) at Fort Bragg, when she barricaded herself in her house near the post. She had called 911 threatening to harm herself, and for several hours, police outside her home spoke to her over a PA system, trying to persuade her to come out. The officers entered the home after hearing a gunshot and found Monique dead, along with her unborn baby boy.

Jessica Harp, a twenty-seven-year-old Army wife, lit up the Internet with the suicide note she posted to the blog *(Mis)Adventures of an Army Wife*: "If you are reading this, you should know that I am dead. At least I hope I'm dead. It would be awful to fail at your own suicide," but others intervened before she took her life.

There's a clear link between the incidents of Army wives attempting suicide and the deployment tempo of their husbands, according to a study published in the *New England Journal of Medicine*.[41] However, military spouse suicides typically aren't made public, so the extent of the problem isn't known. The Army doesn't

----

41. Mansfield et al., "Deployment and the Use of Mental Health Services," *New England Journal of Medicine*.

track suicides by military family members because most occur "off post or involve [family members of] reservists or guardsmen," said Army spokesman Lieutenant Colonel Christopher Garver on July 5, 2009.[42] After the wife of a soldier deployed with the 172nd was suspected of committing suicide on post in Schweinfurt, Germany, where her husband was stationed, Army officials launched an investigation into her death, according to Lieutenant Colonel Eric Stetson, 172nd Infantry Brigade rear detachment commander.

In 2010, senior spouse Deborah Mullen blew the whistle on the growing incidence of suicides and suicide attempts by military family members, and the military's failure to respond. This time, when she asked Army leaders to release records on military spouse suicides, she went public with their answer:

"I was stunned when I was told there are too many to track," said Mrs. Mullen.

---

42. Robson, "Some Seek Mental Health Checks," *Stars & Stripes*.

CHAPTER FOUR

I Am Not the Enemy

"WHO HASN'T BEEN STRANGLED by their husband?" asked one of the dozen or so Army and Marine Corps spouses on the conference call, all of whom were also wives of multiply-deployed active-duty and Guard combat veterans. After several moments of silence, during which each of us was very likely reliving the moment it happened, another wife whispered, "I know, right?"

After a few more seconds of empty air space, we resumed talking about an upcoming event for spouses in DC and whether we could afford the plane fare. All the while, I was waiting for someone to say something more, wondering why I didn't. I used to facilitate a support group for victims of domestic violence, but I still couldn't talk about what happened that night. I tried to, initially, but was told "I don't want to hear it," or asked, "What did *you* do?"

What I had done was tell my husband that, during his last deployment, another man had come on to me. It began when I was lobbying on the Hill and testified before the House Committee on Veterans Affairs. Afterward, Congressman Bob Filner (D-California), the committee chair, grabbed me in his office and gave me a quick peck on the lips. I was stunned speechless. Filner scuttled to the other side of the room while I sat there, flustered. I spent the next year trying to avoid physical contact with the congressman while keeping in touch via phone and email. He knew I was married, that my husband was serving his second tour in Iraq, and still he made the occasional comment with sexual overtones. I'd ignore them, or dance around them. Sometimes I'd remind him that his emails and voice mails left an electronic trail and tell him to stop, but he didn't seem to care. I was trying to advance legislation and was deeply concerned about not offending one of the most powerful people in the veterans' community. But Filner had a pay-to-play policy, and I refused to pony up, effectively ending my advocacy work with the House Veterans Committee. Filner later lost his Congressional seat, but was elected mayor of San Diego in 2012. After less than a year in office, he resigned when multiple women made allegations of sexual harassment. Filner pled guilty to charges of false imprisonment and battery.

Many years before, the man who supervised my company's government contracts put his paws on me. Lorin and I had been dating for a while, and when I told him about it, he got mad. But that time he had gotten mad at my harasser. This time he turned on me.

IT HAPPENED ABOUT A year or so after Lorin finished that last deployment in September of 2009. He was supposed to move to Medford then, but during his post-deployment leave he was asked if he'd like to spend a year on Active Duty Orders (ADOS) and he jumped at the chance. He didn't have a civilian job to go back to, and as much as I wanted him with me and out of the Army, the uniform had a stronger hold on him than I did. If this was what he wanted, and was going to make him happy, what was another year apart? At least he'd be in the neighboring state, and not in a combat zone half a world away.

Lorin started ADOS at Joint Base Lewis-McChord, First Army, Division West, tasked with training soldiers for deployment to Iraq and Afghanistan. About once a month, he'd drive or fly to Medford, and I went up to our place in Kent a couple of times. By this point, he had about six weeks remaining on orders, and had already turned in his resignation paperwork. When he was done at the end of November 2010, he would hang up his uniform after twenty-seven years. He'd come to Medford on a long weekend pass, and it was the night before he had to leave and go back to post.

We were relaxing on the couch after dinner, drinking wine, laughing, trying to catch up. We both wanted one perfect night; as if one night could begin to make up for all of the nights we had missed. And then talk turned to war, his *and* mine. I mentioned the Filner thing in an off-hand, happened a long time ago, how weird was that kind of way, but Lorin lunged across the couch like he was on fire. The next thing I knew, he had me pinned down and was strangling me. His thumbs were digging into either side of my windpipe, bearing down, cutting off my air. His face was maybe four inches from mine and he was yelling. I knew he was, but I couldn't hear him. All I could hear was a pounding, roaring noise, and I didn't know if it was coming from him or inside my head. Then the first few flickers of black passed before my eyes.

Oh my God, I could die. What do I do?

Don't move, don't say a word. You just lay here like your life depends on it.

Don't *look at him! Who is that?*

Who is *that?*

Don't move, just hold on, hold on . . .

Then: *Oh, Christ, what will they tell my dad? Oh Daddy, I'm sorry—*

And he let go and got up.

I stayed exactly where I was. *Where's Kobe* (my Chow Chow)*? I swear to God if he hurts the dog I will kill him. Where are his weapons?* Lorin was raging, cursing me, stomping around, and slamming doors and drawers and walls. He opened the back door.

I vaulted off the couch, fumbled for my keys and cell phone, and raced toward the bedroom, where my dog was sleeping on the floor. I grabbed the cat from the foot of the bed and locked the bedroom door. I ran into the master bathroom and locked that door, too. I crouched in the far corner of the bathroom, between the toilet and the wall, vibrating with fear, listening for the sound of his footsteps in the hall. I took short, shallow breaths, trying to be as quiet as possible, waiting for him to break down the door.

If I called the police, it would be the end of his career, the end of us. And maybe it already was, but I couldn't call the cops. So I called my battle buddy in the middle of the night. Her phone rang, no answer. I disconnected and tried again, same result. On the third call, at 2:12 a.m., she picked up.

"If you don't hear from me in the next twenty-four hours, call the police," I said as quietly and urgently as I could and hung up. She called back—I didn't answer. I turned the ringer off. No time to talk, and I didn't want him to hear it. I spent the rest of the night on lock down. The next morning, Lorin apologized repeatedly, but I was having none of it.

"Pack your shit and go. I cannot stand the sight of you right now. You could have killed me last night."

"I know," he said. "I'm sorry."

"Sorry doesn't cut it; sorry doesn't *begin* to cut it. I don't want to see you or speak to you until you've gotten help. Leave."

I barricaded myself in the bedroom again until he was gone. I went to my computer to see what resources I could pull up and checked my email. There was one from my battle buddy: *I cannot, for the love of God, imagine what you were thinking when you called last night. Please tell me.*

I called her and said, "Lorin tried to strangle me last night. I called you from the bathroom. I locked myself in with the pets. I didn't want him to hurt my puppy. I'm sorry I called. I was just so scared, and I didn't have anyone else to call. I couldn't call the cops."

"How are you now?" she asked. "Where is he?"

"I'm okay, but my throat hurts a little. He's gone. I made him leave this morning. I told him I didn't want to hear from him until he had talked to a counselor or gotten into some kind of treatment. I said that I didn't feel safe with him, and I couldn't . . . I wasn't . . ." I sobbed, hiccupping out words, "I wasn't sure if I ever would again . . . Goddamn it. Goddamn this war."

I called my battle buddy a lot over the next several days. Mostly I talked, and she listened. I spent much of my time at home, shell-shocked and alone. I went to a civilian counselor a few times, but she just kept telling me to leave, lecturing me on the typical cycle of domestic abuse, the power and control wheel, and the escalation of intimidating, threatening behaviors. I explained that this wasn't typical, and then gave up and tried to find someone who understood the military and veterans.

I called the military chaplain at Fort Lewis and the commanding officer of the Badger Battalion Lorin was attached to and left several messages, but they never called back. I called the White City VA and asked if they had support programs for wives of combat veterans. They didn't. I called Military OneSource, the free counseling assistance program provided by the Department of Defense. When I told her what had happened, the lady at the other end of the line started to cry.

"I'm sorry," she sniffled. "I get these calls all the time. I can't help you. Unless you authorize a report, I can't authorize assistance. There are so many of you going through this, and we just can't help if you won't file a report."

"I called the chaplain and the CO, but nobody ever calls me back. I don't want to file a formal report right now, so what am I supposed to do?" I asked.

"I don't know. I'm sorry."

I thanked her and she was still crying when I hung up.

I reached out to a friend who was married to an Afghanistan war veteran. She said she and her husband had gotten into so many screaming matches, hitting and throwing things at each other, that the cops had been called several times, and once she ended up going to a domestic violence shelter. Staff at the shelter told her that her husband made too much money for her to stay there, and they didn't have programs for wives of veterans, anyway. I got the same answer when I contacted a local agency that worked with victims of domestic violence and asked about services specific to veterans' partners. So I didn't know what else to do. I hadn't spoken with

Lorin for a week. Sometimes I wasn't sure I wanted to. But when he finally called, I picked up.

"Hey," he said, "how are you?"

"About as well as can be expected, given that you tried to strangle me," I snapped. "I am so hurt, and so furious with you. I still can't believe you did that, and everything I know tells me I should leave."

"I'm sorry, I am so, so sorry. I never wanted to be that guy, and now I am."

"Yeah, you are that guy. You became that guy when you tried to kill me. What are you going to do about it?"

"I called a domestic violence hotline here and told them what happened. She asked if it had happened before, I said no, and she had a bunch of other questions. She said there's a men's group for abusers, but that I didn't really fit the abuser profile, so she didn't think I needed to go. I'm checking around, but I'm working about ten hours a day and I can't call from work. I checked with the insurance, and they said that since I'm active duty, on post, they won't pay for me to see a private therapist at night. I have to see someone at the base medical center, and there's no way I'm doing that. My only other option is the VA, but I can't really sneak off for three hours in the middle of the day."

"Look, I know you don't fit the profile, but you better figure something out," I insisted. "You scared the hell out of me the other night, and you made me something I never wanted to be, either. And just so you know, I called the chaplain, and I also left a message with the CO. I haven't filed a report, but I'm thinking about it."

THE DoD PROVIDES TWO reporting options for victims of domestic violence: restricted and unrestricted. Restricted reports are not shared with law enforcement and command, and there will be no investigation or administrative action taken against the offender. Once a report is filed with a Family Advocacy Program (FAP) victim advocate, clinician, or supervisor, or a military health-care provider, the victim can receive victim advocacy services, medical care, counseling, safety planning, and information about military protective orders and military and local civilian community resources. Restricted reporting is not an option in the event of child abuse, or where the victim is deemed to be at imminent risk of serious harm. In those cases, the branch of service will provide emergency relief funds to enable the victim and any children to relocate.

Unrestricted reports initiate an official investigation of the abuse, and can be made with the service member's command, the FAP, or law enforcement. It provides the victim all of the same support services available when filing a restricted report while also allowing for command participation in supporting and protecting the victim and gives command the discretion to take administrative action against the offender.

Most family victims of veteran violence don't file reports with the police or with command. Most of us don't file them at all, and virtually never after the first incident. I didn't, because I didn't want his nearly three decades of honorable service tarnished at the very end of his career. I didn't want that one awful act to define him, and us. I didn't file because I hadn't waited for so many years, and sacrificed so much, for things to end like this. I didn't file because he promised me he would get counseling for his PTSD, and because whoever was behind his eyes that night was not the man I married. I didn't file a report because he'd been to war, and I hadn't, and in the fall of 2010, returning veteran violence was a conversation few were willing to have.

The military is stepping up domestic violence programs and education at military installations, but the tacit pressure on spouses within the active-duty and retired military culture and from much of the civilian population to remain silent is especially intense during a time a war. In addition to the potential loss of income, housing, health and retirement benefits, and other services, speaking out about veteran violence at home seems to be perceived as more of a betrayal than the violence itself.

Four Fort Bragg wives were killed over a six-week period in the summer of 2002, three of whom were married to Special Forces operatives recently returned from Afghanistan. After the initial spate of press, their deaths dropped off the radar and from the country's consciousness. Each time a military spouse was murdered, there'd be a blurb about it in the local news, but it rarely received national coverage. Even when the war came home as hard as it did in October of 2006.

Zackery Bowen was a twenty-eight-year-old Iraq war veteran who, by all accounts, redeployed a profoundly changed person. As documented in *Shake the Devil Off*,[43] Bowen was diagnosed with PTSD, and he grew increasingly moody and volatile as his marriage unraveled. He became romantically involved with Addie Hall, a bartender in New Orleans, Louisiana, who went missing about a week before Bowen jumped to his death from a hotel rooftop in the Big Easy. In Bowen's pocket was a suicide note directing police to his apartment. "LOOK IN THE OVEN," was spray painted on the

---

43. Brown, *Shake the Devil Off*.

wall in Bowen's unit, and when the New Orleans homicide officers lowered the oven door, they discovered roasted human legs. Bowen had murdered Hall and tried to get rid of her body by cutting it into pieces, stashing her torso in the fridge, and boiling her head in a pot. We talked about the horror of it in hushed tones in my little circle of military spouse friends, sickened, angry, and afraid of what these wars were doing to our men. And what it might mean for us.

Since 2003, there has been a 75 percent increase in reports of domestic violence in and around Fort Hood, where the number of soldiers diagnosed with PTSD rose from 310 in 2004 to 2,445 in 2009. As mentioned by Karen Houppert in *Mother Jones* in 2005, between 2002 and 2004, Fort Bragg alone documented 832 victims of deployment-related domestic violence.[44] Equally telling was the 2010 Military Family Lifestyle Survey, the second annual poll conducted by Blue Star Families of military families with a loved one currently in the service. That survey included a slate of questions about returning-veteran violence. I don't think there was a single question on that topic on their first poll. Maybe there was and I wasn't paying attention, because it didn't pertain to me then. Now that it does, maybe I've got a bad case of Baader-Meinhof (or Blue Car) syndrome: the experience where an idea or thing you just found out about suddenly seems to show up everywhere. Or maybe it's just that I remember that night. I always will.

After that night, I was more careful. I watched. I felt like I was always watching. When he would get mad, I would watch like my life depended on it. I looked for whatever it was in his eyes that

---

44. Houppert, "Base Crimes," *Mother Jones*.

in an email. "I'm not proud of my decision, but I had no choice but to stay. I had cancer and needed help. I told him if he did it again we were done."

For more than five years, Karen tried to forgive and forget. She went to counseling but her husband refused, although he lay off the booze for a while. His drinking became an issue again in 2012, when he was arrested for a drunken bar brawl. Several months later, Karen was in their bedroom texting a girlfriend when he barged in and accused her of texting another man. Things escalated quickly, and in the fight that ensued, her husband of more than two dozen years punched her reconstructed breast and slammed her head and arm in the door.

"This time," she said, "I called the police. He was arrested and one week later I filed for divorce."

Mary Hamm[47] thought about divorce in the year or so since her husband brutally attacked her, but told me that, "[I]f he would initiate the divorce it would be so much easier. My husband never wanted to resolve things by getting counseling. He said he would, but it never was a priority. He didn't want to get in trouble, and I don't want him to be punished either."

Mary's husband is Army aviation, and he was diagnosed with PTSD during a deployment to Afghanistan that began in 2012. His psychological issues downrange were so severe he was shipped back to the States at the urging of the military chaplain. Mary said her husband was prescribed an array of medications to help him deal with depression, anger, insomnia, and other symptoms of PTSD, but the military did not mandate counseling. According to Mary,

---

47. Name has been changed to protect identity of victim and children.

nearly two decades when her husband served a fifteen-month tour in Afghanistan. When he came back in 2007, she immediately saw a change in him. Karen contacted me several years later, long after his hostility and drinking had begun to escalate. She had initially reached out to the local VA for help, hoping to get her husband into counseling, but he was put on a three-month waiting list. During that time, Karen was diagnosed with stage 2 breast cancer and discovered that she carried the faulty BRCA gene. A bilateral mastectomy was recommended, and she began a course of chemotherapy prior to surgery scheduled for the end of the year.

It was Christmas Eve, a week before her surgery, and she was getting one of her two daughters ready for bed. She started the shower for her nine-year-old, sat on the ledge of the tub, and began to sob. (PTSD combat vets tend to remain calm when another veteran gets teary, but frequently become highly aggressive when their spouse or child cries, so most of us learn to hide it.) Infuriated by her crying, her husband, who had been drinking all evening, barged into the bathroom and threw her against the wall, threatening to kill her until their daughter started yelling that the water was cold. Karen and the girl put out a plate of cookies for Santa, and then Karen tucked her into bed. When she walked out of her youngest child's room, her husband was waiting and dragged her down the hallway. He told Karen that she would ruin their daughter's Christmas if she called the police and punched his fist through their bedroom door, repeatedly threatening to kill her if she called the cops.

"He was so drunk and out of control that I made an excuse to get away and called our friend, a military chaplain. He left his family and stayed with Randy all night calming him down," wrote Karen in an email. "I'm not proud of my decision, but I had no choice but to stay. I had cancer and needed help. I told him if he did it again we were done."

For more than five years, Karen tried to forgive and forget. She went to counseling but her husband refused, although he lay off the booze for a while. His drinking became an issue again in 2012, when he was arrested for a drunken bar brawl. Several months later, Karen was in their bedroom texting a girlfriend when he barged in and accused her of texting another man. Things escalated quickly, and in the fight that ensued, her husband of more than two dozen years punched her reconstructed breast and slammed her head and arm in the door.

"This time," she said, "I called the police. He was arrested and one week later I filed for divorce."

Mary Hamm[47] thought about divorce in the year or so since her husband brutally attacked her, but told me that, "[I]f he would initiate the divorce it would be so much easier. My husband never wanted to resolve things by getting counseling. He said he would, but it never was a priority. He didn't want to get in trouble, and I don't want him to be punished either. "

Mary's husband is Army aviation, and he was diagnosed with PTSD during a deployment to Afghanistan that began in 2012. His psychological issues downrange were so severe he was shipped back to the States at the urging of the military chaplain. Mary said her husband was prescribed an array of medications to help him deal with depression, anger, insomnia, and other symptoms of PTSD, but the military did not mandate counseling. According to Mary,

---

47. Name has been changed to protect identity of victim and children.

"I knew he was out of control based on our conversations and his coldness toward me. He was a different person. They gave him more meds. I thought he was better."

They had a baby girl a little less than a year later, and when the infant was about two months old, Grandma babysat and the couple went to a friend's house for a party. They both had too much to drink and went into the guest bedroom to sleep it off. Mary awoke several hours later, alone, and discovered her husband vomiting in the bathroom.

"All of a sudden he grabbed me by my throat and told me that it was my fault he did this," wrote Mary in an email to me on February 25, 2014. "I was shocked and I didn't lash back but instead said 'sorry' as he strangled me. He let go and I continued to clean up. When I was done we were walking down the stairs and he was still being mean and rough. I told him to stop and that I was sorry. He slammed me by my throat again onto the staircase. My head hit hard, [and] I blacked out for only a second. He told me to get up and I was slow to move. I cried and asked him to please stop. He told me no and that he was going to kill me tonight."

Mary ran out the front door and to the street, her husband on her heels. He caught up to her, hitting her on the side of the head, and then grabbed her arm and dragged her back toward the house. When she told him she was scared and wanted to go home, he beat her unconscious. When she came to, she warned him that, "If we don't go inside and calm ourselves that the cops will come. He blamed me, and said that I'm going to cost him his job. That the cops will shoot him, and our daughter won't have a mother or a father. I was terrified."

The next day, her husband claimed he didn't remember a thing. Mary can't forget.

"I'm crying all the time and having nightmares. But at the same time he's been through so much and I know he's not the typical wife beater. I'm heartbroken because everything I read says to leave him and that he's a monster and will do it again. I'm aware I could've died. My head still aches and it's been a few days, and my body is sore. I had a C-section and it could've been bad had I struggled against him, but I let him batter me around. Up until this point I felt very loved and respected. He still tells me he loves me and he's sorry and will do what it takes to fix it. I don't want to leave him but I always told myself I cannot tolerate someone who abuses others and I would never stick around like all those other women. But now that it has happened I'm torn and find that my situation *is* different. He's not a repeat offender and he swears it was the alcohol and he will never drink again. I don't know what to do."

Mary ultimately made a restricted report with the Family Assistance Program on post, confiding in them about both the violence and the PTSD. The FAP told her that she was too emotionally unstable and that her husband was better off with the baby. She was denied her request for marriage counseling, and the FAP requested a thirty-day no contact order without informing either Mary or her husband. Mary said, "They overstepped their boundaries, and used the domestic violence *against* me. The FAP worker who was making all these calls was rightfully let go."

Mary has let the incident go, too, and put it behind her as much as she can. She's got a toddler and the family recently PCS'd (permanent change of station) to a post in Georgia, where she has no friends or relatives or community support. Mary refuses to ask for help again from the military, which is losing the battle to get out in front of the unprecedented rates of service-related (or service-connected) domestic violence. And that's how we should be categorizing abuse by troops with deployment-related mental health problems.

The military classified the 2006 suicide of Air Force Sergeant Jon Trevino, a medic diagnosed with PTSD after multiple tours in Iraq and Afghanistan, as "service related." He killed his wife before he killed himself, making her murder "service related," too. The exact numbers of service-connected domestic violence are unknown, even to the Pentagon, whose data only reflects child abuse and domestic abuse reported to the DoD FAP and criminal offenses in the Defense Incident-Based Reporting System for active-duty service branches. They do not include Guard/Reserve or reports filed with civilian agencies. Given that all domestic abuse is self-reported, it is generally accepted that it is underreported. Only one-quarter of the 1.3 million American women who suffer intimate partner violence every year report the assault to the police, according to the National Coalition Against Domestic Violence (NCDV).

"In family-style cultures that promote loyalty above other concerns, victims are often disinclined to seek safety," said NCDV executive director Ruth Glenn. Nowhere is that more true than in the military, and the accuracy of DoD statistics on domestic violence has been debated by advocates, the Government Accountability Office, and even military officials. But the spouses know what's happening in military homes. I received an email from one Army wife that read:

> [T]he sad fact is that domestic violence is epidemic among military families. It is so bad that when my husband returned from Iraq, I would get a weekly call on my cell phone from a social worker within the military who was calling me for the sole

reason of making sure that I was not feeling endangered by my husband . . . [who has] never abused me. I have gratitude to the military for bothering to contact me to make sure that he wasn't, and for sending me information on how to get help if I need it. But how many other professions need to have employees whose job it is to call the wives of other employees to make sure they're not getting beat?

When troops are in garrison during peacetime, military rates of domestic violence may be comparable to civilian rates, although some studies, including one by Heyman and Neidig in 1999, suggest that active-duty males perpetrate domestic abuse more frequently than their civilian counterparts. But even as the overall frequency of domestic abuse in the United States was on the decline, falling 64 percent from 1994 to 2010, according to the Department of Justice, levels of intimate partner violence within the post-9/11 military and veterans' communities began to explode. Before 9/11, the Army received roughly thirty-five to fifty cases of domestic abuse a month. By 2005, they were fielding approximately 143 cases a week, a twelve-fold increase. As documented by Karen Jowers in an *Air Force Times* article on October 31, 2005, the Pentagon reported that there was also a demonstrable escalation in the severity of violence between 2001 and 2005. Some studies have found a direct correlation between the length of the deployment and the level of brutality. Researchers have also found that there is a significant probability of aggression for soldiers who had deployed as compared to those who had not.[48] It stands to reason that the studies that will be conducted—and that are likely under way—on the incidence and

---

48. McCarroll et al., "Deployment," *Military Medicine*.

severity of spousal aggression by soldiers who have served anywhere from two to twelve combat tours, ranging in length from ten to twenty-two months, will show astounding levels of both.

CBS News reported on January 29, 2009, that rates of domestic abuse in Killeen, Texas, home of Fort Hood, had risen by more than 75 percent since 2001, and of the 2,500 cases reported to Killeen cops in 2008, fully half of them involved military personnel. According to the 2010 United States Census, the city's population was 127,921, and the population of Fort Hood was 29,589. Calls to the National Domestic Violence Hotline from people affiliated with the military more than tripled from 2006 to 2011. According to the *New York Times*, between 2006 and 2009, the number of soldiers at Fort Carson near Colorado Springs, Colorado, charged with domestic violence, rape, and sexual assault spiked by nearly 275 percent.[49] A 2010 DoD report showed that domestic abuse in the Army skyrocketed by 177 percent as an increasing number of soldiers returned from lengthy, repeat tours in Iraq and Afghanistan and levels of PTSD began to rise.

As stated in a 2008 *New York Times* article by Lizette Alvarez and Deborah Sontag, research has found veterans diagnosed with PTSD are "'significantly more likely to perpetrate violence toward their partners,' with over 80 percent committing at least one act of violence in the previous year, and almost half at least one severe act," including strangulation, stabbing, and shooting.[50] This is more than fourteen times higher than the general civilian population.

---

49. Alvarez and Frosch, "A Focus on Violence," *New York Times*.

50. Alvarez and Sontag, "When Strains on Military Families Turn Deadly," *New York Times*.

Traumatic brain injury, which is considered the signature wound of the post-9/11 wars, also increases the likelihood of aggression and impulsivity and is linked to veteran domestic violence. And that violence has markers that distinguish it from the cycle of violence perpetrated by batterers, under the standard definition of domestic violence recognized nationally and internationally.

Unlike typical civilian domestic violence, VIPV often occurs in the absence of an attempt to exert financial control; it is an explosion of violence, rather than an escalation. There is generally no "honeymoon" period after the event, as the veteran withdraws in shame, and the violence is more likely to be lethal or potentially lethal in severity. They are, after all, trained to kill and use lethal force, and a combat veteran very likely already has.

There is a direct correlation between PTSD severity and intimate partner violence severity, according to April Gerlock, PhD, who has conducted VA-funded research of veterans and their partners. She's one of the nation's leading investigators of veteran interpersonal violence, has worked for the Veterans Administration for three decades, and is married to a Vietnam veteran.

"I have a lot of empathy for the veteran," said Gerlock during an interview with me, but she is concerned that the couples' counseling available through the VA sends a message to the spouses (who are frequently the primary caregivers) of wounded warriors that: "You need to put up with this because this person's disabled." Gerlock continued, "The VA is in a fantastic position to address all of this, but there is nothing systemic available."

They are working on it. In January of 2014, Jennifer Broomfield, LISW, JD, was hired as the VA's first domestic and intimate partner violence program manager. Broomfield's job involves coordinating and providing training and services, including a continuing education seminar titled Understanding Domestic Violence/ Intimate Partner Violence (DV/IPV) for Caregivers. It's delivered online through the VA's eHealth University, and I was enrolled, along with what appeared to be thirty or so other caregivers, mostly wives, based on the chat room activity.

"The VA DV/IPV assistance program is in its infancy," said Broomfield, "but eventually there will be DV coordinators in every VA hospital who will assess, screen, and educate veterans, caregivers, and staff, and provide referrals to community resources." As part of the VA's Plan for Implementation of the Domestic Violence/Intimate Partner Violence (DV/IPV) Assistance Program, which was disseminated to VA network directors on September 11, 2014, the VA will be piloting a program for veterans who have engaged in DV/IPV. Plans are also under way for a specialized couple's therapy program for vets who have committed situational couple's violence, the kind of intimate partner violence that occurs when a disagreement becomes an angry argument and then escalates into violence.

Broomfield has said, "IPV isn't a diagnosis; it's a social phenomenon," a statement that acknowledges the link between IPV and poorer physical and mental health, including possible PTSD. The percentage of Iraq War veterans diagnosed with PTSD is already more than double that reported in Vietnam War vets. While the VA has treatment programs for veterans suffering PTSD, there are no such programs for veterans' caregivers who are suffering PTSD as a result of veteran domestic violence. As of now, the VA lacks a functional plan to provide in-house help for victims of veteran partner abuse. But if veterans' issues are so unique that they require an institution whose sole purpose is to serve them, and if VIPV is so distinctive and prevalent and has service-specific mitigating factors, then it makes sense that the VA would be providing programs for the caregivers, too.

The confluence of unprecedented levels of TBI, PTSD, and other mental health disorders—conditions requiring assistance from the majority of caregivers—puts this newest generation of veterans at extremely high risk of perpetrating violence in the home. Throw alcohol into the mix, and VIPV becomes a probability rather than a risk.

Xenia Zimmerman was warned she was at risk by the men who served in her husband's platoon in Afghanistan. They pulled her aside after they got home and told her that her husband was "crazy, he did some crazy shit over there, and you need to get away from him."

But she stayed and was strangled to the point of unconsciousness. Then he held a gun to her head, twice, and still she refused to leave. It wasn't until he "popped [her] child" that she packed up her twenty-month-old son and a few of their belongings, filed for divorce, and relocated within the state. The staff sergeant was already awaiting trial for stalking, harassment, domestic abuse, and a violation of the protective order, which also covered "the child of the protected person." But Xenia's estranged husband still had visitation rights, although the transfer of the child would be "determined on a case by case basis and will be conducted at a neutral location with local law enforcement present or with a social services representative present." So she couldn't leave the state, and she couldn't refuse visitation, and she'd spent what little money she had to pay the attorney who filed the divorce papers.

Xenia had been unemployed since the baby came; she didn't have the money to hire another lawyer. She'd reached out to social services, to Court Appointed Special Advocates, and other advocacy groups, like the Louisiana Chapter of Bikers Against Child Abuse. They all said the same thing: "We're sorry, but we can't help you." So she called me one afternoon (I'd received an email from her many months earlier and replied with my phone number, but hadn't heard from her again), scared witless because her husband had found out where she was staying and was making threats against her and her family.

"Is there a local women's shelter you can go to?" I asked.

"We've already been there," she replied, "but his doctor said that my son's immune system is so weak that if we go back to the DV shelter, he'll end up in hospital, so we can't go back. I can't leave the state because of the visitation rights, but after he sees his dad, he always comes home crying. My baby cries when he sees men in uniform."

I started reaching out to every resource I could think of, including Rosemary Freitas Williams, the Deputy Assistant Secretary of Defense for Military Community and Family Policy. Rosemary suggested I tell Xenia to call Military OneSource, and then directed me to contact the Military Spouse JD Network and drop her name and see if they will help. They would not, so I contacted another half-dozen groups, posted on Facebook, and had a friend in New Orleans put out a call for aid on the church grapevine. I was more than a thousand miles away, and there wasn't much more I could do.

Xenia's estranged husband liked to tell her that he could kill her and get away with it because he "has a PTSD card in his back pocket, and he'll use it." In between two combat tours, the staff sergeant had racked up six criminal charges, including assault, criminal mischief, and vehicle theft since he enlisted in 2006, but he's still wearing the uniform. The military was well aware of his charges, but the court-martial system was back-burnered while conducting war on two fronts. A September 2010 article in the *Army Lawyer* stated that, whether at home or away, "commanders and judge advocates exercised all possible alternatives to avoid the crushing burdens of conducting courts-martial. . . . By any measure—numbers of cases tried, kinds of cases, reckoning for service member crime, deterrence of other would-be offenders—it cannot be said that the American court-martial system functioned effectively."[51]

The staff sergeant was considered dangerous enough for the Army to issue emergency relief funds for Zimmerman to get away, according to a memo written by Major Hollywood, JA, Special Victims Prosecutor. But like nearly 87 percent of soldiers found to have committed spouse abuse and child abuse and neglect over a six-year period, according to a 2010 Army report, he was never referred for counseling, and he can still carry a weapon. The military has a zero-tolerance policy on domestic violence, but every year, more than eight thousand military families file complaints of domestic violence with the military, according to DoD data. Thousands more show up on the police blotter, and it's likely that many thousands more are never reported or recorded. (The VA has no tracking mechanism for victims of VIPV, whose numbers must be mind-boggling.) But cases of spouse abuse at Fort Bragg still reached the danger zone in January of 2013, when reports spiked to more than two

---

51. Rosenblatt, "Non-Deployable," *Army Lawyer*.

times the Army rate, according to data compiled by the Fort Bragg Community Health Promotion Council. I cannot get precise figures on exactly what the Army rate is, but I do know this: That is not what zero tolerance looks like.

A 2010 Yale study on the effects of war on men and the American homefront found that Vietnam combat vets were almost 4.4 times more likely to have abused a spouse or partner than other men. They were also 6.4 times more likely to have PTSD. The researcher's logarithm concluded that combat veterans are responsible for almost 21 percent of domestic violence nationwide, mediated by the development of PTSD. This is comparable to the fact that veterans alone account for 20 percent of suicides in the United States. When service member suicides surpassed combat casualties, the military mandated a Stand Down on Suicide. This country calls the problem of veteran suicide an "epidemic," funding research, convening conferences, creating new programs, hotlines, and therapies aimed at prevention, intervention, and reducing the stigma of seeking mental health care. But we don't talk about VIPV at all, effectively ensuring that the catastrophic consequences remain largely unacknowledged and unaddressed. There have been days that service-connected domestic violence deaths on the homefront have surpassed troop deaths on the war front, but there's yet to be a Stand Down on Domestic Violence by the DoD or VA.

The Pentagon maintains it can revamp itself and convened "two multi-day-long Rapid Improvement Events, one on child abuse and neglect in November 2013, and one on domestic abuse/intimate partner violence in January 2014," according to Lieutenant Commander Nate Christensen, a DoD spokesman. Commander Christensen was responding to my request for information about how the military was handling the rapid rise of serious domestic violence by service members, and stated that the events were "a Department initiative based on the desire to increase prevention efforts across the nation's military community."

That's a good first step, but prevention should include targeted outreach and tailored interventions for the Iraq and Afghanistan veterans struggling with PTSD and alcohol abuse, 54 percent of whom had engaged in "acts of physical aggression . . . or severe violence," including prolonged physical assault, and often involving the use or threat of using a knife, gun, or other deadly weapon in the preceding twelve months. That's seven times higher than veterans without those issues, according to the joint study by VA and University of North Carolina researchers,[52] and if we can allow for underreporting of abuse by victims, I think we can assume under-reporting by perpetrators as well. The VA/UNC study acknowledged that, had researchers relied solely on veterans' reports, they would have missed "20 percent of cases positive for violence toward others."

Congress has to get serious about moving the Pentagon and the VA from a zero-tolerance policy to practice on service-connected domestic abuse. Because in the debate about whether returning troops with PTSD who commit domestic assault deserve compassion or conviction (how about both?) we seem to have lost sight of the fact that these are violent crimes, and that a PTSD diagnosis shouldn't come with a "Get Out of Jail Free" card like the one I gave Lorin when I made "wounded veteran" synonymous with "victim." There is empathy and then there is enabling, and trying to find

---

52. Jaffe, "How Should Military Treat Those with PTSD," *Washington Post.*

the line for someone you love who's been injured while wearing the uniform can be exhausting. It can also be deadly, as Kryn Miner's family found out.

Miner was a forty-four-year-old chief warrant officer 2 with the Vermont Army National Guard with two and a half decades of service, including eleven military deployments in seven years, most recently Afghanistan in 2010. Every combat tour escalates the likelihood of developing PTSD, so after eleven tours, the question is less whether there's PTSD than how severe it is. National Guardsmen have been found to have rates of PTSD as much as three times higher than active-duty troops after combat. Guard vets also report more alcohol abuse, suicidal ideation, and incidents of aggressive behavior. The vast differentials in mental health outcomes between reserve and active duty are primarily due to: the lack of post-deployment unit support; markedly poorer post-deployment mental health services and follow-up; and the rapidity with which citizen soldiers return to civilian life after combat. Factor in a TBI, which also often increases aggression and reduces impulse control, and you've got a recipe for deadly domestic assault in the veteran's home.

In this case, it was Kryn Miner's home, in Essex Junction, Vermont, on April 26, 2014, when Miner's teenager was forced to fatally shoot his father in self-defense after he threatened to kill the family. Media coverage stated that Amy Miner, Kryn's widow, disclosed at least one previous incident where her husband had become agitated and threatened her and their four children with a gun. She was able to talk him down, but she didn't report it, which is pretty typical. Those of us who fell in love with our spouses before they went to war know *they weren't like this before.* We know that the battle buddy who had their back over there isn't here, so it's our job to look out for them now, because we aren't going to lose one more thing to this war. We know that we are the firewall between our veteran and homelessness, and even in the midst of this awful dark sickness, we believe there might be a light waiting for us somewhere on the other side. So we stay.

Kristy Huddleston stayed with her husband, Bourne Huddleston, a USMC veteran, while he served multiple tours in Iraq and Afghanistan. She loved being a Marine spouse, and during the years they were stationed at Camp Lejeune, North Carolina, she pursued her passion for nursing. After Bourne got out of the service, they moved to southern Oregon to be close to Kristy's family in Klamath Falls. She was selected to serve as the first caregiver support coordinator at the SORCC in April of 2011, and Bourne began an internship in a different department at the same VA. Kristy and I first met in early 2012, and I'd visit her in her office in White City, Oregon, and we'd bond over conversations about shoes, purses, and being married to a vet with combat trauma. We also had several months worth of discussions about providing equine therapy programs and peer support services for caregivers and were in the initial stages of drawing up contracts for my nonprofit, the Sanctuary for Veterans & Families. PTSD can cause physiological changes in the brain, and the equine movement that occurs during therapeutic riding positively affects brain chemistry and neural connections, thereby advancing neurodevelopment and neural recovery in veterans. I was providing a workshop on it at a horse expo in Albany, Oregon, in late March of 2012. My phone rang as I was heading out of my hotel room.

"Hey, good morning pooches! What's up? I'm just leaving for the expo."

"Are you in your room still?" Lorin asked.

"Yeah," I said. "Why? What's going on?"

"Your friend, out at the VA, you know, the one who's doing those contracts, is her name Kristy?"

"Mm, yes . . . why?"

"Is she married to an OIF/OEF vet?"

"Yeah, Bourne, I haven't met him yet. I'm going to be late. What's going on?"

"Turn on your TV, see if you can get Channel 5." Lorin paused. "I'm sorry. Kristy's dead. They're saying her husband killed her."

CHAPTER FIVE

The New Normal

"HOW DO YOU GRIEVE for someone who isn't dead?" asked the wife of a severely wounded Marine. It's something we've all wondered, but it's a question so loaded with guilt, failure, and betrayal that we beat ourselves up for even thinking it. To say it aloud was verboten, but now that she had, shame and sadness fought on her face, and she dissolved into tears. We worried about our service member being killed over there. It never occurred to any of us at the retreat for families of veterans that they'd be injured so badly as to change who they were. Some of our vets looked the same. But others, like the husband of the woman who posed the question, are barely recognizable. Her vet was blown up by an IED, and was slumped in a wheelchair, missing chunks of his legs and part of his head. The traumatic brain injury to the frontal lobes was so acute that his language skills were those of a very bright six-year-old, his short-term memory was nonexistent, and his emotional control wasn't much better.

Since he came home, she'd been providing round-the-clock care, serving as the sole parent of their three children and taking care of her ailing mother. She had no time for herself, no time to think, feel, or mourn, like another wife of a wounded warrior who was so desperate for an hour of her own she went to Fred Meyer once a week, dropped the kids off at the store's daycare for customers, and wandered the aisles. The Marine spouse's husband's injuries were such that she couldn't do that, or she couldn't allow herself to do that. She couldn't give herself permission to mourn the man he was because it felt disloyal to the man that is. After all, he's still alive; she just wasn't prepared for so much of him to be gone.

Advances in military medicine have more than quintupled the wound-to-kill ratio as compared to earlier wars, according to CRS Reports and DoD personnel statistics. Grievously injured post-9/11 troops who would have died on the battlefield before are surviving with wounds that will require a lifetime of care.

"Nothing can really prepare you for when it's your own child," said Chris Smith, sitting in the small conference room adjacent to his office, where he pulled double duty as an executive for Dreamz Work, which provides supported living assistance for adults with disabilities, and Wilderness Trails, a Christian camp for children. I'd first met Chris more than three years ago when I interviewed for a job with Dreamz Work. Midway through the interview, we realized we were both military family members and the conversation jumped the rails to talking about that. Several weeks later, the whole hiring process was sidelined when Chris's youngest son, Cody, twenty, an Army private first class with the 101st Airborne Division, was shot in the lower back during an insurgent attack in the Kunar Province of northern Afghanistan.

Chris and I had talked on the phone a few times since, but I hadn't seen him since he got the call on February 17, 2011, telling him his son was in very serious condition at Bagram Air Base. As the military worked to get Cody stabilized enough to fly him to Landstuhl, and then to Walter Reed Army Medical Center, Chris and his wife, Vicky, worked the phones, informing close friends, family members, and their church that Cody's L5 vertebrae had been shattered. They called the Army hospital in Germany twice daily for medical updates. The doctors informed Chris that Cody's L5 vertebrae had been completely rebuilt, and they had put braces on either side of his spine and inserted rods into his pelvic bones to help hold the weight of his torso.

"They basically told us Cody would be able to wheel himself out to the front porch and watch traffic go by," said Chris. "That was our first indication that he was paralyzed and the doctors didn't expect him to walk again."

They also called Cody, but for the first four days, Cody wouldn't answer; he didn't want to talk to them. On the fifth day a nurse asked Cody if he'd be willing to talk to his parents, and he relented, staying on the phone just long enough for Chris to tell him, "We love you, and will see you in Washington." The Army flew Chris and his wife to DC, and two of Cody's siblings were flown in with a combination of Army and charitable funds. Chris marveled at the military's efficiency, how they had a soldier at Dulles holding a sign with his name, how they got right into that SUV, were whisked to the hotel, checked in, and given debit cards for meals and incidentals from the Department of Defense.

"I was so impressed with how they handled everything," said Chris. "It was clear they'd had a lot of practice. When we got to

Walter Reed, the very first thing, someone came up to us and said, 'This is the new normal. We want to talk to you about dealing with your soldier's injuries and the emotional impact.'"

After the briefing, Chris, his wife, and two of their kids made their way to Cody's room on the third floor.

"That was pretty devastating," recalled Chris. "But you have to remember that when you show up at Walter Reed, you see things that . . . you're just not prepared for in the halls, and everywhere. People in wheelchairs with legs missing, and arms missing, and . . . you know . . . I mean . . ."

Eventually, Chris continued, "Because the major injuries go there, which, we didn't know that. I'm Army ignorant. We just realized that this whole hospital is filled with severely injured guys. By the time you've walked three floors, you've seen a lot of that. We got to Cody's room, and he was so bloated from IVs for a week straight. He didn't even look like himself, and all you can do is just hug him. But there were four family members that walked into that room, and all of us were taken aback."

Five weeks later, having improved enough to begin physical therapy, Cody was transported to the Palo Alto, California, VA's Spinal Cord Injury and Disorders Center, where he would reside for the next three months. Chris bought a brand new SUV so he and his wife could drive down there every other weekend, taking Cody's brother and sister and grandparents and other family members. Sometimes teammates from Cody's high school football squad rode along, and Chris loaned the car out to extended family members and friends to make the commute, putting more than twenty thousand miles on the odometer in less than three months. While in Palo Alto, the family stayed at Fisher House, where, Chris says, they had "amazing support, while learning the endless inefficiencies of the VA system."

Chris and his wife met with the VA doctors, who told them their son would always need a wheelchair, and they began figuring out how to get their 1912 two-story home ready for Cody's return.

"As a father, you go into a 'take care of the next thing on the list' mode," said Chris, explaining that the cost of converting the first floor into a handicapped accessible studio apartment was estimated to be more than $100,000. The Smith family has lived in southern Oregon's Applegate Valley for decades; they're active in their church and respected in the community. Chris is solid and good, and being in his presence is to be calmed and reassured that, for as long as fathers like this exist, the American family is doing just fine, thank you. Cody was an all-conference high school football player in a town where Friday nights in the fall are a living time capsule of stadium lights and pom-poms and Styrofoam cups of steaming hot chocolate. So when Chris started talking to a local construction crew about working out a payment plan for renovations, the foreman interrupted.

"Chris, that's not the way we're gonna do it."

Three months and nearly $150,000 in donated materials and labor later, Cody came home.

"From day one, my son has always gotten progressively better, but the whole family dynamic changes," said Chris. "Suddenly, Cory, my son who is mentally challenged, he's two years older than Cody, and Cody had always taken care of him, now Cory is taking care of Cody." And sometimes, that made Cody mad.

"The family," said Chris, "they take it out on the family. I'd think to myself, *really? Is this what it's going to be like?* And there wasn't anyone I could talk to about it. It's hard for people to know how to support you until they've been through the same struggles. Honestly, the most supported we ever felt was when Vietnam vets came to our house to do some work."

Cody was determined to walk again, and approximately one year after coming home, he did, with the help of a walker. But if it was one step forward physically, it was two steps back psychologically, and after a while, Chris came to understand that they were "no longer dealing with the same person."

Cody was struggling with depression and combat trauma, but refused treatment. For the next year or so, Chris and his family tried in vain, "taking hold of Cody's finances, trying to keep track of him and hold him accountable."

Cody slid further into an addiction to opioids, disappearing for hours—and then days—at a time, emptying his bank account, lying, denying, and lashing out at his family. The crazier things got, the more Chris struggled with feeling isolated.

"There are some things that you can't talk about to anybody. There are some things that happen when you're living with a veteran that you don't even *want* to talk about. Because there's no way people can understand. *I* don't understand," said Chris. He focused on logistics, the things he could do to help. But as Cody deteriorated, sometimes Chris would be driving and in the stillness of his car, the tears would come. Slowly, at first, and then he'd be crying so hard he'd have to pull to the side of the road and park.

Cody got an apartment in town and started selling drugs and his guns to feed his habit. Finally, an exhausted Chris laid down the law.

"I can't let you and your problems ruin our whole family. You've already caused so much damage. We've been lied to so many times, and this is ruining not just me, but your mother, and your relationship with your grandparents and your siblings."

Cody checked in for treatment in the White City VA's Substance Abuse Treatment Program, spent ninety days, and seemed better. He was better for a while. And then the old lies, the old behaviors, the old hateful, hurtful, addicted Cody came back, and Chris confronted him again.

"I just couldn't babysit him 24/7. You can't help people that don't want help. I told Cody that it's a spiritual battle, and that I couldn't fight it for him."

That was the first week of September 2014, and Cody agreed to go back to treatment. Two months later, he hadn't yet completed the inpatient program, and I asked Chris how his son was doing. Chris stared out the picture window for a few seconds before he replied.

"Every once in a while I've just got to remind myself how fortunate we are. But it's nearly four years later for Cody, and he's still struggling, he's still searching for a direction in life. What's he supposed to do for a career when he can only be on his feet for an hour at a time? He needs help setting and achieving goals, and we're on the second round of dealing with addiction. . . . There's more to taking care of our veterans than just sending them a disability check."

The VA has proven a particularly tough nut to crack for parents whose child is suffering from PTSD. According to an account posted by Richard Sisk at the *War Report Online*, Cheri Caiella, of Syracuse, New York, had nowhere to turn when her son, a Marine Corps scout sniper, came back from Iraq after serving during the troop surge in 2007.

"I think he was sober maybe three days," said Caiella of his visit during Christmas. Her son came home for good when he got a bad conduct discharge in March of 2008.

"He didn't sleep. He holed up in the basement. He hardly ever came out," Caiella said. One of his few forays from the house ended up with him totaling the family car. Caiella began to understand that her son was a different kid than the one this country sent to war. But help wasn't available from the Marines, and the VA also denied assistance, telling Caiella that her son's "bad paper" disqualified him from receiving services. More than one hundred thousand troops have left the armed services with bad paper since 2001, including many who saw combat. Some received medals before they were convicted of crimes or violated military discipline regulations. The "less-than-honorable" discharge means no VA services, no disability compensation, no GI Bill, and it's a red flag for potential employers. Bad paper vets aren't welcomed at most veterans' service organizations, some landlords refuse to rent to them, and a lot of private sector jobs programs for vets will work with honorable discharge only.

At home, Caiella and her son fought. Sometimes, she'd find him collapsed at his computer desk, and, fearing he was dead, would gently touch him, provoking an attack.

"He thought I was the enemy," Caiella said. More than a year later, the VA finally consented to treat her son.

"I understand we're in a war. But I did not expect my son to get as damaged as he did and then they put the burden on the family."

Post-traumatic stress disorder and traumatic brain injury are considered the "signature wounds" of these wars. Both are invisible. Both are challenging to treat, and often impossible to cure.

Both fundamentally change the veteran in ways that are complicated and perplexing—to the wounded themselves, as well as their
families. PTSD can also change the attachment characteristics of
combat veterans. Attachment theory asserts that we are geneti-
cally oriented toward relationships as a matter of survival. In their
book, *Attached*, Amir Levine, MD, and Rachel Heller, MA, describe
this tendency:

> [T]he need to be near someone special is so important that the
> brain has a biological mechanism specifically responsible for cre-
> ating and regulating our connection with our attachment figures
> (parents, children, and romantic partners).[53]

The behaviors and emotions that comprise our attachment system
keep us connected to and protected by our primary relationships.
The majority of the population endorses a secure attachment style,
evidenced by trust, intimacy, openness, and warmth. Combat vets
with PTSD largely skew toward an avoidant attachment style hallmarked by withdrawal, rejection, belittling, intentional instigation
of irresolvable conflicts, and other distancing strategies. Because
this is the most-married military force in history, many service
members live with a spouse and kids after war, and too often the
combat veteran makes them the enemy so they have an outlet for
their anger and pain that facilitates the avoidance of intimacy.
That behavior comes at the expense of their loved ones, who learn
to live with the insults, bullying, unpredictability, and abuse, but
are too ashamed to let anyone know. "PTSD due to combat exposure

---

53. Levine and Heller, *Attached*.

has more disruptive effects on interpersonal and family functioning than trauma from other sources."[54]

According to the VA, over 75 percent of returning veterans reported family readjustment issues. While stress and anxiety levels in the civilian spouse tend to drop when the soldier comes home, "parental combat deployment has a cumulative effect on children, which remains even after the deployed parent returns."[55] Researchers found no significant difference between the anxiety levels of children with a parent currently deployed and those with a parent recently returned. They did find that child distress is extremely high in the aftermath of a service member's injury, and both physical and behavioral changes were alarming for military kids.

"It's not like they've spent a year at Disneyland," said Margaret Eichler in an interview. "There are huge gaps of families being able to be together, but they have an additional layer of not really being able to talk about what happened." Eichler holds a PhD in counseling and educational psychology and a master's in marriage and family counseling. Her father was a World War II pilot, and she's been volunteering an hour of her time every week as a provider for the Returning Veterans Project (RVP) in Portland, Oregon, since 2006. RVP provides free counseling and somatic services to post-9/11 veterans and their families who live in Washington or Oregon. The Returning Veterans Project was founded by Carol Levine and other board members who wanted to make sure that the families were not forgotten.

---

54. Renaud, "Attachment Characteristics," *Sage Journals*.

55. Lester et al., "The Long War," *Journal of American Academy of Child & Adolescent Psychiatry*.

One of those family members is Belle Landau, whose son served in Iraq and who is also the executive director of the organization. Belle and I first met when she helped me stage the Portland, Oregon, premiere of *Homefront 911* in the summer of 2011. I'd called RVP to ask for their support, and wasn't even done describing the play when Belle said, "Absolutely." Belle pitched in with publicity and helped at the rehearsal, during the performance, and with the reception. She's smart, funny, and committed to helping our vets and families, and I fell in love a little bit. We've stayed connected, and collaborate on the occasional project, and she put me in touch with Eichler.

"Every family is different, and has its own pre-deployment dynamics," said Eichler. "But when they come back, things are different, and that's insurmountable in so many ways. It's called 'the new normal,' but that's misleading. It's not normal. Nothing's the same."

Eichler treats all manner of military families and couples, including LGBT, years before Don't Ask, Don't Tell was repealed in 2011. She's found that much more important than sexual orientation is if the couple met pre-service, because there's a much "wider gap when they come home, and the dissonance is much greater."

A growing number of spouses married to active-duty veterans are fighting tooth and nail to bridge that divide. Many have held down the fort while their soldier served anywhere from two to twelve heavy-combat tours. The psychological distress of bearing the burden of war at home during multiple deployments is compounded by the difficulties of readjustment, and recalibrating your relationship with a troubled service member. Approximately 20 percent of active-duty and 42 percent of Reserve veterans of the

Iraq and Afghanistan campaigns require mental health care, and the numbers are about the same for family members of the veterans. A significant proportion of those vets have some level of PTSD, and the more severe the veteran's PTSD symptomology, the poorer the family functioning.

Mental health professionals are beginning to recognize that PTSD is highly contagious. The most recent edition of the *Diagnostic and Statistical Manual of Mental Disorders* acknowledges that PTSD can develop in family members of people who've encountered violent trauma. Multiple studies on the Vietnam War and the war in Croatia in the 1990s show that caring for and living with a partner with PTSD for an extended period of time is a potent predictor of developing PTSD indicators as well, including flashbacks, nightmares, and panic attacks. Due to the nature of the marital relationship, combat PTSD takes a particularly heavy toll on the spouse, who typically serves as a buffer between the veteran and the children.

"The spouse internalizes the veteran's pathology. Each day that you have to make a choice that the veteran's needs are more important than yours takes a toll on your sense of self and your ability to have basic needs met. The daily, extreme disregulation of complex PTSD trauma creates secondary trauma in the spouses, which also has physiological elements," according to Dr. Eichler. These elements include elevated blood pressure and susceptibility to infection. Depression, anxiety, and acute stress reaction and adjustment disorders are among the mental diagnoses associated with secondary traumatic stress.

"When something terrible happens to someone you love, it is going to affect you," explained clinical psychologist Dr. Laurie

Pearlman in an interview about the mental health crisis in military families. Dr. Pearlman played a lead role in identifying the effects of secondary trauma. "The person comes back and your life is completely altered. You live according to their trauma.[56]

"There's a lot of research to show that partners and spouses and kids suffer from secondary PTSD," said Tom Berger, a senior analyst for veterans' benefits and mental health issues for Vietnam Vets of America. CBS News reported that Abigail Barton was six when her dad, Army National Guard Specialist Aaron Barton, deployed for the first of two back-to-back tours in Iraq, which left him with injuries to his brain and spine and PTSD. The resultant changes, the terrifying fits of rage, depression, and withdrawal, changed Abigail and her older brother, Alex, as well.

"I would get so angry," said Abigail, now fifteen. "I would just think, *This is what Iraq did to my father*. I'd start blaming it on America's military, you know? I would be like, 'You guys stole my father.' . . . I developed depression over time and a lot of anxiety."[57]

Abigail's school offered no support, she said. "I haven't gotten any help through school. All of my, I guess, depression and anxiety help, it's come from other places—through our family doctor."

Abigail's mom, Wendy Barton, said that for older brother Alex, it has been "devastating, devastating, to see the changes in his dad, and to feel helpless." After several years of distress, seventeen-year-old Alex attempted suicide in 2013, and very nearly succeeded. He spent four days on life support.

---

56. Lazare, "The Military's Hidden," *Al Jazeera*.
57. CBS News, "Collateral Damage."

"I don't think that America is intentionally neglecting these kids by any means, but I think that they need to wake up," said Wendy Barton, "because this is a real problem, and it is certainly not just my children that are suffering."

Children may adopt maladaptive behaviors and mirror the anger and depression they see in their parents. Other common symptoms of secondary trauma include emotional exhaustion, detachment, difficulty concentrating, fearfulness, shame, physical illness, and chronic fatigue. This adds another layer of trauma to family members who are likely already struggling with the unresolved stress of the ambiguous loss of their loved one.

Ambiguous loss theory, first proposed as a relational disorder by Pauline Boss, PhD, in 1999, includes two types of loss: "ambiguous absence, in which a family member is absent physically but present psychologically (i.e., a missing child or a deployed parent), and ambiguous presence, where a family member is present physically but absent psychologically."[58] Research conducted by military spouse and therapist Jennifer Daniels, PhD, and others has found that living with a partner (or parent) who is emotionally unavailable can generate painful feelings in the spouses and children.

"Rife with ambiguity, losses that cannot be clarified or verified become traumatic," posits Boss on her website. "[An] ambiguous loss—an unclear loss that defies closure . . . is the most stressful kind of loss. It defies resolution and creates long-term confusion about who is in or out of a particular couple or family. With death, there is official certification of loss, and mourning rituals allow one to say good-bye. With ambiguous loss, none of these markers exist.

---

58. Daniels, "Burden of Care."

The persisting ambiguity blocks cognition, coping, meaning-making and freezes the grief process."[59]

Boss and other researchers have found that community conversations about the nature of ambiguous loss can promote meaning and hope, and formal and informal social support can help mediate the negative effects of living with someone with PTSD. But nobody is talking about this; there aren't any public health forums or monthly meetings for families of veterans. There are all kinds of clubs and organizations for veterans, but there's no such thing as an American Legion or VFW or Order of the Purple Heart for veterans' families. The White House convened a Summit on Veterans and Military Families in the fall of 2013, and one of the presenters was Bonnie Carroll, president and founder of the Tragedy Assistance Program for Survivors (TAPS). Two years after her own husband, Brigadier General Tom Carroll, died in an Army C-12 plane crash in 1992, Bonnie began TAPS to provide peer support, "grief and trauma resources and information, casualty casework assistance and crisis intervention for all those affected by the death of a loved one serving in, or in support of, the Armed Forces."[60]

Bonnie spoke about how TAPS convenes the families of the fallen for retreats, and one of the activities involves creating a circle for each family member to acknowledge the loss while tying it to the reason for their sacrifice. That ritual would be no less powerful for the families of the wounded; my beautiful husband was gone, and he and I seemed to be the only ones who were aware of it. There had been no ceremony to sanctify the passage of pre-war Lorin. So after the summit I asked Bonnie

---

59. www.ambiguousloss.com.

60. www.taps.org.

and TAPS executive vice president Dr. Lynda Davis to please consider expanding their mission to include veterans' caregivers and kids.

"Of particular concern," said Ron Astor, a professor at the University of Southern California's School of Social Work, "are the children of veterans." Only the veteran is eligible for mental health help through the Department of Veterans Affairs and vet centers. If the veteran is in treatment and provides consent, sometimes the spouse can go to couples counseling with the veteran (most typically in the aftermath of the veteran abusing the spouse) or attend a monthly support group for spouses. Even that is hard to come by, and if a veteran's "kid comes in suicidal or has other issues—primarily because of the separation and deployment of the war—they don't get VA services," said Astor in an interview with Liz Dwyer that was published on the social action website *TakePart*.[61]

More and more of the men and women who've served in Iraq or Afghanistan will transition out of the military in the coming years, and by 2025 the overwhelming majority will have left the service. This means a growing number of veterans' kids will be enrolling in public schools and accessing social services, and those institutions should be ramping up to receive them. But with less than half of 1 percent of Americans having served in Iraq or Afghanistan, and fewer than 5 percent of Americans having a family member who did, veterans' families are not in this country's consciousness.

"They're just invisible. They're not appreciated," said Astor. "Your family goes through all this, and it seems like it doesn't matter." I kept trying to convince myself that the past decade of service and sacrifice mattered. I needed to persuade myself that the PTSD

---

61. Dwyer, "A Staggering Percentage," *TakePart*.

and TBI Lorin got in combat were worth it, even if I still didn't know what "it" was. I wanted to find a way to justify what we'd lost with some equal, if not larger, gain and find some greater good that would bind my broken heart. I would like for there to have been a point. Maybe then it wouldn't bother me so much that my husband doesn't touch me anymore.

That's what I miss the most after the easy comfort of physical intimacy during all of our years of being together. After leaving the Guard and moving down to Medford, he seldom kissed me, or hugged me, or even held my hand. He would if we were out with friends, or having dinner at Tracey and Karl Haeckler's house, another post-9/11 veteran couple, when I effectively forced myself on him. It was all kinds of awkward if he pushed me away, and he wanted people to think everything was okay. So I got as much contact as I could in those situations, which were becoming increasingly rare. He was becoming increasingly reclusive, and I was beginning to resent this public farce. He would say he loved me, and I supposed somewhere that was true, but it was a somewhere he wasn't willing to go. He angered easily and often, a bewildering new trait in someone formerly so easygoing I used to call him Sergeant Sweet Bear. Mad he could do. That's a visceral response that worked well in war. Love, though, lives in the heart, right next to pain, and to embrace one is to welcome the other, so he welded the whole thing shut.

I kept telling myself to give it time, because that's what the Yellow Ribbon Reintegration brochure suggested. I was encouraged to be patient, and supportive, and forgiving, and not to expect too much. As long as we took it slow (and I had no needs whatsoever of my own), eventually he'd get readjusted. But if he didn't, it was my job to watch out for that, and see to it that he got help.

"I need your help," said Lieutenant General Jack Stultz, the Army Reserve's top ranking officer, speaking to a group of spouses of soldiers recently returned from Iraq in the fall of 2010. At the Yellow Ribbon Reintegration Program weekend, Stultz said, "I need you to help me convince your soldiers, if they need counseling, if they need help, it's OK."[62]

Lorin had been retired for almost a year, so there was no one I could go to. Even if he'd still had a command, it's unlikely they would've tried to convince him to get treatment. The Army had five years after the initial PTSD diagnosis to convince him; instead, they deployed him again, and not once had mental health counseling been mandatory, if it was even discussed. I had hoped Lorin would get counseling when his Compensation & Pension review came back with his rating. He'd gone through a battery of tests and examinations at the VA to determine his level of service-connected disability.

Six months later, a thick envelope arrived with the results: severe PTSD, bilateral hearing loss, tinnitus, hypertension, respiratory airway disease, back and neck conditions, degenerative disc disease, and discoid lupus that had mysteriously appeared during his burn pit exposure at Joint Base Balad in 2004–05.

The DoD authorized the use of burn pits in Iraq and Afghanistan to incinerate human and medical waste, trash, plastic, tires, and other debris that created potentially harmful emissions when incinerated. The Pentagon "had been aware [of the health risks] for years," said John Sopko, special inspector general for Afghanistan reconstruction, in a 2015 report by Patricia Kime for *Army*

---

62. Miles, "General Provides," *American Forces Press Release.*

Times. Sopko characterized the persistent use of burn pits—even after policies were adopted to restrict it—as "disturbing."

Thousands of troops have reported medical problems they believe are linked to living and working near the pits, including cancer, rare pulmonary diseases, and unexplained rashes. While the DoD was publicly dismissing the possibility of burn pit–related health hazards for military personnel, the Naval Health Research Center was conducting a study that investigated, among other things, the "Odds of Newly Reported Lupus Among Deployers in Relation to a 3-Mile Proximity to a Burn Pit."[63] The research stated that "the elevated and statistically significant association between newly reported lupus and deployment within 3- and 5-mile radii of the burn pit at Joint Base Balad (JBB) may be of concern."

I was concerned when Lorin came back after a year at JBB in early 2005 with a slowly growing whitish bald spot on his scalp. I was concerned enough that I badgered him to go to Madigan, where the military's best medical providers diagnosed it as eczema and sent him home with a tube of ointment. The cream didn't stop the thing from spreading, so I kept pushing Lorin to get it checked out. The correct diagnosis of lupus was not made until the latter part of 2009, when Lorin returned from his second tour in Iraq and the doctors at Fort McCoy examined the lesion and had it biopsied during his post-deployment physical.

Lorin was later also diagnosed with mild TBI; apparently it never occurred to the VA doctors to test him, a mortar platoon

---

63. Jones et al., "Newly Reported," *Journal of Occupational and Environmental Medicine.*

sergeant who had been in the blast vicinity when the HMMV in front of him rolled over an IED. The thirteen double-sided, single-spaced, black-and-white pages documented some of what the war had done to him, and what he'd done at war—things he never told me. Things that told me we'd be living with this war for the rest of our lives. The VA uses the "combined rating table," which Lorin calls "VA beer math," to calculate the level of service-connected disability. It's a complicated logarithm that "considers the effect from the most serious to the least serious."

The 80 percent disability rating was more than we expected. But the $1,652 monthly benefit couldn't begin to make him better. The money couldn't bring those parts of him back, the ones he carried downrange that never came home. It wasn't nearly enough to make him let go of the parts and pieces of bodies that he picked up at war and may never put down. It would not heal his permanent scars, and I laid my hands on the ones I could touch, willing him whole and unmarked by this war.

I wrapped my life around the wounds beneath his skin, needing to believe that I could love them away. But I couldn't, and I felt like a failure because of it. Cash for casualties can't buy back those years. There's not enough money in the world to finance his freedom from the blast that took those soldiers' lives, reverberating in his brain, sending shock waves to his soul. Or to purchase peace from the order he gave that killed children by mistake. Buried is not dead, because they came home with him too. They lived in our house, and they clung to the walls. Combat residue. How could I clean that up? How could I let him know I didn't blame him for this, when I knew he blamed himself? How could I fix him when sometimes I felt like I was broken, too?

The VA could not tell me what to do about that. Their decision decided nothing about how to find a new way to love in the "after" when I fell in love with "before," before I learned how to hide my shame when I begged for his touch and he turned me away. Before I learned how to swallow my fear when he flew into a rage at some imagined slight. Before I learned that the smallest thing—or nothing at all—could set him off. His anger wasn't always aimed at me.

One day, he tagged along when I went to return books at the local library. Lorin was planning on using the GI Bill to go back to school and get a degree, and while we were there, he decided to apply for a library card. He hadn't switched his driver's license to Oregon yet, and hadn't thought to bring along a piece of mail with our Medford address, without which, the librarian explained, she couldn't issue him a card.

"Are you kidding me?" he demanded. "Here's my military ID. Just give me the card today, and I will come back later with identification."

"I'm sorry, sir, but I can't do that. I have to see some sort of proof of local residence."

"I just fucking moved here!" he bellowed. "I don't have any with me. I'm a combat vet. I served my country, and this is how you thank me?"

As he escalated, the librarian shrank behind the counter, and a small crowd began to gather in the lobby.

"Lorin, shhhh, it's okay, honey," I said. "Let's just go. We can come back."

"I don't fucking want to come back. Fuck it. I ain't coming back. Fucking library."

"Okay, that's fine, whatever you want. It's okay, we can just go now."

I hustled him out before someone called security, and when we got outside, he said he needed a smoke. He went to the smoking area at the corner of the building and I snuck back inside, face hot with humiliation, to apologize. I explained to the librarian that he wasn't like this before. Who would explain to me how to live in the "after"?

After he retired, my military spouse support network virtually disappeared. I was no longer a Blue Star wife, and it was disorienting to be cut loose from the gravitational force field of that life. It wasn't that I wanted to go back to it, I just had never thought about what would happen when it was over and I was no longer a member of the sisterhood fluent in the super secret squirrel code of military spouses during wartime. We never once discussed *American Idol*, and when new acquaintances or coworkers started talking about it, I was stumped speechless. All of those years have rendered me incapable of water cooler conversations. That's not the place to bring up what it was like living with Lorin's PTSD, but I only knew four local women who were married to veterans, and we weren't close enough yet for that conversation. They may not even have been living with it. Most veterans' spouses aren't, either because the vet never saw combat or, if he did, he didn't develop trauma as a result of it. Or, they are the veteran's second, third, fourth, or fifth wife and the earlier wives did the heavy psychological lifting until finally, surveying the wreckage of relationships in which the only common denominator was him and his war, the vet got help.

I tried to broach the subject with a few close civilian friends and family members who knew Lorin back when, but none had ever lived with a combat vet. They clearly didn't get it (I didn't either, until I did), and when they learned that Lorin's disability claim had gone through, they said, "Gee that must be nice." Like we'd won some scratch ticket, and a little irritability was nothing if you were getting money in return.

So I signed up for a Wounded Warrior Project (WWP) Retreat, really, really hoping it would be different. WWP is among the dozens of nonprofits created to serve post-9/11 veterans, but they're one of the first, and the largest. From time to time, they provide retreats for family members and caregivers, and there were probably thirty of us—all women—at the event in Colorado. We'd been flown in and put up at a gorgeous hotel, with a free spa service of our choosing over the course of the weekend. During the day, we attended seminars and peer support groups, and at night, after a big dinner buffet, we got to sleep, which had become a luxury for many of the women who were there.

Lack of rest, support, friends, and free time are common concerns, but nobody's talking about sex. Given the number of women with small children, and those currently expecting, it didn't seem to be a problem for them. I was reluctant to bring it up, but if I didn't say anything, hoping for some guidance, then I would have wasted my weekend and the donor's money.

"My husband hasn't been willing to have sex for nearly two years. Anybody else have that problem?" I asked.

"I wish," said one pregnant woman, while a few other wives rolled their eyes and nodded their heads in agreement. In the ensuing silence, it became clear that it either wasn't an issue for anyone else, or they weren't willing to admit to it. PTSD has been referred to as the "elephant in the bedroom" by some spouses and mental health professionals. Medication can contribute to lack of desire, and impotency often has a strong biological component, including low testosterone, but Lorin refused to take any medications and all of his blood work came back normal. He also refused to consider the possibility that his untreated war trauma was coming between us in the bedroom. Matthew Tull, PhD, has stated that rates of sexual dysfunction in Vietnam vets with PTSD have been found to be as high as 80 percent.[64] A study of OIF/OEF male vets in treatment for PTSD at the Veterans Affairs Pacific Islands Health Care System found that almost 90 percent had some sort of sexual dysfunction. Nearly three-quarters reported reduced sexual desire, and virtually half had erectile dysfunction (ED). As noted in a 2014 *Military Times* report, "the incidence rate of ED among active-duty personnel more than doubled from 2004 to 2014."[65] Factors known to contribute to ED include depression, anxiety, and PTSD.

Military sexual trauma (MST) can also interfere with sexuality and intimacy. Being severely sexually harassed or abused by another service member or your commander is a violation of the code of honor and conduct. It is a betrayal of the brotherhood and sisterhood of the service that makes the United States military unique. I'd spearheaded a therapeutic retreat for women veterans in 2009, and during the long Sanctuary Weekend nearly two-thirds of them spontaneously disclosed some sort of MST. But women aren't the only victims, and incidents of MST rise precipitously during a deployment, particularly when the initial invasion has morphed into an occupation, as it did in Iraq. So I worked up my courage and asked Lorin, as gently as possible, if that had happened. I conveyed

---

64. Tull, "Sexual Problems in Veterans with PTSD," *About Health*.
65. Kime, "ED Cases among Troops," *Military Times*.

to him that if it had, it wasn't his fault, and he had been hurt, and we would get help for him together. He laughed and sloughed off the question, "Nope, never happened." One more question that I never thought I'd ask.

I'd done it again at the retreat, and regretted opening my mouth. I blinked away the sting of tears, thinking I might be the biggest loser. I hadn't gained weight (not that that should necessarily be an issue), but I seemed to be the only one wondering why their husband no longer found them attractive. While I was chafing in my chair, one of the WWP executives sitting in on the counselor-facilitated support group half-seriously suggested I get a prescription for Viagra, slip it into Lorin's drink, and then take advantage of him after he fell asleep. (There's a reason this guy's not a therapist.) That missed the point: sexual intimacy is the exclusive dialogue of the relationship, and my husband wasn't willing to "talk."

"Good luck," he said, and the topic changed. I sat there, waiting for the session to end so I could leave. The guy pulled me aside afterward to acknowledge how hard living with PTSD was, and that he didn't have any answers.

"I'll tell you this, though, almost nobody gets divorced because of physical injuries."

Military couples were divorcing because of lengthy deployments, and if the enlisted service member had been deployed twelve months or more to a combat zone, it raised the risk nearly 30 percent.[66] "Fifteen-month deployments are designed to destroy marriages," said a mental health specialist serving soldiers in Iraq

---

66. Rand Corporation, "Lengthy Military Deployments."

and Afghanistan.[67] Female veterans are nearly three times more likely to lose their marriages, as are troops who married before the September 11 attacks.

"We're providing a lot of couples counseling," said Belle Landau, the executive director of the Returning Veterans Project (RVP). "But there's only one male out of 125 partners and spouses. I am getting a lot of quarterly reports from the counselors that say the veteran is no longer participating, but the wife will continue to receive services. That tells me they're probably getting divorced."

Problems in relationships quadruple after a deployment, and fully one-fifth of returned married troops were planning a divorce, according to a survey by Strategic Outreach for Families of All Reservists, which provides counseling and support for dependents of Guard and Reservists. As noted by David Wood in the *Huffington Post* in 2013, active-duty military divorces rose by 42 percent from 2000 to 2011, but virtually all of the divorces (97 percent) were filed after the soldier came home.[68] There's a code among the spouses that you just do not serve them papers while they're at war.

* * *

Twenty-year-old Army specialist Clay McGarrah had been asking Emily to marry him for seven years, according to a report by Greg Barnes in the *Harrison Daily Times*. She kept saying "No," until he got his orders for Afghanistan. Less than two weeks before he was supposed to ship out, they had a quick ceremony at the courthouse,

---

67. Army's Mental Health Advisory Team (MHAT) Report, February 2008.
68. Wood, "Military and Veteran Suicides Rise," *Huffington Post*.

with Emily wearing a simple white eyelet wedding dress. The fancy formal gown would wait until the big wedding when he came home. The couple went out for dinner afterward, and Emily wanted to change out of her dress, but Clay pleaded with her to keep it on. Soon after he deployed, Emily left Fort Bragg and went back home to be with her family and work as a nurse's aide at a hospital in Branson, Missouri.

Clay called as much as he could, and Emily was expecting to hear from him one day around noon when her supervisor approached. She was crying, but wouldn't say why. She told Emily there was someone waiting for her in the office. Emily followed her boss down the hall, feeling like her heart was going to explode. When she saw the casualty notification officers, it did.

Hundreds of people came to Clay's funeral. When they drove from the church to the cemetery, people lined the streets, and dozens upon dozens of Patriot Guard Riders parked their motorcycles along the side of the road, the American flags fixed to the back of their bikes floating in the breeze and the bright July sunshine. The Patriot Guard convenes at the funeral services of fallen troops, veterans, and first responders at the invitation of the family. They come to pay their respect to the deceased and shield the bereaved from potential protestors. They've been at every military funeral I've attended, and when the Patriot Guard rumbles into position around the perimeter of the parking lot, it's as though the hands of God have cupped the church. But it was just Emily and Clay's parents in the darkness at Dover Air Force Base as Specialist McGarrah returned to American soil less than a month after he'd shipped out. When Emily's husband came back in a coffin, she wore her wedding dress to welcome him home.

The Patriot Guard Riders were at Oregon's Evergreen Aviation airfield to welcome the body of Army Sergeant Michael Vaughan, twenty, and provide escort to the Newberg funeral home.[69] Sergeant Vaughan was assigned to the 5th Squadron, 73rd Cavalry Regiment, 3rd Brigade Combat Team, 82nd Airborne Division out of Fort Bragg. He had been serving as a scout in Iraq when he died in an IED explosion on April 23, 2007. Sergeant Brice A. Pearson, Sergeant Randell T. Marshall, 1st Lieutenant Kevin J. Gaspers, Staff Sergeant Kenneth E. Locker Jr., Staff Sergeant William C. Moore, Specialist Jerry R. King, Specialist Michael J. Rodriguez, and Private First Class Garrett C. Knoll were also killed by the blast. The 82nd would send an honor guard to lead the funeral procession, but on his first night home, Michael Vaughan's mother, Debra, wanted to see him.

Michael was in his dress uniform, lying in the casket, with white gauze wrapped tightly around his head to hide his crushed skull. Debra wept long and hard next to the body of her boy while her husband, George, stood by, fixing his gaze on his son's white-gloved hands.

Both parents struggled with depression after they buried their only child. George had been retired for a while, but went back to volunteering, and Debra eventually resumed work at the post office. Most of her time at home was spent in Michael's room amidst medals, photos, flags, and plaques commemorating his service. A little more than a year after Michael's death, George, a Gulf War veteran, was asked to present the Oregon Honorable Service Medal at the Field of Honor memorial. Debra attended, but left prior to the

---

69. Sullivan, "Measures of Sacrifice," *Oregonian*.

presentation, telling George she'd meet him at home. When George got there, Debra was nowhere to be found, and he called her on her cell. Debra told him she loved him, and said that if she failed, she didn't want to be on life support.

Then she pulled the trigger.

Several days later, the Patriot Guard got ready to ride again, posting the new mission on their website:

> 04 Oct 08
> Ladies and Gentlemen,
> It is with great sadness and heavy heart I post this mission. We have been invited to honor Debra Vaughan, a Gold Star mom, and a veteran who served in both the Army and Air Force, at the St. Augustine Catholic Church in Lincoln City on Saturday Oct 4th at 10am. Many of us were present to try to give comfort to Debra at the mission for her son, Sgt Michael Vaughan in April 07 and remember her, even in her grief, walking the flag line thanking each of us for taking the time to be there. Debra fought that grief long and hard, but lost the battle this past weekend. She is again walking with her son.[70]

Debra was buried next to Michael. George gave up after that. For a very long time, it was him, thoughts of suicide, and what felt like one-sided discussions with God, wondering if he was somehow to blame, asking why? When the answers didn't come, George got involved in search-and-rescue efforts, looking for those who were lost.

A few states over, Rory Gavic had vanished. Rory was stationed at Hill Air Force Base in Layton, Utah. He'd served two tours,

---

70. www.patriotguard.org/archive/index.php/t-311312.html.

including one in Iraq, as a K-9 handler. He had earned numerous commendations, a nomination for Airman of the Year in 2008 among them, and developed PTSD after his deployments. Rory phoned his mother, Linda Sawatzke, on November 14, 2009, worrying her with the tone of his voice, according to a *USA Today* article by Kirsti Marohn. After he hung up, she called back repeatedly. Rory wouldn't answer. The next call she got was from Utah officials who were searching for her son. The call after that was to let her know that they'd found her son's truck in Antelope Island State Park. Rory's body was discovered the following day.[71]

Four years after her son's suicide, Sawatzke duplicated his death, shooting herself in the heart, as he had, using his 9mm handgun. Her obituary and directions for her funeral were left on the dining room table of her home in Buffalo, Minnesota. Mother and son are buried side by side in a small hilltop cemetery. The statue of a military service dog sits guarding the graves.

There is a river of grief that runs through the families of the veterans who've been wounded or killed in these wars, or who killed themselves when they came home. The families of military casualties, particularly the suicides and those with nonlethal injuries, have few resources and scant support. We tend our wounds in private, if at all, desperately holding on to what was, even as we struggle to accept what is. Most of us fumble our way forward, but when the river runs too wild and deep, some of us cannot.

---

71. Marohn, "Veteran's Suicide Devastates Those Left Behind," *USA Today*.

CHAPTER SIX

Who's Caring for the Caregiver?

I DIDN'T GET TO decide to be a caregiver. I didn't get to decide that my husband would reenlist with the Guard, or when he went to war. When he was injured, I didn't get to decide where he received treatment, or whether he would participate in his own healing. Becoming a caregiver was the consequence of a series of choices I never made. I was thrust into a role where the options available to me were phenomenally few, but had major repercussions nonetheless. As my husband's condition deteriorated, my caregiving responsibilities grew.

By the fall of 2012, Lorin's Global Assessment of Functioning (GAF) score was hovering around 50 out of a possible 100. The GAF scale is a subjective measure used by mental health clinicians and physicians to gauge the social, occupational, and psychological functioning of adults. The numeric rating reflects how well a person navigates daily life, and the majority of adults register well into the 70th percentile or above. A score of 50 is considered severely symptomatic, and is indicative of serious impairment in social, occupational, or school functioning. Lorin had been working the graveyard shift as a social services assistant at the SORCC for more than a year and a half without a problem. He was also taking classes at Southern Oregon University and made the Dean's List one quarter. Work and school are highly structured, contained environments that have an intellectual format and clear, measurable expectations. Success is dependent on left brain prevalence, and the dissociative element of trauma serves as an adaptive mechanism that keeps the right brain dormant.

Males are generally left-brain dominant to begin with, and have less connectivity between brain hemispheres than women. The corpus callosum—a bundle of nerves linking left and right brain hemispheres—is thicker in women, which enables greater ease and fluidity in moving back and forth between the intuitive right brain and the rational left brain. PTSD has been shown to shrink certain brain structures, and it may impair neural networks, so, as long as it was task- or tech-oriented, Lorin was successful, but he had no social life or friends of his own, and he was falling apart at home. It became my job to put him—and everything else—back together.

When he forgot to pay the bills and spent his money on tools or toys, I put several months' worth of missed payments on my credit card to keep the lights on. When the collection agency called, I paid the balance so his car wasn't repossessed. We'd always kept separate bank accounts, and he was understandably unwilling to give that up. I wasn't going to ask Lorin to relinquish control in yet another domain, even if it meant more work for me. When he was unable to move his laundry from the washer to the dryer, I made sure he had clean clothes. When he didn't remember to go to appointments at the VA, or put the ointment on his scalp to keep the discoid lupus from spreading, I went with him to the doctor, and applied balm to his head. I scheduled his appointments, reminded him of meetings, and tried to cajole him into taking the dozen or so medications gathering dust on the shelf. When I found burners left on, I turned them off and took over most of the meal preparation. When he could no longer remember what chores needed to be done, I wrote them down on a large calendar mounted on the wall. When he avoided sleep for twenty hours at a stretch, I got him into bed; and when he dozed through the alarm, I got him out of it so he could get to work. On the days the nerve damage and back problems flared up, I assisted him with sitting up, getting moving, and getting dressed. I didn't worry about him when he was at work, but I worried when I was.

I had accepted a position as veterans program manager at a large nonprofit based in Medford that had recently been awarded a handful of HUD-Veterans Affairs Supportive Housing (HUD-VASH) contracts from the VA. The VASH case management contracts were part of the Obama administration's effort to end veteran homelessness by 2015, and I oversaw a clinical supervisor and ten case managers in six cities throughout the Pacific Northwest. These contracts, combined, consisted of 250 vouchers across Oregon and Washington, covering a geographic region that spanned nearly five hundred miles along the I-5 corridor. Our program placed chronically homeless veterans into subsidized housing, which required troubleshooting multiple barriers to getting them leased up: mental illness, substance abuse, prior evictions, poor employment and rental histories, and criminal convictions, including murder.

After years of burning bridges beyond repair, many of the vets had no friends or family left. Some of them were placed in the local supportive housing complexes owned by the company. But it was Mary Pico, the clinical supervisor, and the case managers on the front lines in their respective communities who did the hard work of securing housing for upward of 95 percent of the veterans we served. Keeping them housed often meant constant crisis management. So I'd do that at the office, and then do it at home. It was a twenty-minute drive from door to door, and I learned to go slow.

* * *

When I got to the house, it was already dark, and Lorin was standing in the kitchen, trying to figure out what he was doing there.

"Hey, what's up?" I asked.

"Uh, nothing," Lorin replied.

"Did you eat yet?"

"No," he said. "I'm not really hungry."

"Well, you need to eat something, so let me get changed, and go see the animals, and then I'll get dinner together."

I'd gotten two wether goats, a dwarf Nigerian and a Nigerian-Lamancha cross, to keep my horse company. Turning them out of the barn in the morning and mucking their stalls before work, and then putting them to bed at night, were often the best parts of my day. I changed out of my work clothes and went to the barn, with Lorin trailing behind. After everybody was grained, I threw the horse a flake of hay and switched off the barn lights on my way out. Lorin was still shadowing me, which was unusual, so I asked him again, "What's up, buddy?"

"Um, there's something you should maybe take a look at . . ."

I braced myself, because that statement has never prefaced anything good.

"I was pounding in some T-posts and had a little accident," he said. "I had the fence post pounder above my head, and brought it down really hard, and it bounced off and hit me."

"Lorin! Where? When did this happen?"

"This afternoon . . ."

God damn it. I had specifically and repeatedly asked him *not* to do anything potentially dangerous or involving ladders, fire, chainsaws, or heavy equipment unless there was someone else on our five-acre property with him. Ever since the TBI and PTSD, his balance was a little off, and he's much more accident-prone. He's suffered second-degree burns on his arms, he trips and stumbles on completely flat surfaces, and has some body part sporting a bandage more often than not. All evidence aside, he maintained that since the military had entrusted him with millions of dollars of equipment and executing tasks that included burning excess mortar charges and putting up triple-strand concertina wire, I should as well. I pointed out that the military never once had him do anything alone.

He pulled off his skullcap when we got back inside and bent down so I could see his scalp. Ivory skull glistened in the three-inch-long gash, which was weeping blood and clear fluid although it had been nearly five hours. I wanted to smack him and clutch him to me, but instead I forced him to go to urgent care, where they stapled his head closed and shot him up with antibiotics and painkillers. Another late night of worry and fear, followed by a few hours of restless sleep: rinse, repeat.

A few days later he had a meltdown while I was on my way out the door to work. I broke my own rule and talked to him on my cell on the drive in. I checked in with the receptionist to see if there were any messages for me, and thankfully, there weren't. As soon as I was settled in at Outpost Bannerman (the nickname for my corner office at the end of a very long, dark, unoccupied hallway) I called Lorin back and spent most of the morning on the line with him, doing emotional caregiving. That meant listening as he vented and raged and then talking him down, comforting him as he worked through whatever memory had surfaced, and consoling him as he struggled with feelings of guilt and shame and worthlessness.

I never used to be the kind of wife who called her husband several times a day, but then I had to so I could take his emotional temperature and reassure myself that he was still alive. If he noticed the change in my behavior, he never said a word. He just called every day around noon (his phone was programmed with a reminder) for the Highway 234 horse report and daily briefing. I had asked him to under the guise of letting me know how Corporal Hickory (horse), Specialist Grizzly (goat), Chief Warrant Officer 2 Biggie G (goat), and Private Kobe (dog) were doing. If Sergeant Bannerman (husband) wasn't doing well, it'd be a very long lunch.

I had let my employers know the situation with Lorin, in very general terms, and that I was his caregiver. The boss was a Vietnam-era veteran, and the office was incredibly supportive, allowing me to take sick leave time to care for Lorin and accompany him to VA appointments. It was a small change for a big company but it made a huge difference in whether or not I could continue to work. And I had to work; we had a new mortgage on our first home. And I needed something to call my own. I had a master's degree and more than two decades of progressive experience, and I wasn't going to give up my job and arrange my whole life around taking care of my husband.

"I get to have a life, too," said Tammara Rosenleaf, my friend and battle buddy of more than eight years. She's also caring for her husband, Sean Hefflin, a service-connected disabled OIF vet, while working full-time. Like me, she had earned a master's degree prior to her marriage. The lower the level of education and income, the more likely a person is to be a caregiver, but when your husband comes home hurt, having gone to graduate school doesn't mean you won't take care of him. What it means is that you'll likely work outside the home while you're doing it. The post-9/11 generation of military caregivers, estimated to be 1.1 million, is the first in which many are employed at least part-time. It is also the first in which tending to the pervasive, debilitating mental health or substance abuse condition of the veteran is a primary responsibility.

Roughly fifty thousand troops have been physically injured in Iraq and Afghanistan, and approximately one million sustained head injuries or are suffering from post-traumatic stress, depression, or other mental health problems. All else being equal, it is widely acknowledged by the VA and mental health professionals that the care and support provided by spouses and family members is the single most important factor in determining how well those veterans do. Tasks associated with taking care of them include assisting with activities of daily living (ADLs), such as eating, bathing, dressing, walking, or using a wheelchair. Military caregivers typically take over all household maintenance and management responsibilities, handling the bills and the budget, and acting as the advocate for the veteran on virtually every front, from financial, to legal, to medical.

The VA assigns a case manager to the veteran, but close to 90 percent of caregivers do some aspect of that job, whether it's coordinating treatment plans, finding providers, identifying community resources, or negotiating care systems. Because we are in the trenches with our veteran, we know first and best what's happening with them. The world sees our veteran's game face; we see them in the locker room.

Lorin kept getting shuffled to new doctors and nurses and referred to different departments and private specialists, so it was relatively rare that he'd meet with the same VA provider more than a few times a year. Those appointments usually lasted about fifteen to thirty minutes, and when Lorin or I would ask them if they'd actually looked at his file, the vast majority of doctors, nurses, and licensed clinical social workers readily admitted that they had not. Over and over and over again, I had to educate the medical staff about my veteran's health needs and issues while simultaneously trying to keep an irritated Lorin from stomping out of the appointment.

* * *

In between taking care of her husband and working a sixty-hour week as a case manager for dual diagnosis clients with mental and developmental disabilities, Tammara carved out a little time at the gym. She was jogging one week in early November and overheard two women on the treadmills next to her bitching because they were going shopping and wanted to get cash, but the banks were closed. One of them asked, "What's the holiday, anyway?"

"Veterans Day," said Tammara. "It's Veterans Day for my disabled husband that you don't give a shit about."

Tammara fled the gym, got into her car, and cried all the way home. But she got it together before she walked in the door. She holds it together because he's coming apart. Because she loves him and she made a promise. She doesn't know how she's going to get through it. All she knows is that she will. She must. Sean was a combat engineer during a four-year stint in the Army, which included a yearlong tour in Iraq. His contract was extended by stop-loss orders, and he was honorably discharged in 2009 with a 60 percent disability rating due to hairline fractures in his feet. The military attributes the breakage to the weight of his body armor, pack, and gear, and there's been speculation that it's exacerbated by exposure to depleted uranium (DU). Several Gulf War veterans groups have been alleging for years that chronic or toxic exposure to DU weakens bones, and there's some evidence that links DU to a dysfunction in the body's ability to efficiently metabolize Vitamin D. The damage to Sean's feet has required several surgeries that left him unable to walk for weeks at a time, and he's also suffering from a TBI and PTSD.

Sean's been unable to find a job since he got out. Some days, he's unable to find the post office. He doesn't tell Tammara what he's no longer capable of; oftentimes he doesn't know himself. Or he forgets.

Tammara only learned about the problem locating the post office when late notices and collection letters began arriving for bills she knew she'd paid. She'd given Sean a $1,000 deposit to mail, along with several other stamped envelopes containing house and utility payments. Now they were all missing or delinquent. When she asked Sean what he had done with the mail, he said he didn't remember. Tammara searched the house, tearing apart her desk, and the junk drawer in the kitchen. She rummaged through boxes in the garage, feeling crazier and crazier, beginning to question whether she had actually written the checks and stamped the envelopes. Then she saw the deposit envelope and several other letters and packages on the bench seat of Sean's truck. So that got crossed off the rapidly shrinking list of things that Sean could do to help out around the house.

Cooking was out of the question; Sean had boiled pans dry, left gas burners going, and set kitchen towels on fire too many times. So Tammara would make him lunch, and before she left for work, she'd park him in front of the TV or his computer, and that's where she'd find him when she came home. She'd also find that the dogs hadn't been fed or let out of the house, the dishes hadn't been washed—not a single thing would be different from the moment she'd left, nine or ten hours earlier.

"It's like he ceased to exist when I was gone," she said. "If there's no one here to define him, he's undefined. It's like he's turned off. I still cannot get used to him being different. I understand that he *is* different, but I still expect he can do things normally."

Tammara was convinced the dramatic change in her husband was the result of a TBI he'd sustained when a bomb blasted him off his seat and into unconsciousness during his Iraq deployment in 2005. Congress didn't pass legislation mandating comprehensive TBI testing until 2007, long after Sean and thousands of other soldiers needed it. Four years later, the military was still struggling to develop and execute the test. The Fort Harrison VA in Helena, Montana, denied Sean's claim for a TBI after he forgot to go to several screening appointments. By the time Tammara got involved, Sean had been assigned to a different doctor, and the whole process had to be started over, beginning with an appeal. Tammara handled the paperwork and paid for him to be examined at two private clinics.

"Outside neuropsychological reports support my diagnosis [of a moderate to severe TBI]," said Tammara, "and the fucker who said it wasn't a TBI has been fired for pronouncing on what he knew nothing about."

The VA assigned a therapist to work with Sean on memory and retention.

"Sean, you have moderate to severe deficits in executive functioning," said the VA clinician at the first session, "and these injuries are old enough that the window of opportunity to repair them is closed. They are permanent. There are coping mechanisms you can learn that can help you, but outside of that, nothing else is possible. And those depend on your being willing to both accept the situation, and habitually use the tools we can provide."

"Nothing I didn't know," said Tammara, but hearing it was "devastating nonetheless. [I was] vindicated and destroyed in the same paragraph."

Like any other injury, early intervention is best, and even when that occurs, there's only so much that can be done to improve brain functioning. Once that plateau is reached, the veteran may hold steady for a while, but over time, their cognitive capacity often takes a long downward slide. Sean's impairment was such that the therapist ordered him a couple of Livescribe pens, which sync written text directly onto a phone or computer, automatically converting whatever is jotted down into organized, searchable content. Tammara calls them "magic pens," and maybe they are, but the VA never taught Sean how to use them. His therapist quit after the first few sessions. And several hundred taxpayer dollars worth of electronic wizardry rides around town on the seat of Sean's truck, gathering dust.

Lorin was also bounced from one primary care provider, and color-coded care team, to another for more than a year. The constant shuffling and re-shuffling of VA providers is a systemic issue that has yet to be addressed in any meaningful way. There's a huge amount of turnover because the VA is basically a training facility where health-care professionals build their resumes before entering the much more lucrative world of private practice. The VA is also grotesquely understaffed and unprepared for the sheer number of veterans suffering the signature wounds of these wars—TBI and PTSD. At one point, the White City VA had just 1.5 full-time equivalent psychologists for tens of thousands of veterans, so the southern Oregon VA campus and many others are increasingly sending vets to civilian providers. That's where Sean and Tammara ended up, but the private therapist spent the appointment instructing Tammara on what *she* needed to do to help him, rather than how Sean could help himself. They didn't go back.

Tammara didn't see the point of going to a counselor who wanted her, rather than her husband, the patient, to learn new skills. She didn't need one more professional shifting one more thing onto her overflowing plate. She was already working, taking care of Sean, the house, the yard, and their five rescue dogs, while handling all of the paperwork for pursuing the TBI claim. The more the VA providers piled on her plate, and the more times they were wrong or dropped the ball, the angrier she got, delivering blistering verbal attacks on whomever happened to answer the phone or be sitting behind the desk when they showed up for an appointment.

"The VA will not work with me," she said. "It's gotten to a point where I've been so fucking fed up and nasty with them that they don't want to work with me. And I don't blame them."

She had been seeing a counselor from time to time, but said that she'd lost the will to fight anymore, for her husband or for herself.

"I used to cry and rage; now I'm just so tired. I just don't have the energy any more. I've got a good reason for being depressed, but medication won't help, because it can't change the reason why I'm depressed. Between Sean being in Iraq and dealing with him afterward, I've just given up."

She knows it could be worse. There are days, though, when she doesn't know exactly how, because it felt pretty damn bad already.

"I feel like I've already died," she said. "I just haven't lain down yet."

She knows she's not supposed to be angry, but she is. She's angry at the institutions that failed her husband and now are failing her. She's angry at her family, who doesn't begin to understand what she's living with, and doesn't seem to want to try. She had two uncles that served in Vietnam, and they're both dead from Agent Orange poisoning and the accumulated toll of combat injuries that got worse, not better, with time. But her family's past war hasn't translated into the current one, and she's both frightened and furious to be speaking a language they cannot comprehend. Tammara remembers being at her grandma's house when her uncles were in the jungle, and how her grandma dropped the laundry basket when a black car parked in front and two men in uniform got out. They walked past the house, and knocked on the neighbor's door; it was their son who had been killed in action, not her grandma's. But it was clear to anyone who could see that something had died in Jimmy and Sammy too when those boys came home. And Tammara is livid now that she's left by herself to deal with the fallout from a war she didn't even want.

She's angry at the people who said they wanted to volunteer at a veteran's shelter, but when she said, "Come to my house," they didn't. She's angry at the people for whom Veterans Day is nothing more than a great day to shop.

"We are already angry," writes Torrey Shannon in a blog post for the *Huffington Post* entitled "Beware of the Wounded Warrior's Wife."

> We accept responsibility for marrying a military man, but we do not *easily* accept having a different man than we married coming back from war. Some of our husbands do not remember our own children's names. They don't remember how to dress themselves, the route to take to pick the kids up from school, or how to cook a simple meal. . . . We are not angry with THEM about these things: We are furious at the cards we were dealt and indignant that such a horrible thing had to happen to our husbands in the first place. We are angry about the loss of the marriage we were supposed to have, and we never truly stop mourning. We're angry at the doctors who blow us off when we give our input, or the VA who puts him into a backlog. . . . We hold a grudge against anybody who ever failed us as we tried to make sense of this chaos. We are also furious at ourselves, because we constantly feel like we're not doing enough to help.[72]

We're furious too at the constant crushing pressure placed on us by health-care providers and communal expectations that it's our job, *our* duty, our *obligation* to keep our veteran alive.

---

72. Shannon, "Beware of the Wounded Warrior's Wife," *Huffington Post*.

"At one point," one caregiver said, "I was ready to [leave my husband]. . . . The doctor said, 'You realize if you leave, he's not going to make it.'"[73] We are mad, and scared, and tired of this socially sanctioned codependency that guilts us into responsibility for someone else's survival.

With that responsibility, however, also comes a sense of reward for many military caregivers who don't want someone else taking care of their loved one. Most injured veterans don't trust strangers enough to let them into their homes, much less tolerate having them help with things that they resent not being able to do for themselves.

So we fight. We fight with ourselves and for our spouses. We fight for their benefits, their treatment, and sometimes, their lives. We fight for them to have access to programs, services, buildings, and events. We fight with our community, and sometimes with Congress, to make sure our veterans receive what they were promised. We fight to help our friends and family members understand what it's really like at home, and why their support is so important, and how sometimes we get bone-tired of fighting and need sanctuary ourselves.

Torrey was in the process of creating that for herself and her husband, Staff Sergeant John Daniel Shannon, who was critically injured in a gunfight in Iraq in 2004, resulting in a traumatic brain injury from a gunshot wound to the head. The pair has three children, and the whole family struggled in the aftermath of that battle, spurring Torrey and her husband to successfully advocate for congressional action and improvements in the military healthcare system. It also led to Torrey being nominated as one of the

---

73. Tanielian et al., "Military Caregivers," Rand Corporation.

twenty inaugural caregiver fellows of the Senator Elizabeth Dole Foundation.

Senator Dole launched the Elizabeth Dole Fellows Program as the focus of the foundation's work after her husband, Senator Bob Dole, spent nearly the whole of 2010 at Walter Reed. During that time, Mrs. Dole spoke with hundreds of injured troops and their caregivers. Troubled by just how challenging it was for the caregivers, she was determined to provide them a voice and draw upon their expertise in informing programs and policies. The Dole Foundation is the only private organization in the country dedicated to raising awareness and support for military and veterans' caregivers, particularly the post-9/11 cohort, whose needs and realities are markedly different from caregivers of civilians, and even caregivers of veterans from previous conflicts.

"Military caregivers helping veterans from earlier eras tend to resemble civilian caregivers in many ways," according to a 2013 Rand report commissioned by the Dole Foundation. The Rand Corporation is a research organization often used to conduct studies for the Department of Defense. The report reinforced earlier findings that military caregivers of all eras consistently experience poorer physical and behavioral health outcomes, greater stress in family relationships, and more workplace problems than non-caregivers. The study also found that post-9/11 military caregivers already fare worst of all in all of those categories. And that's a problem because they've only been at it for a decade or so, and right now, it's as good as it's going to get for a very, very long time.

Speaking at a National Press Club luncheon in November of 2014, Secretary Robert McDonald, appointed by President Obama to head up the VA in the wake of Shinseki's resignation, said that he anticipated the needs of OIF/OEF veterans would peak in about forty years. I suspect it may be closer to thirty for three reasons: first, post-9/11 veterans started out as the oldest aggregate veteran population this country's ever seen. At the start of the war on terror, the average Guard soldier was in his thirties, and active-duty troops were in their mid-twenties. In previous wars, the typical GI was nineteen.

Second, these veterans are getting sicker faster than earlier generations due to multiple, lengthy deployments with no front lines and skyrocketing rates of PTSD, TBI, and polytrauma. The disabled veteran population grew by nearly 50 percent from 2000 to 2013, and the ratio of veterans with disability ratings above 70 percent almost doubled.[74] Both of those figures are expected to continue to climb for the foreseeable future.

Third, between 20 to 40 percent of today's combat veterans are struggling with PTSD, and an estimated 10 to 20 percent have TBIs, figures that are certain to increase in the coming decades. PTSD has been linked to early aging, and VA scientists have found indications of premature aging and progressive brain damage in OIF/OEF vets who were exposed to bomb blasts, as reported in the June 2015 issue of *Brain, A Journal of Neurology*.[75] Given the physiological implications of PTSD, including increased rates of heart attacks, strokes, gastrointestinal problems, substance abuse, depression, and dementia, it can be anticipated that the ailments of those vets will accelerate over time. And the heavy burden of caring

---

74. Zoroya and Hoye, "Veterans' Disability," *USA Today*.

75. Trotter et al., "Military Blast Exposure," *Brain, A Journal of Neurology*.

for post-9/11 veterans will become staggering for those who carry the load.

Nearly 100 percent of veterans' caregivers are women, and in our highly gendered culture, they are expected to step into that role readily. Whereas only 6 percent of civilian caregivers who assist civilian family members are providing care to a significant other, at least 70 percent of veterans' caregivers are helping their husband or partner, which profoundly changes the relationship dynamics. "Of those who are currently married, separated or divorced, nearly three-quarters say caregiving or the veteran's condition placed a strain on their marriage."[76] When a spouse shifts from a partner role to a parent role in taking care of a wounded warrior, the libido of both can take a hit.

"Sex isn't great with someone you're responsible for," said Marshele Waddell in an interview with Lee Woodruff of CBS News that aired January 3, 2010. "It seems incestuous."

Marshele's husband, Commander Mark Waddell, a US Navy SEAL, retired after twenty-five years of service with a TBI and PTSD that gave him "a very short fuse, with no tolerance for the unpredictable." The camera captures the two of them sitting side-by-side, and while he appears calm, reflective, and at times upbeat, Marshele's face is a study in loss, tension, and disbelief that her husband can joke about how, as the result of his invisible injuries, "it's kind of like getting to date a new girl again."

Tammara also felt squeamish about having sex with her husband, because she "didn't have sex with children." It is the childlike quality of many vets with moderate to severe TBIs that

---

76. National Alliance for Caregiving, "Caregivers of Veterans."

frequently makes intimacy difficult, distasteful, and in many cases, impossible.

"I'd say that cognitively, he's about like a ten-year-old," said Debbie Sanford in November 2012. "We don't have real conversations. He can't do anything that requires a sequence of more than two steps."[77] Debbie quit her job to take care of her thirty-one-year-old husband, Brandon, after he spent a year undergoing treatment at a neuro-rehabilitation center in Texas, trying to restore some of the cognitive function that had been lost in Iraq. Brandon was wounded in three different explosions, but the extent of the internal damage didn't become evident until after the Army staff sergeant came home. Prior to Brandon's discharge, one of the neurologists had a conversation with Debbie, trying to impress upon her just what the future held. Debbie maintained that she was ready for it. She was not.

"Suddenly I was doing a job that fifteen different people had been doing before," Debbie said. "I thought he'd get better, but he actually got worse. He had terrible panic attacks and nightmares. He wouldn't leave the house."

Debbie was on call around the clock, making his meals and driving the daily hour-long commute to the nearest VA for her husband's rehabilitation therapy, tracking everything in a journal so that Brandon can see what he's learned. Because of Brandon's seizures, she had to keep an eye on him at all times. Ever since Debbie started bringing him to the nail salon and other gatherings, her girlfriends have gradually disappeared.

---

77. Daum, "Caregivers: Celebrating the Invisible War Heroes," *Redbook*.

"The women I used to get pedicures with, I don't really see them anymore," she said. "Brandon comes everywhere with me. It's like, 'Come on, Brandon, I need to go pull the weeds.' 'Come on, Brandon, we're gonna garden now.' If I go to the nail salon, he comes with me. And I guess they got tired of that."

Overwhelming social isolation is a defining characteristic of the post-9/11 caregiver population, over half of whom have no caregiving network to support them, according to a Rand report. There are a handful of programs that provide services to caregivers, but they are in their infancy, and almost all are focused on the veteran. Veterans' caregivers have been so invisible for so long that agencies have only recently begun to try to understand their needs and tailor programs and services to meet them. This country has a huge stake in getting that done right and getting it done right now, because the general consensus, which is supported by reams of research, is that the well-being of the caregiving spouse is the main predictor of the well-being of the veteran and the family.

I attended a few VA-sponsored caregiver support groups, but when the nurse facilitator said she "got some of her best ideas from Dr. Phil," I quit going. I had watched a couple of his shows with wounded veterans, and always ended up yelling at the screen. Dr. Phil interacted with the vets, but seemed oblivious to the fact that sitting next to every one of them was a wife or a mom with tears streaming down her face. We get used to being ignored, and we, in turn, learn to ignore ourselves. Studies on military caregivers show that they "tend to put their own concerns last,"[78] with the majority reporting "declines in their own healthy behaviors, such

---

78. Tanielian et al., "Military Caregivers," Rand Corporation.

as exercising (69 percent), good eating habits (56 percent), and going to one's own doctor and dentist appointments on schedule (58 percent)."[79]

Caring for a veteran with a disability rating of 70 percent or higher can be a full-time job, often to the detriment of the caregivers' own employment and financial stability. At least half of veterans' caregivers give up educational goals and professional careers, sacrificing current and potential earnings, losing something of themselves in the process. But quitting school or work or taking an early retirement can be better than the alternative. Caregiver Virginia Peacock wrote in *The State* that she had to leave her job to save her life. Peacock had worked as a nurse for nearly twenty years when she became her husband Dave's caregiver as well. The damage done by eleven deployments included PTSD and a TBI, and Dave was medically retired in 2012. A few years later, his wife said, "I had not been taking care of myself. I became depressed—so depressed that I began having suicidal thoughts."[80]

A study on caregiver burden among partners of vets with PTSD stated that nearly half of the wives "felt as if they were on the verge of a nervous breakdown."[81] A Rand report revealed that 38 percent of post-9/11 military caregivers, and 19 percent of pre-9/11 military caregivers, have major depressive disorder (MDD). Another investigation found "high levels of psychological distress with elevations on clinical scales at or exceeding the 90th percentile. Severe levels

---

79. Ibid.

80. Peacock, "Military, veteran caregivers need our support," *The State*.

81. Beckham, Lytle, and Feldman, "Caregiver burden," *Journal of Consulting and Clinical Psychology*.

of overall psychological distress, depression and suicidal ideation were prevalent among partners."[82]

I WAS STRESSED AND lonely and exhausted. I was bewildered by what my life, and my husband, had become, and regardless of what I did, I couldn't change it. I couldn't make it stop. My dad, Russ Hersrud, and stepmom, Jean, drove down for Thanksgiving 2012, which had always been the best holiday for us—a long, lazy day of food and family and watching Gonzaga basketball. Lorin and I hadn't seen them for over a year, since Lorin wasn't willing to travel, and I thought he was looking forward to their visit, too. But when they arrived, Lorin disappeared. He picked up extra hours at work, and then came home and scuttled to his workshop in the back of the two-car garage, which had effectively become his bunker. I had to hunt him down to get him to join us for Thanksgiving dinner, whereas before, he was right in the middle of it, making the turkey and stuffing, drinking a glass or two of wine, laughing and talking. My folks and I and a few friends of mine were already seated when Lorin finally grabbed a chair. He wolfed down his food, disparaged my cooking, and was aggressive, irate, and unpleasant. When Lorin got like this, when he became "General Dickishness," I just kept my head down and let it pass, because I knew that Lorin was looking for a fight that I could never win.

My dad was disgusted by Lorin's behavior, and when Russ called him on it, the two of them began to argue. Lorin threw down

---

82. Mire et al., "Psychological Distress," *Journal of Nervous and Mental Disease*.

his silverware and stormed upstairs, slamming the door of his office. He'd made it into a shrine for his service, hanging yards of digital camouflage material on the door and one wall and painting the trim Army green and the remaining walls infantry blue. Stacks of boxes, papers, and books, mounds of unopened mail, and piles of dirty clothing and military gear covered the floor so that you had to choose your steps carefully. The screensaver on his computer scrolled through hundreds of photos of his time in Iraq, many of them featuring blood-spattered vehicles, both military and civilian. The room was the physical manifestation of being stuck in a psychological sickness, and I avoided it altogether. We didn't see him for the rest of the night.

At the Black Friday brunch the following day it was the same, but worse. I had made a tater-tot hot dish and a cheesecake that Lorin loved, but he sat at the table and proclaimed the casserole "gross and disgusting," and then rambled on about a really great cheesecake he'd gotten from a local bakery. He continued to pick me apart as my friends and family grew increasingly uncomfortable and sent me sympathetic glances. That bullying, abusive behavior is pretty common in vets who haven't dealt with their PTSD, and I had gotten used to Lorin saving up his frustration with work, school, and the world and vomiting it on me. But lately it had become malicious, almost malignant.

After my friends left, I walked down to the pasture and cried. My folks cut their visit short, and just before they departed, my dad glared at Lorin and said, "Be civil." After he returned to Coeur d'Alene, Idaho, Russ told me they wouldn't be back, not for that. I was saddened but not surprised. I wasn't going to invite my family or friends again anyway. It hurt too much to be humiliated in my own home.

Studies show more than two-thirds of people cut back on time spent with family and friends after assuming the caregiver role. Between work and Lorin, I just didn't have as much time, and when he quit wanting to do anything away from home he wasn't getting paid for or graded on, I kind of quit, too. Avoidance is one of the symptoms associated with PTSD, and Lorin could steer clear of reminders of the trauma by keeping to himself.

I didn't want to leave him alone any more than I had to, and I got weary of explaining his absence at social events or running interference and rationalizing his behavior when he attended. Lorin had no social filter whatsoever, but he really wanted to go to my office Christmas party, and I really didn't want to go alone. So I introduced to him one of the owners during pre-dinner cocktails and Lorin promptly began badmouthing the boss's protégé who worked in the suicide prevention program at the VA. I pulled Lorin away and ushered him to our table, and General Dickishness sat down. We couldn't leave until dinner was over, so the next few hours were a not-so-festive exercise in damage control for my husband's appalling behavior. All the while, I was dying inside, trying to figure out who the stranger was in the seat next to mine. I just got tired of the constant confrontations, with Lorin and other people, and how every single one of them forced me to look into the well of my own bottomless grief. I excused myself during dinner and went to the women's room, locked the stall door, and wept.

I couldn't count on Lorin any more for solace. He was incapable of providing emotional support, and he maintained that he "wasn't ready" to get treatment for his PTSD.

"But Lorin, what happens if I'm done before you're ready?" I asked.

"How come you don't understand that I can't?" he'd demand, never waiting for an answer.

"There's a world of difference between won't and can't," Kat Causey blogged. "Living in between is a purgatory of its own. . . . Some days, I want a TBI to manifest itself into something human so I can punch it in the face. Repeatedly. And often. I'll take the physical disability hurdles over the mental ones *any day*, a million times over, and I reckon Aaron would, too. . . . We have a lot to be grateful for, but it doesn't make what we will *never* do again hurt any less. Stupid war." [83]

Kat's husband, Sergeant First Class Aaron Causey, explosive ordnance disposal, was conducting dismounted counter-IED operations in southern Afghanistan when an IED detonated while he was working on it. SFC Causey lost both legs above the knee, two fingers, and a testicle. After three years of treatment and rehabilitation that included more than forty surgeries on his legs, hands, arms, abdomen, and backside and multiple skin grafts, he went home to his wife and their baby girl. Roughly one-third of veterans' caregivers have minor children at home, and over half of those kids are having difficulties at school or struggling emotionally. More than two-thirds of caregivers report having spent less time with their children than they would like, primarily because of the demands of invisible injuries.

Ever since a car bomb exploded in Iraq more than ten years ago, Alex Guad-Torres has been trying to balance the needs of her

---

83. www.afterblastwarriorwife.com.

three kids with those of her husband, Axel Guad-Torres. An October 4, 2014, article in the *Gazette* reported that the thirty-year-old Air Force master sergeant needed assistance with bathing, walking, taking medication, and most other ADLs. His wife makes his doctor's appointments, sees to it that he gets to them, and keeps an ever-expanding collection of medical records and notes and files. When their insurance claims get rejected, she handles it, along with all of the household bills, maintenance, cooking, and cleaning. One night, she had supper on the stove and put her husband in a chair to keep an eye on the rice. As the pan began smoking on the stove, a panicked Axel screamed at his wife.

"He didn't know where he was," she said.

That can happen with PTSD or a TBI. More than once, they've had to make a hasty exit from restaurants when the sudden shouts and impulsive movements of kids being kids put Axel on red alert. "Chuck E. Cheese is out of the question," said Axel.

His wife has been looking for the man she married in her husband's face for more than a decade. "Nobody talked to me about what to expect about having him home from a war zone. I had no clue. . . . Every once in a while, he comes out for a little while and I'm reminded why we got married. That keeps me going."

Alex, in turn, keeps her husband going.

"I thought I had it hard," he said. "I thought that what we faced in Iraq was hard. But it's harder for the spouse. It's harder for the spouse when we come home. Without my wife, I would be dead. That's all there is to it."

Family caregivers keep veterans alive and off the streets, saving US taxpayers billions of dollars. According to the VA, homeless veterans are at least three times as expensive to care for as veterans in stable housing, and behavioral health counseling for veterans has been found to be much more successful when the family is involved. The VA Caregiver Program that was implemented after the passage of the Caregivers and Veterans Omnibus Health Services Act of 2010 provides post-9/11 caregivers who qualify (the veteran's injury must have been assigned a disability rating of 40 percent or more) with a monthly support group, formal training focused on physical health care, and access to occasional videoconferences on topics such as PTSD, TBI, and self-care.

After both the caregiver and the veteran are approved for program participation, the caregiver may also receive a monthly stipend depending on the how much time and support the veteran requires each week. There are three tiers of care, ranging from ten to forty hours per week, although most caregivers are on call around-the-clock. The rate of compensation is determined by the average wage paid for caregiver services in the local economy, typically between $9 and $10 dollars an hour, slightly more in major metropolitan areas. The Rand report estimated that the actual duties and services provided by post-9/11 caregivers are worth approximately $3 billion annually (in 2011 dollars). In fiscal year 2014, the VA Caregiver Support Program, including staff, services, and stipend, cost about $350 million,[84] netting the nation well over two and a half billion dollars in free services for veterans. Those services are being provided by a miniscule proportion of the population—roughly one-third of one percent—that is shouldering the bulk of the burden of a national obligation by themselves.

---

84. Shane III, "Critics," *Army Times.*

The massive cost savings provided by veterans' caregivers often comes at great expense to the caregivers themselves. The price paid includes a level of caregiver burden—exhaustion, stress, and other psychological symptoms experienced by nonprofessional caregivers who assist mentally ill and physically disabled family members at home—that has consistently been found to be more than double that of civilian caregivers. Spouses caring for veterans diagnosed with PTSD have even higher stress levels than those caring for veterans without the diagnosis. Veterans' caregivers also have high rates of financial hardship, particularly if the veteran has a mental illness or a TBI.[85] Caregivers are less prone to have health insurance than non-caregivers, and postponing their own medical treatment means increasing the likelihood of higher out-of-pocket expenses for urgent care services.

Veterans' caregivers are often footing the bill for their veteran's co-pays as well, since the VA is increasingly referring this newest generation of vets to civilian health-care providers. OIF/OEF veterans are legally entitled to five years of free VA health care for service-connected injuries and illnesses, but the White City VA's OIF/OEF/OND program coordinator kept directing Lorin to go to doctors and specialists in town at twenty-five bucks a pop. Lorin refused to pay the co-pay as a matter of principle, and after it went into collection, those bills became my responsibility. When reminded that it was the VA's responsibility to provide free care, the program coordinator replied that Lorin could either wait for a very long time, or go to a civilian.

---

85. Calhoun, Beckham, and Bosworth, "Caregiver Burden," *Journal of Traumatic Stress.*

"Besides," he said, "you're probably going to get better treatment there, anyway." That aggravated the hell out of Lorin, who wanted to turn every fuck-up and false step into a congressional inquiry, to the increasing annoyance of the staff at the small VA.

I had applied for the VA Caregiver Program, and after I was denied Lorin went into the program office in White City, yelling at the program coordinator and demanding to know why it was that we hadn't been approved, when he knew—and worked with—vets with the same level of disability, or less, whose wives had been admitted to the program. By all accounts, it was not pretty. The nurse on duty that day worked with PTSD vets all the time, but this went beyond even what she was used to. And since then she's had no particular love for Lorin. I appealed the decision, and after several rounds of documents was accepted at the lowest tier level of support.

Once a quarter, the VA conducts a home visit where a nurse comes out and spends a few hours. This was the third visit, and the third nurse or social worker, forcing me to dredge up the whole history of everything and go over it again. It's a bastardized version of Prolonged Exposure Therapy, and I could see why Lorin hated it so much and quit going after four sessions. The social worker of the month asked: What is a typical day like? What do you do for your veteran? Do you feel safe? Does he get violent? Can you give me an example?

I answered her questions, but what she failed to understand was that they made me relive and remember things I had been trying to forget. I hated going back to those memories, picking them up and rolling them around in my soul. I kept papering over the holes this never-ending war was tearing in our lives and the Caregiver

Program personnel kept making me rip it off. After about two hours of recalling and reenacting the most painful, awful moments of my marriage, she left me raw and weeping. Lorin was long gone; he bugged out if he caught the scent of my tears in the wind. I couldn't go to him anyway; the only place I could go was the barn. It was my safe place before, when my birth mother's bizarre, abusive behavior made being in the house unbearable. I went outdoors or to the barn when I hurt, but my little herd wasn't in there today. I walked to the pasture where Hickory and the goats were hanging out by the water trough.

I sat heavily on the twenty-five-pound salt block and hung my head between my knees, crying in the dirt. It felt like I would be crying for the rest of my life, and I looked at Hickory, about three yards away, and pleaded, "If you can talk, now would be the time to say something." He meandered over, stopped, and dropped his head so that his left eye was level with mine. One clear, shimmering tear descended from the corner, and he turned his head and did it again. I was alone on this planet, except for my horse.

CHAPTER SEVEN

The Biology of the War at Home

I F THIS NATION'S MORAL compass has retained any magnetism whatsoever, the biological collateral damage of combat in the family members of veterans should point it toward ending endless wars. The psychological toll of war on military families has been documented, but the physiological implications of those problems have largely been ignored. Based on accumulating evidence that emotional problems, particularly trauma and stress, are linked to physical illness, and extrapolating from the mounting research indicating that those problems are heritable, America may well have consigned the caregivers, children, and grandchildren of today's wounded warriors to sadder, sicker, shorter lives. Military kids growing up in the shadow of more than a decade of war are suffering higher levels of child abuse, neglect, maltreatment, and psychological disorders than any previous population sampling, according to data from the *Journal of Developmental and Behavioral Pediatrics*, the *Army Times*, and elsewhere.

More than half a million children of active-duty troops are under the age of six. They are emotionally dependent on adults, and their brains are particularly susceptible to high levels of stress, depression, and anxiety in the household. Severe emotional trauma in children has been shown to change the size of several parts of the brain, including the hippocampus, which is where memories are processed. Researchers at McLean Hospital in Belmont, Massachusetts, found that portions of the hippocampus were reduced in size between 5.8 and 6.5 percent in people who had suffered abuse or neglect, whether it be physical, emotional, or sexual, major grief, or significant parental conflict.

Prolonged stress and anxiety during childhood seems to increase both the size and synaptic connections of the amygdala, which is associated with aspects of perceiving, learning, and regulating emotions. Stanford University researchers discovered that "the larger the amygdala—and the stronger its connections with other regions of the brain responsible for perception and the regulation of emotion—the greater the amount of anxiety a child was experiencing."[86] And the more likely they were to be consigned to chronic anxiety, adulthood depression, and possible development of an autism-spectrum disorder. According to recent research, autism may be rooted in structural irregularities in brain development that occur in the womb. A study of the donated post-mortem brain tissue of autistic children found that more than 90 percent had "recurring patches of abnormal development in layers of the cerebral cortex that form

---

86. Bergland, "The Size and Connectivity," *The Athlete's Way.*

during prenatal development," according to the March 26, 2014, report on *Autism Speaks*.[87] Those areas of irregular growth were evident in less than 10 percent of the children without autism.

The cerebral or prefrontal cortex where the patches were discovered is the most evolved region of the brain. It is also the most susceptible to the detrimental effects of stress. Early childhood maltreatment is linked to a reduction in the temporal and prefrontal cortexes of infants. During the first year and a half of life, the actual cellular growth and functioning of the prefrontals is reliant on appropriate stimuli from the environment.[88] When the early childhood environment is defined by parental stress and prolonged exposure to traumatic events, including parents displaying symptoms of PTSD or a TBI, brain growth will likely be retarded, stunting everything from social relationships to SAT scores.

The prefrontal cortex is responsible for our highest-order cognitive abilities and is hypersensitive to in utero stress, including increased heart rate, blood pressure, and cortisol levels of the mother. When a pregnant woman (or any person) perceives a threat, whether physical or psychological, the hypothalamus, a small region at the base of the brain, sounds an alarm. The "fight, flight, or freeze" response triggers a surge of adrenaline and cortisol that permeate the placenta. In the midst of this hormonal flood, the immune, digestive, and reproductive systems not essential in dangerous situations are suspended or suppressed. Over time, fetal exposure to stress results in architectural changes in

---

87. "Direct Evidence that Autism Starts During Prenatal Development," *Autism Speaks*.

88. Pearce, *The Biology of Transcendence*.

prefrontal dendrites. This creates impaired stress signal pathways in unborn children that can yield symptoms of severe prefrontal cortical dysfunction connected to mental illness. According to a study conducted by Professor Matti Huttunen of the University of Helsinki, acute stress may be associated with markedly higher rates of behavior disorders and schizophrenia in adult children born to World War II widows.

Severe stress is caused by events that pose an immediate threat to one's life or the life of a loved one: the unexpected death of a close family member, a terrorist attack, or war. As the result of unending war, the military community has been living with extreme and chronic stress for more than a dozen years. This severe stress has been linked to elevated cortisol levels in pregnant women that are evident in their children for years after their birth. Post-deployment pregnancy raises the risk of maternal onset of depression, anxiety, and post-traumatic stress in female veterans.[89]

More than three hundred thousand women have served in Iraq or Afghanistan, and at least a third of them have suffered military sexual trauma or PTSD, as well as the attendant depression and anxiety common to both diagnoses. Maternal depression and anxiety predisposes the developing fetus to a host of physical and behavioral problems, such as low birth weight, premature birth, more reactivity to stress, difficulty sleeping, and higher rates of impulsivity and hyperactivity. Prenatal factors combine to produce offspring whose biological resources have been configured for physical survival in the presence of a constant threat, rather than

---

89. "Women War Veterans Face Higher Risk of Mental Health Problems During Pregancy," *ScienceDaily*.

children who are wired for the optimal intelligence, creativity, and social connectivity that would support success in an environment of relative calm. To a remarkable degree, whatever we are subjected to in the womb is what we are physiologically geared for in life.

Nowhere is the in utero susceptibility to stress more evident than in epigenetics, the alteration of gene expression that "can occur transgenerationally, developmentally, or in response to environmental stimuli such as stress exposure."[90] Epigenetics—from *epi* or "on top of" genetics—focuses on how what happens outside of the gene influences the way the gene performs. Epigenetics is the intersection of nature and nurture.

Maia Szalavitz is a neuroscience journalist for Time.com. She explains some of the potential ramifications of childhood trauma. "By either silencing or activating genes, epigenetic changes can influence everything from brain development and functioning to the risk for certain diseases."[91] Maternal diet and prenatal stress both cause epigenetic changes, but parental stress and abuse in early childhood have also been shown to change children's patterns of genetic activity through their teen years, and possibly beyond. Many of the post-9/11 military kids have lived with a significantly stressed parent, either the returning service member or the civilian spouse, and sometimes both. Growing up with a mentally ill, chemically dependent, abusive, or neglectful parent affects brain development, hormonal and immune systems, and DNA function. A high level of childhood exposure to these painful events triples the potential for heart disease and lung cancer and reduces life

90. Hodes, "Sex, Stress," *Biology of Sex Differences Journal.*
91. Szalavitz, "Abused Children May Get Unique Form of PTSD," Time.com.

expectancy by two decades, according to Dr. Nadine Burke Harris on *AlterNet*.[92] A significant subset of the military child population has also experienced child neglect or abuse, all of which have physiological implications.

Research available through the National Center for Biotechnology Information found that some of the genes that were influenced—typically they were deactivated—by parental stress were ones involved in DNA repair. The impact of parental stress also appeared to change two of the proteins involved in how their child's brain develops and performs, changes that may well be permanent.

Writing about "how stressed parents scar their kids," for the *Daily Beast* on September 12, 2011, Sharon Begley stated, "although the adult brain retains enormous powers of plasticity, the window when the basic wiring takes place tends to slam shut by early adulthood.... Some DNA changes, particularly those in genes that choreograph brain development, may have a lifelong legacy."

Childhood abuse appears to create an epigenetic pathway for the development of PTSD when trauma is experienced again later in life. In a study of people with PTSD who had suffered major traumatic events in adulthood, those who also had a history of child abuse had twelve times the level of epigenetic changes of those with no early abuse.[93] PTSD-imposed epigenetic changes may last for multiple generations, being passed on from grandparents to grandchildren. Epigenetic studies of humans are still relatively scarce, but transgenerational epigenetic inheritance of early stress, adverse conditions,

---

92. Harris, "Doctor: Childhood Trauma Can Destroy Your Health," *AlterNet*.

93. Mehta et al., "Childhood Maltreatment," *Proceedings of the National Academy of Sciences*.

and "emotional trauma" of the "first generation" that altered gene expression in subsequent generations has been demonstrated in mice, rats, and a variety of other animals, plants, and even bacteria.[94] A similar intergenerational transference of trauma-induced mutations in genetic expression likely occurs within humans.

Evidence to support this is found in multiple studies that have discovered PTSD symptoms and increased stress hormones in second-generation survivors of the Holocaust. Rachel Yehuda, PhD, professor of psychiatry and neuroscience, is an expert on the molecular biology of intergenerational trauma. She founded a clinic exclusively devoted to treating Holocaust victims, anticipating a flood of calls from survivors. What she got was a tsunami of inquiries from their middle-aged children who were living the effects of a horror that happened before they were born.

Yehuda's initial research on Holocaust offspring revealed that the children of PTSD-stricken mothers were three times as likely to be diagnosed with PTSD as control group members. Rates of substance abuse, depression, and anxiety in children of parents with PTSD were up to three and four times higher. Cortisol levels in grandchildren of Holocaust survivors were also negatively affected. The same was true for infants whose mothers had been pregnant and near the Twin Towers on 9/11, according to Yehuda. She is the director of mental health services at the Bronx VA and works at Mount Sinai, where she continues to investigate the transgenerational transmission of PTSD, the subject of an increasing amount of research.

---

94. Kellerman, "Epigenetic Transmission," *Israel Journal of Psychiatry and Related Sciences*.

Studies also suggest that PTSD manifests differently depending on the parental source. For example, according to Judith Shulevitz, "maternal PTSD heightens the chance that a child will incur the kind of hormonal profile that makes it harder to calm down. Paternal PTSD exacerbates the possibility that the child's PTSD, if she gets it, will be the more serious kind that involves feeling dissociated from her memories."[95]

Maternal PTSD, including secondary PTSD, can powerfully affect offspring in the womb and during infancy and early childhood, making it difficult to isolate the genetic contribution. But, Yehuda argues, paternal transmission is more clear-cut, and believes that her findings on fathers suggest that PTSD may induce epigenetic changes to sperm. Yehuda's colleague at the Mount Sinai Medical School, Dr. Scott Russo, is a biological psychologist studying neurobiology and depression. Dr. Russo has been researching the paternal transmission of stress vulnerability traits, and the results implicate "a role for epigenetic modifications in the paternal germ line."

I interviewed Dr. Russo about the mechanisms by which traumatic events become biologically embedded in specific genes. During our conversation, it became apparent that PTSD most powerfully alters the genes that regulate the immune system. In the first large-scale investigation of trauma-induced differences in the genes of people with PTSD, DNA samples revealed that "participants with PTSD had six to seven times more unmethylated genes than unaffected participants, and most of the unmethylated genes were involved in the immune system," reported *ScienceDaily* on May 5, 2010. Methylation is a basic epigenetic control mechanism used by cells to lock genes in an "off"

---

95. Shulevitz, "The Science of Suffering," *New Republic*.

position. Changes in methylation, such as unmethylation and hyper-methylation, produce dysfunctional changes in gene regulation. Errors in methylation are linked to a variety of devastating consequences, including cancer.

"PTSD is a full-body disease. We need to treat it like cancer or heart disease," said Dr. Russo. "If you catch it and treat it aggressively and early, you'll have your best prognosis." The longer you wait, "the more damage it will cause, becoming less likely to respond and go into remission." That damage may well extend to the cellular level, according to a study showing that susceptibility to stress may be transmitted epigenetically by changes in germ cells (sperm or egg) that consequently influence the behavior of the progeny for up to three generations.[96]

Genetics are a key factor in the heritability of mental illness and susceptibility to addiction. In a sampling of adult children of combat veterans with PTSD, more than 80 percent demonstrated hypervigilance, 65 percent began using alcohol during childhood, and over half reported drug use. A report published by the Australian Institute for Health & Welfare in 2000 revealed that children of Vietnam vets are more likely than children of nonveterans to suffer depression and die of accidental death.

Maureen Wildes's husband served in Vietnam, and she participated in the study. Their adult son is one of an alarmingly high number of children of Vietnam vets struggling with a mental disorder.

"There is something wrong with our children," said Maureen. Suicide rates of children of male Vietnam veterans, most of whom

---

96. Franklin et al., "Epigenetic Transmission," *Biological Psychiatry*.

served a single tour, are triple that of civilian youth. Time will tell if multiple tours raise that rate even higher in the children of veterans who served in Iraq and Afghanistan.

* * *

Ariana del Negro lost twenty-five pounds in one month, and friends said she looked great. They wanted to know what she'd done. "My husband got blown up," she told them. Second Lieutenant Charles Gatlin was a scout/sniper and reconnaissance platoon leader of the 25th Infantry Battalion in northern Iraq. On September 28, 2006, a vehicle-borne IED detonated less than twenty yards from where he was standing outside his forward operating base in Kirkuk. He was medevaced to Joint Base Balad for treatment, and Ariana got the call informing her that her husband had an acute brain injury. Ariana managed the cardiology site on the Web MD Medscape and immediately began researching brain injuries. The Sharp Institute's Community Reintegration Program in San Diego looked to be the best treatment facility, and in 2007, that's where he went.

"I got the horse to water, but I couldn't make him drink. It was up to him to maximize the opportunity," said Ariana in a phone call. She and I had been electronically introduced by another military family member whose son was gearing up for his sixth deployment as an Army Ranger. While Charles was working on getting better, Ariana was working up to fourteen hours a day, but "I couldn't concentrate at work," she said. "I was so engrossed in what was going on with him." She gave up her job and six-figure salary in 2009 to focus on her husband's support and recovery.

It was "no longer a husband-wife relationship, [but] we're the fortunate unfortunate ones," Ariana said. "Holy shit, my husband's an officer, we're financially independent; how hard is it for others?"

Charles was permanently medically retired with a rating of 70 percent disability due to his head injury and awarded a Purple Heart. His TBI claim was rejected by the Fort Harrison VA in Helena, Montana. Ariana first challenged their findings in August of 2011, the beginning of a more than three-year-long battle that would eventually get her called before the US Congress in April 2014. In her opening remarks to the House Committee on Veterans' Affairs about the VA's persistent pattern of denying TBI claims, Ariana testified that "there is evidence that the gross malpractice and undercutting of the Veteran and his/her family that we have witnessed is indicative of policies and procedures routinely endorsed within the local system and may even reflect current practice at many VA's throughout the nation."

Ariana continues to advocate for her husband and others, and like most of the spouses who have taken the fight to the Hill on behalf of our veterans and our families, she doesn't get paid for that work. They were separated for a while and are struggling to adapt to the changes in their relationship.

"He probably resents me," she said. "He's only admitted two times that he appreciates what I'm doing. The most important person [who can] provide feedback is him. I don't get it. . . . There's no validation from anyone.

"I'm in therapy; he's not," said Ariana. "I'm thirty-nine, but I feel older."

She probably is. Several studies have linked chronic stress, caregiving, and PTSD to significantly shortened life spans in both the veteran and the spouse. Research by Nobel laureate Elizabeth Blackburn found that female caregivers who reported very high levels of stress had markedly shorter telomeres in key cells of the immune system. Telomeres are recurring DNA sequences that function as kind of cellular timer, and after roughly fifty replications, cell division stops and aging starts. Dr. Blackburn's research of civilian caregivers found that the immune system cell truncation was equal to a decade of additional aging as compared to women with low stress levels.

Since veterans' caregivers consistently report a dramatically higher level of burden than nonveterans' caregivers, their aging process may be exponentially accelerated. Even after accounting for differences in health status, all caregivers have nearly double the occurrence of chronic conditions as noncaregivers, and higher mortality rates.[97] Telomere length is also detrimentally affected by childhood exposure to violence or other traumatic events in the home, according to research by the Tulane University School of Medicine, providing further evidence that emotionally hazardous home environments can permanently affect chromosomes and quicken biological aging.

Extreme stress or grief can also have a devastating physical impact. There is a biological basis for the widely held belief that people can die of a broken heart. In the days after a loved one dies, the risk of heart attack skyrockets by twenty-one times. Emotions have a significant role in the development of chronic disease, and social stress appears to be at least as damaging to immune function as physical stress.

---

97. Tanielian et al., "Military Caregivers," Rand Corporation.

Social stress "disregulate[s] the immune function," said Dr. Russo. In his research, he found that "the white cell count shot up as the system dumped huge amounts of proinflammatory cytokines into the bloodstream." These molecules instigate inflammation, a physiological process that repairs tissues in response to internal or external aggressors. But if that threat is constant, it can produce a chronic state of inflammation, which has been associated with a greater risk of cardiovascular events, arthritis, type II diabetes, susceptibility to infection and skin problems, and may be a factor in pathophysiological aging mechanisms, including neurodegenerative disorders such as Alzheimer's disease.[98]

Prolonged social stress, such as watching someone close to you experience stress or living with a hostile, physically or psychologically abusive veteran, keeps the body in a constant state of inflammation. More than two-thirds of veterans' caregivers reported that their veteran experiences depression, anxiety, and/or PTSD. According to an article on Today.com, the early findings of a study of family caregivers published in the journal *Biological Psychiatry* revealed that "something goes awry in the caregivers' white blood cells, leaving them less responsive to inflammation and raising their risk of illness." Other research has found that socially stressed animals were twice as likely to die as those that were biologically stressed, i.e., subjected to extended periods without food and water. If that stress is coupled with the social isolation common to veterans' caregivers, the negative health impacts may be multiplied.

---

98. Michaud et al., "Proinflammatory," *Journal of the American Medical Directors Association.*

Social isolation correlates with increased inflammation and changes in T cells, which help fight infection. One study conducted over a period of nearly two decades found the risk of heart disease shot up a stunning 76 percent in women who reported feeling lonely most of the time.[99] The increased mortality risk of significantly socially isolated persons is about that of smokers, and nearly twice that of people with obesity. Social isolation also impairs sleep, and, as stated by Jessica Olien on Slate.com, lonely people "were far more prone to micro awakenings, which suggest the brain is on alert for threats throughout the night, perhaps just as earlier humans would have needed to be when separated from their tribe."[100] Seventy-seven percent of veterans' caregivers cited sleep deprivation as an issue,[101] which has been linked to obesity, hypertension, diabetes, and a host of other physical ailments. When combined with high levels of stress, "a lack of close friends or family can significantly reduce life expectancy," writes Daniel Goleman in a December 7, 1993, article for the *New York Times*.

One study cited by Goleman found that having substantial "concerns about a family member, being forced to move, feeling insecurity at work, and [having] serious financial trouble" tripled the mortality rates among those with no social support. Many caregivers of combat veterans constantly struggle with at least two of those concerns, and often three, which may help explain their impaired health. Subsequent research has shown that social

99. Good HouseKeeping, "Heart-Health Guide."
100. Olien, "Loneliness Is Deadly," Slate.com.
101. National Alliance for Caregiving, "Caregivers of Veterans."

isolation initiates a biological chain reaction that creates malfunctions in the immune response at a molecular level.[102]

I'd been laid off in September 2013 when the VA began to roll back the HUD-VASH contracts and staff them in-house because it was more cost-effective. The financial hit was partially moderated by the increased caregiver stipend that had been awarded after a case review several months earlier. The upside of losing my job was that I was no longer working seventy-some hours a week between the office and home. Taking care of Lorin was taking even more time and energy from me; I kept telling the case managers and nurses at the VA that something was wrong, *really* wrong.

"He's getting worse," I'd say. "There's something going on with him, and I don't know what it is, but it scares me." I had been afraid for the better part of a year. Something had come into our home, a third entity or energy that felt like Hell. It was a hard, metallic frequency of raw animosity that was fueled by destruction. I began locking my bedroom door at night, terrified by something I could not see or name. Work, at least, had given me thirty-two hours a week where I could try to forget, and P. J., who was willing to help me do it. Patty Trepanier, "P. J.," had moved to Medford from Bend, Oregon, a few years earlier and had been working at the company almost that long. Her job title was housing specialist, but I called her office CENTCOM because she handled everything from ordering cars, cell phones, and laptops to arranging property and vehicle maintenance to billing. She cheerfully did whatever she was asked to do, and being around her immediately made me feel better. P. J. had a coupon for everything, so about once a week we'd go to lunch,

---

102. Medical News Network, "Social Isolation."

get pedicures, see a movie, or go shopping, a few hours of respite before I had to go home.

*　*　*

Crimson splatters the size of quarters began blooming on the leaves, faster and faster, and by the time I registered that they were coming from me, blood was streaming from my nose. I tipped my head back and pinched below my nostrils, but the bandanna was drenched within a matter of seconds. I lay down in the dirt, hoping that would stem the flow. I wondered at what point I might need to get some help. It finally stopped about ten minutes later. I cautiously sat up and felt something slither down the back of my sinus cavity. I spat out a tube of coagulated blood the size of a pen. I'd had nosebleeds before, but not for decades, and never like that.

I mentioned it a few days later when I saw my doctor because of another skin infection. This was the third one in a year, three more than I had ever had in my life. During the visit, my doctor said I'd probably had an arterial nosebleed. They are caused by the accumulation of excessive stress over a prolonged period of time, in combination with high blood pressure. Increased blood circulation is one of the changes the body makes in an effort to cope with increased mental strain and anxiety. Lorin's blood pressure readings had plummeted since we'd moved to the country, but mine had been ticking up steadily. My normal readings were around 96 over 70-something, but now they bordered on hypertension. An abnormal rise in blood pressure can damage the fragile arteries that supply blood to the entire nasal cavity, and they bleed profusely when ruptured. Unlike most other nosebleeds, those that are stress-induced start without any warning signs. I wasn't taking aspirin, anticoagulants, or any other medication; I hadn't been injured when mine started. I had just discovered we had defaulted on our home loan, which was going into foreclosure.

Every month I gave my husband money for the mortgage, and every month he assured me that it had been paid. The letter from the mortgage company said they hadn't gotten a payment for more than two months. Now my home was in jeopardy and I had proof he had lied. Again. I had been warned that "veterans lie, that's just what they do," by some program heads at the Washington State Department of Veterans Affairs years ago, when Lorin had lied about getting tested for PTSD.

I wanted to ask him what had happened to the payments, but I had no idea where he was. Lorin had taken to disappearing for hours on end, not answering his phone when I called, and coming home long after I was in bed. I left multiple voicemails on his cell phone, telling him that I knew he hadn't paid the mortgage, and that he needed to get home now. He showed up a few hours later, looking defensive.

"I fucked up," he said. "I'm sorry. I fucked up, but nobody died."

It was that last little dig, which had become his go-to comment—a free pass for any and every offense—that lit my fuse.

"Lorin, what you have done is so far beyond fucking up that fucking up isn't even *visible* from here," I said. "It doesn't even *exist* in the space-time dimension of the black hole you have created that even now is sucking the light from our lives."

He opened his pie-hole and I thrust my palms toward him to stand down now.

"You have created a shit-storm that makes the previous shit-storms you created look like a gentle spring rain. I am not sure if or how I can get past this and all of the lies, the betrayal, and the damage to my credit. I have been so careful for so many years. You are jeopardizing my home, the home for my beloved animals, my future financial stability and ability to get credit and loans." I inhaled deeply and continued.

"You just lie. Repeatedly. About major fucking shit. That car you call your life is on the verge of crashing—just like Dr. Tiffany said. And he said I should back off, and ultimately I did. And you bitched and whined and moaned and complained, when all I wanted was to support you and us in making a new life together. And now *this* is the life you think I deserve? You are going to crash and crash hard—and I am not sure I want to be in that vehicle when you do. It's been a long hard road already. I don't have any answers—and this isn't mine to fix. And if there was such a thing as a 'we,' well then *we* wouldn't be here, would we?"

He made another move to interrupt, and I held up a finger for him to wait.

"We are here because of you. And whatever comes next is squarely on *your* shoulders, *your* conscience, *your* soul for the rest of your life. I am so profoundly hurt and angry and sad. And tired, tired, *tired*, of always having to forgive; always having to be as close to perfect as I can be, because I can't afford to fuck up since you do all the time. And I think it just might be killing me."

Lorin stammered something, but I was crying so hard I couldn't hear him. He saw that and shut up, looking relieved. I shook my head, still sobbing, and walked back to the barn. Lorin disappeared again, but he called from work that night to ask if we're still on for couples counseling the next day.

"Well, jeez, I don't know, do you think we need it?" I asked, not waiting for a reply. "Yeah, I'll be there."

So we went, and talked about the mortgage situation, and the counselor helped us troubleshoot it. Then she said to me, "If Lorin has been having money problems for a while, it's going to take a long time to turn the ship. So you need to be patient, because this will probably happen again."

So I needed to be patient. As if I hadn't been patient for years. As if I hadn't been patient these past months watching the clock tick while I waited for him to show up for our counseling sessions. Half the time he'd arrive late and then sleep through most of the appointment; sometimes he just never came. He was working forty hours on the graveyard shift, occasionally picking up extra nights, and going to school, so the counselor and I were inclined to be forgiving, but he was making a travesty of marriage therapy. I hadn't even wanted to do it, not until after he began some sort of PTSD treatment, and stuck with it. He'd started pushing for marriage therapy several months earlier.

"Don't you think that's kind of like having a broken leg and wanting me to go on a cross-country hike with you?" I'd asked when he brought it up again. "I'll be happy to, but get your leg fixed first, or it's going to be painful and miserable for us both, and I'll have to carry you all the way."

"You seem to think it's so easy, but it's not," he said. "It's *not* a broken leg, and it's not so easy to fix."

"I know that, Lorin, I was trying to make a point. You are a good man with a bad injury. One that's a lot harder to heal than a broken leg, and will probably take a lot more time, which is why I wish you'd get started. Just because you can't see it doesn't mean that it doesn't hurt. It doesn't mean that you don't need help. I can't help you; you need to find someone who can. I will do it *with* you, honey, but I cannot do it *for* you."

"If we could just communicate better, a lot of these problems would go away," Lorin replied. "I just need you to listen to me. You don't listen to me."

Lorin maintained, as he always had, that the PTSD wasn't the problem, I was. If only I would leave him alone. If only I understood what it was like for him, how hard it was for him.

"Have you ever killed any kids?" he'd demand, thrusting his face a few inches from mine. "You go kill some kids and then tell me what it's like."

Lorin had weaponized his war trauma so that it became a deadly tool to be engaged when I asked questions he didn't want to answer. He bludgeoned me with it, telling me that it was my fault because I expected too much. So I caved and agreed to couples counseling even as Lorin resisted addressing his PTSD.

"I just need you to quit pressuring me," he whined when we got home after the post–mortgage default counseling session. "I'm trying so hard that I keep fucking up.

"I don't shit money," he spat, ignoring that I had given him money, and that his monthly net between payroll, the GI Bill housing allowance, and disability was around $5,000 after taxes and health insurance. Lorin admitted he'd never been good with money, but his financial mismanagement had become epic and constant. But when I offered to take over handling all of the household accounts payable, Lorin got furious and accused me of trying to steal his money.

Control issues are endemic in combat veterans, and when traumatized people are triggered by something that reminds them of the past, they relive that past as if it were happening now, with the attendant rage, fury, terror, or fear.

"After the emotional storm passes, they may look for something or somebody to blame for it. They behaved the way they did because *you* were ten minutes late, or because *you* burned the potatoes, or because *you* 'never listen to me.'" writes Bessel Van Der Kolk, MD.[103] Spouse-blaming by vets with PTSD is so common that it's talked about on virtually every caregiver blog and most of the websites created by veterans' wives. It's so culturally accepted within the veterans' family community—and even expected—that when I called USAA a few weeks after the counseling session to make changes to the auto insurance policy, the customer service agent brought it up.

USAA provides home, life, and auto insurance for members of the Armed Forces and their families, as well as online banking and investment services. "Ninety-two percent of their customers plan to stay with them for life," according to the company. And there's a reason: they are simply the best. (USAA could get the VA squared away in six months, tops.) So I'm on the phone with the agent while she's updating the incorrect information Lorin provided about the title and registration for my Jeep Wrangler.

I sighed, and said, "I'm just coming along behind him, cleaning up his messes. He starts projects, and leaves them half-assed done.

---

103. Van Der Kolk, *The Body Keeps the Score*.

There are piles all over the property. But god forbid that I ask if he's going to finish them, because he will rip my head off and shit down my neck if I do. So I either do it myself, or pay someone to come out and clean it up."

I sounded tired and grouchy, and felt a twinge of guilt but was too exhausted to care. Lorin's chaos had been manageable when he kept it contained to his room, office, and workshop, but it had started to take over the whole property. Clutter and disorganization is common to people with depression, and it was depressing me. The agent told me that her husband was also a post-9/11 Iraq war vet with PTSD and a mild TBI.

"I do that, too," she said. "But I hate how he blames me for everything now. It's *always* my fault."

"I hear that," I responded.

"It doesn't matter how many times I tell him something," she said, "he forgets. He won't write it down, though, he'll just come back fifteen minutes later and ask me again. And blame me for not telling him."

"Mmhmmmmm, that's familiar."

"Then he'll go off on me. He can stand there screaming at me and an hour later, he acts like it never happened. He *never* apologizes."

"I know. It's a shitty way to live . . ."

We'd come too close to a dangerous edge. Crossing the line meant telling ourselves the truth about our miserable marriages, and that was a rubicon from which we could never retreat. So we both backed off, putting on the Pollyanna personas we'd created to cope. There seemed to be an inverse correlation between a veteran's bad behavior and a spouse's good demeanor, as though we could singlehandedly will our veterans and our lives to get better by the power of positive thinking. We'd keep telling ourselves that it had to improve, but everything had become a fight for Lorin, and therefore, for me. He seemed to feel better after furiously unloading on me, but I felt worse. I'd get angry, too, but I had to hide it, or risk being the target of his escalating rage. Most veterans' spouses learn to suppress their anger as a matter of survival, but it shows up in the body.

Researchers at the University of Utah compared the emotional and physiological responses of two groups of veterans and their partners during and after a "disagreement task." They found that couples affected by PTSD had higher heart rates and other signs of cardiovascular health risk than the non-PTSD veteran couples. The female partners and spouses of veterans with PTSD had *even greater* increases in blood pressure than the combat veterans themselves.[104]

Researchers were surprised by these findings, but I suspect that if any of them had been married to a combat vet with PTSD, they wouldn't have been. They might have known that the vast majority of PTSD vets have used their partners like verbal, if not physical, punching bags. The stress of the constant conflict that defines many of those marriages, coupled with the stress of the perpetual worries and demands of caregiving, may more than double the wives' risk of dying from cancer, heart disease, or stroke.[105] According to research from Yale, severe stress also shuts off the genetic switch that signals the brain to generate new synapses, which permits communication between brain cells. This creates a reduction in

---

104. Siddique, "Combat Vets' PTSD Symptoms," *Medical Daily*.
105. Jegtvig, "Stressful Relationships." Reuters.

brain volume over time. *MSN Health & Fitness* reported on January 5, 2015, that "there's evidence linking this type of brain shrinkage with higher rates of depression." Partners of PTSD vets report extremely high rates of depression and marital distress, typified by frequent arguments, which have been associated with a doubling to tripling in the risk of death from all causes, according to *Medical News Today*.[106]

"PTSD places intolerable stress on the entire family system. . . . It's like living in hell," said retired Navy psychologist Commander Dennis Reeves, who deployed to Iraq in 2003.[107] Tim Kahlor's son Ryan served several tours in Iraq and came home with a TBI and crippling PTSD. Ryan had gutted his first marriage in a couple of years and divorced in 2007 at the age of twenty-four. After his wife was gone, Ryan's PTSD worsened, and his dad stepped in to try to help, ultimately taking a few months leave of absence from his job as an operations supervisor at the University of California in San Diego.

I met Tim in the summer of 2006 when we and a few dozen other military family members spent nearly three months in Washington, DC, making daily trips to the Hill to advocate for better support for deployed troops and improved post-combat care for returning veterans. In between meetings with members of Congress, we were stationed on the sidewalk in front of the congressional offices with a display of combat boots and photos of our loved ones. We handed out literature about the human cost of the wars to passersby as the sweltering heat and humidity softened the tar in

---

106. Whiteman, "Frequent Arguing," *Medical News Today*.
107. Kime, "Families," *Army Times*.

between the steps of the Russell Senate Building. I'd only seen Tim a handful of times since then, but I had begun calling him occasionally to help keep me together as my life with Lorin was falling apart. I asked Tim how he'd managed to take care of himself while trying to take care of his son.

"I was driving myself to work for the first time after being off," said Tim, "and suddenly I was on the side of the road alone crying like a baby, because I had no idea where I was and how to get to work that day. I totally had a meltdown and realized I couldn't fight this PTSD beast 24/7 anymore."

Tim tried to find some separation between his own mental health and that of his son's, but his stress manifested as clinical depression and anxiety that landed Tim in the hospital for several days with symptoms of a heart attack. Anxiety disorders have been shown to raise the risk of stroke, heart failure, or cardiac arrest by nearly 75 percent. Tim didn't have a heart attack—he had an anxiety attack so severe that the physical symptoms simulated one. That was his wake-up call.

"I had done everything I could," said Tim. "I realized I had to detach some from my son and hope that everything I and everyone involved had done would keep him alive. As parents, we may have to 'divorce' ourselves from our children when we have done all we can to fight that fucking PTSD bullshit."

Parents that "divorce" children who choose not to address their PTSD can do so without jeopardizing their primary intimate relationship, their house, or their financial stability and that of their offspring. But for spouses like Renee Ayres, a divorce would entail the loss of husband, home, financial security, and support for the kids. Child support and alimony can be court-ordered, but that doesn't mean it gets paid, even when a wage garnishment is issued. Securing a legal garnishment of earnings takes time and money, and when you're in crisis, it's likely that you have neither. So Renee learned to live with the stress. She's the wife of retired Marine Corps captain Chris Ayres, and her flashbacks and nightmares of secondary trauma were eventually supplanted by the lived nightmare of her husband trying to strangle her to death, and her subsequent withdrawal from family and friends.[108]

Retreating from social relationships is not the only consequence of intimate partner violence, however. A *US Medicine* report by Annetee N. Boyle stated that "Women who experience intimate partner violence have a 60 percent higher rate of health problems than those who have not." Typical physical ailments include STDs, cardiovascular disease, obesity, stroke, asthma, and ulcers. Partner violence also raises cortisol levels, and increases the risk of depression, PTSD, eating disorders, and substance abuse.

I had been drinking more and more often; many veterans' caregivers report increased alcohol use and substance abuse. I'd taken stock of my marriage in the fall of 2012, and the only redeeming aspect was our home, particularly the barn and pasture. But it was the first home I'd ever had, and my animals were with me and I wasn't going to give that up. I decided to tough it out. I'd just have to drink more. About once a week, I'd pick up a bottle of wine, and seldom stopped pouring until it was empty. I'd wait until Lorin had left for work, because I was too afraid to be impaired when he was at home. Lorin was becoming increasingly volatile, and between that and the constant calamities he created, I had no margin for error.

---

108. Ibid.

I couldn't afford to make mistakes because I was too busy dealing with his. Drinking had become the only way that I could let down my guard. Wine bought me a night of relief from the relentless fear and anxiety; it quieted the persistent sadness and made the intolerable tolerable. And it turned off my mind, because I was just so tired of thinking for two all the time.

Lorin's executive functions seemed to operate at work, but they were useless at home, where I had become his external hard drive for memory and daily tasks. PTSD can impair executive function tasks carried out by the prefrontal cortex, as can a TBI. Executive function relates to the ability to make decisions between good and bad, predict outcomes and likely consequences of actions, make progress toward a defined goal, and exercise social control. Executive functions manage the voice in our head that keeps us from doing the things that, if we did them, would result in social humiliation or exclusion. A *Washington Post* article by Amy Ellis Nutt reported that TBI tissue samples revealed a unique "honeycomb pattern of broken connections" in the brain lobes that govern personality and emotional control.[109] Doing that for the both of us, and trying to troubleshoot for him, was exhausting *my* executive function capabilities, and putting me into constant cognitive overload.

By the end of the very bad days—and they were coming fast and hard in the final few months of 2013—I might have known that drinking wasn't a good idea, but I just had nothing left with which to care or stop.

* * *

---

109. Nutt, "Wounds of War That Never Heal," *Washington Post*.

Lorin had finally given me access to his online bank account. When I logged in to check the balance on Christmas Day, I was blindsided. He'd spent our thirteenth wedding anniversary, December 23, 2013, surfing porn sites. Based on the charges, that's what he had been doing several nights a week for a very long time. It felt like I'd been punched in the heart. A lot of troops start looking at porn online during deployments. In 2010, Navy lieutenant Michael Howard, a licensed therapist, chaplain, and sex addiction specialist, estimated that porn abuse or addiction among military personnel returning from a war zone is about 20 percent, about double the civilian rate.[110] Lorin had avoided intimacy since his last deployment, and I had endured it. I kept telling myself that it wasn't me, it was the PTSD. But maybe it was me, because apparently he *was* interested in sex with other women. Finding months and months and months of fees for porn sites should have made me feel marginally better about my failed attempt to implement a Don't Ask, Don't Tell policy, but somehow it did not.

About six months earlier, after years of abstinence, I had told Lorin that, since he wasn't willing to have sex with me, I would find someone who was. I looked on Craigslist a couple of times, but just looking felt wrong, and I gave up. I lacked whatever it took to make having an affair acceptable. I lacked whatever it was that made military veterans twice as likely to have extramarital sex as civilians, according to a study by Syracuse University. Where's your code of honor now, soldier? A code of honor that is only upheld to get a paycheck is not a code of honor. It is a personnel policy.

---

110. Howard, "Addicted to On-Line Porn," *Army Times*.

I didn't think Lorin was sleeping around, but I hadn't thought he had a porn problem, either. I couldn't bring it up in couples counseling, because the therapist had basically fired Lorin in November and told him to come back when he was ready. I had no clue anymore who I was married to, or what I was living with. But sweet Jesus, how the latest evidence of his rejection hurt. My aching chest caved in, collapsing my shoulders, and I lowered my head to my desk and cried. Psychologists have found that the sheer, visceral pain of rejection is perhaps worse than virtually any other emotional wound.[111] Lorin's rejection of me was also destroying the chemical bond between us that had already been weakened by years of service-connected separation. Hugging, holding hands, and sex releases dopamine, a neurotransmitter that bolsters happiness and self-esteem, and oxytocin, the "love hormone" that promotes bonding and attachment.

"When you're first becoming intimate, you're releasing lots of dopamine and oxytocin. That's creating that link between the neural systems that are processing your facial cues, your voice, and the reward system" of a partner's brain, said Larry Young, a professor of psychiatry at Emory University.[112] He studies the role of oxytocin in social bonding. Oxytocin also lowers stress levels, and improves sleep and immune function.

Several days after stumbling upon Lorin's porn habit, I returned to the urgent care clinic in Eagle Point. I'd gotten an antibiotic shot at the clinic the day before because I had another skin infection, this time above my eye. When the nurse saw the

---

111. Winch, *Emotional First Aid*.

112. Goodman, "How the 'Love Hormone' Works," *HealthDay*.

inflamed skin around my right eye, which was swelling shut, she sent me straight to the ER, which sent me to a hospital bed. I had a severe cellulitis infection the size of a golf ball bulging out just below my eyebrow. The doctors couldn't figure out what caused it, and the initial round of antibiotic injections and pills administered during the first trip to urgent care had failed. The whole upper right quadrant of my face was puffy and inflamed, and the area around my eye burned a deep red. After I got settled in my hospital room, I called and asked Lorin to bring me a bag with pajamas and toiletries and things, which he dropped off, along with the Chinese take-out I requested. I paid him for the food, but he was fidgety and distracted and left a few minutes later. I didn't see him again that day. Or night. No one came.

When I woke up the next morning, the IV antibiotics hadn't kicked in, and the swelling was spreading, getting worse. The doctor arrived and told me that they were pulling out the big guns. He switched me to vancomycin, an intravenous antibiotic reserved for treating severe infections. "We're trying to save your eye," the doctor said. "We should know if this is going to work in the next twenty-four hours. We need to keep this from going into your brain, because if it does . . . well, I'll see you tomorrow."

I bit my lower lip into my mouth and waited for the door to my room to sigh shut behind him. I muffled my sobs with the pillow. I hadn't been able to get ahold of Lorin, and none of my friends or family had called or stopped by since I'd let them know I'd been admitted. A nurse came in a little later to check the IV and my vitals. She entered them into the computer and, as she did, glanced up, clearing her throat.

"I'm sorry, but I need to ask you for your advance directive," she said, then looked away.

I was forty-eight years old and didn't even have to think about my answer.

"Do not resuscitate."

I was released from the hospital two days later with prescriptions for a couple of antibiotics. I drove home to an empty house and got started on my exit strategy.

CHAPTER EIGHT

Standing Down Suicide

A N OLD BLACK VINYL glasses case was sitting on my desk, but it wasn't mine. Lorin was at work, so I couldn't ask him about it. The case held a small aluminum container, the size used for rolls of 35-mm film. That made no sense; Lorin had a digital camera, if he hadn't hocked it yet. He'd been pawning things for the last several months. I clumsily unscrewed the cap from the little canister and extracted a small plastic bag. It was half full of an off-white granular powder with flecks of pastel crystal. I replaced the baggie, put the lid back on the can, and pushed it into the case. My situational Tourette's kicked in and I swore like a staff sergeant as I frantically tried to figure out what to do with what had to be drugs, what to do with the animals, what to do about Lorin, and what to do with myself. Shocked and scared, I could not string together a sequence of thoughts. It was all I could do just to breathe.

I collected myself and dropped the glasses case into a large plastic Ziploc that I then tucked into a Tupperware container. I put on my barn coat, grabbed a flashlight, and walked the property in the dark, searching for a place to hide it. It had to be somewhere the animals couldn't get to it, and where Lorin would never find it. The February thaw was still a few weeks away, so I buried the container under a pile of leaves near the front gate and went back inside to pack. While I threw clothes in a suitcase, I left voice mail messages with Chris Petrone, Lorin's VA case manager, and Michelle at the VA Caregiver Program. I called Tammara, my battle buddy, and told her what happened. She said the coarse powder was probably crystal meth. I Googled crystal meth and the pictures that came up closely resembled what I had found. I packed until I was too tired to continue, and then I locked my bedroom door and wrestled with the sheets for a few hours.

First thing the next morning, I called the Jackson County Sheriff's Department and the Medford Police. I described the substance and asked if they would test it. They informed me they could come out to the property, but if they discovered drugs, they would search the whole place and arrest me. Or, I could bring it in, but if I was stopped while driving, or if I carried it into the cop shop, I'd be charged with possession.

Lorin wasn't home yet, and I had no idea what I would say when he arrived. Michelle called and I told her what was going on. She volunteered to come out to the house so I could show her the drugs. When she got there, Michelle confirmed it was most likely crystal meth and asked me what I planned to do.

"I don't know," I said. "If I get the cops involved, I'll get in trouble, too. I left a message for Chris, but he hasn't called back. All I know is that I have to find somewhere else to stay."

Chris finally called back, and I relayed what was going on and that I was leaving until I felt like it was safe to return. Chris said he would figure out how to handle things with Lorin, given that he's also an employee in the Substance Abuse Treatment Program. Lorin got home around noon. I lied to him with everything I had. I lied with my words and eyes and body. I made my heart lie, too, glossing over the sucking psychic chest wound that would, if I let it, drop me where I stood.

"I think I need some time alone," I said. "I was talking to Michelle from the Caregiver Program, and she thinks it's a good idea. So I'll probably go stay at the Flying L or something."

"Okay," he said, and wandered off to his shop/bunker (drug den?) in the back.

I avoided Lorin for the rest of the day while trying to hide that I was packing for much more than a couple of nights. Cowboy Tim McGinnis, Hickory's farrier, lived a few miles down the road, so I called and had him trailer up Hickory and take him to his place. After Lorin left for work, I loaded two suitcases, a duffel bag, a sleeping bag, two pillows, and four boxes in my two-door Toyota Rav4, along with a few framed pictures. I wedged in a bulging expanding file jammed with the papers and legal documents that I would need in case I could never come home. When I'd found Lorin's crystal meth, I lost the luxury of time to plan an exit strategy. I kissed my cats and hugged the goats, and then drove off the property without looking back.

Karl and Tracey Haeckler let me stow my boxes at their place and crash on the twin-sized bed in their spare room for a couple of nights. They said I could stay as long as I needed to, but I had no idea how long I'd be on the run, and didn't want to wear out my welcome. Over the next two weeks, I divvied up my time between their place, the Flying L Ranch, and the home of a couple I had just met.

I stayed at a cheap motel in Ashland for one night, relieved and disoriented to be paying for a small, grungy room forty miles from my home. I had to make my money last, though, so I spent the next night struggling to sleep in my car, which I'd parked in the corner of the lot of a big box store. How had I become homeless so fast? I spoke with P. J. and swung by her house, but both her boys were in high school, and I refused to contaminate their lives with this horror. She didn't offer me a place to stay, and I didn't ask.

Chris had left several messages saying that he'd been trying to get Lorin to come in for a meeting. Lorin hadn't responded. I talked to Lorin on the phone, to see how the animals were, and coordinate schedules so that I wouldn't run into him when I went out to the house to check on things and use my computer. I didn't have a laptop, and I was looking for work.

I called Republican State Representative Sal Esquivel at his office in Salem to see if he knew of any jobs. When I heard Sal's warm, friendly voice on the phone, I unraveled. I told Sal what had happened and that I was couch surfing and scared.

"Young lady," said Sal, "you are more than welcome to stay at our house in Medford. We're up here in session, which will last another month or so. You'd actually be doing us a favor if you'd be willing to stay there. But you need to get out and take care of yourself. I am really disappointed in your soldier."

We figured out the logistics of getting me the house keys, and he brushed off my gratitude. I would have dozens of thank you notes to write when this was over. I said that to Sabena when I met her for lunch at the Silver Dragon, a Chinese restaurant in Medford. Sabena and I had fallen out of touch after she testified in support of my Military Family Task Force bill. She was busy taking care of five kids under the age of sixteen while her husband, Stephen Moriarty, worked as the area director for the Oregon National Guard Military Funeral Honors detail. We hadn't spoken for a year or so, but when I called out of the blue, we picked up where we'd left off, talking like our last conversation had been the week before.

"I just want you to know how much I appreciate your support." We had been speaking or emailing regularly since I'd stumbled across the meth a couple of weeks ago. I had just started staying at Sal's house, and Sabena wanted to make sure that I was okay and that I knew I wasn't alone.

"Everybody has been so great. Thank you so much for being here. I really, really appreciate it . . ." I said and then looked away. "I must be the dumbest person in the world, though. Lorin must think so, too, because he told me that the drugs weren't his. He was just 'holding them for a friend.' I can't believe he'd try something that didn't even work in high school."

Chris and I had finally connected on the phone, and he'd told me Lorin had come in to his office and come clean—after a lot of denial. Chris kept pressing Lorin to tell the truth, reminding him that his job was at stake, and finally Lorin caved and admitted he'd been using meth for more than a year. Chris gave him a few days to take a urine analysis and think about where he wanted to go for treatment. When that time was up, Chris talked to Lorin's boss. Lorin's urine analysis was dirty, and Chris made clear that Lorin would need to go to treatment in order to keep his job. He consented, and Chris put in a referral for admission to the Walla Walla VA substance abuse treatment program. A few days later, Lorin learned that they would have a bed ready for him in about six weeks.

Social services assistants at the VA are exempt from mandatory drug testing, but Lorin was getting tested regularly now in order to keep his job and his place in line for the treatment program. I started staying at our house again a few days before he was scheduled to leave. The night before, he futzed around the property. I didn't say much, because there wasn't much to say. His plate was already full, and he wouldn't be able to hear—or handle—what I had to tell him anyway. I no longer owed him the truth.

Lorin came into my bedroom around 3:00 a.m., waking me from a restless sleep. He was sobbing and staggered to the side of my bed, where he collapsed to his knees. Straining to speak, but finding it impossible, he reached a hand tentatively across the comforter, fumbling in the darkness for mine. He cried like his soul had broken. I scooted over to make some room and patted the bed. Lorin crawled up and curled onto my chest. I held him and let him sob.

"I'm sorry, I'm sorry," he gasped. Over and over and over again. I laid there with my arms around him as he wept, remembering the last time he had allowed me to hold him this way. It had been zero dark hundred of the day he left for his first deployment to Iraq. I stroked Lorin's back and stared up through the skylight over the bed until the stars disappeared. He took off later that morning and called from Walla Walla.

"I have to stay in a homeless shelter," said Lorin. "I didn't make it in time, and they won't let me check in until morning. I don't have any money." He paused, most likely waiting for me to jump in and save him, tell him to find a motel and call me and I would put it on my credit card.

"That's too bad," I said, "but that's probably your future. I hope not, for your sake. I hope that you will take the opportunity you've been given and do whatever you need to do to get better. Please call tomorrow morning after you've been admitted."

He did, and then over the next six weeks he called about once a week. During these brief conversations, he relayed snippets about treatment and said that he was feeling better and learning a lot about moral injury in the context of war. Moral injury is an evolving concept pertaining to the profound existential pain of seeing, or being involved in, events that betray deeply held moral and spiritual values. There may be overlap between PTSD and moral injury, but trauma typically stems from frightening events that jeopardize your life. Moral injury results from events that jeopardize your soul, and in combat, those events often involve hurting or killing a noncombatant. The VA is among a growing number of service providers and research facilities working to develop meaningful methods for treating it.

I was glad Lorin seemed to be getting what he needed, but I would've liked some treatment for what I'd been through. I would've liked to go to a place where they fed me and did my dishes and helped me try to make sense of things. I'd have liked to spend some time on the government's dime with other wives of combat veterans so that we could talk about *our* war wounds and get help with healing them in the wake of living with our loved one's PTSD and addiction. When I said that to Chris, he suggested I go to the Vet Center up in Grants Pass, about twenty-five miles away, or find a local provider. I called half a dozen counselors, but when I described my situation, they were hesitant to take me on as a client. Two of them had worked with veterans, but none of them had ever treated the spouses of vets with severe PTSD. When I outlined why I was seeking counseling, one therapist said, "Your situation is too complex for me."

Chris and I were playing phone tag, so I sent him an email that said, "I guess you forgot that I cannot get services at the Vet Center unless my veteran is getting services at the Vet Center. And of the local mental health providers that are in the BCBS federal network, not a one has any experience whatsoever serving wives of PTSD vets. Square one, meet Stacy. I believe you know each other."

After I sent it, I kind of wished I could take it back, or explain to Chris that it wasn't so much him that I was frustrated with as the whole situation. Chris was doing his job, and he'd thrown Lorin a life raft, but I was still drowning. I was tired of chasing my tail and running around looking for resources that did not exist. Resources the VA knew were desperately needed for the people who often provided the most significant support for the veteran.

The VA moderator of a cyber seminar on women readily acknowledged the importance of social support for veterans with PTSD, "especially from the spouse or intimate partner. [T]hat support in and of itself may counteract or reduce some of the PTSD symptoms. . . . That positive affect may be time limited because of the impact of living with someone with PTSD."[113] According to the VA moderator, there is a "body of literature" that "really looks at partner distress of these partners who are living with someone with PTSD, and looking at their distress whether it is secondary traumatization in terms of living with someone with PTSD, or maybe a primary trauma themselves secondary to their victimization at the hands of the loved one for whom they are also often a caregiver."

But the VA does not offer those caregivers any sort of residential or outpatient programming or therapeutic retreats to help them

---

113. Veterans Administration Spotlight on Women Cyberseminar Series.

recover from caregiver burden, secondary trauma, veteran violence, or the inevitable nuclear fallout of living with a combat veteran with an addiction.

A study of combat veterans with PTSD conducted by Herbert Hendin and Ann Haas found that 85 percent developed significant drug and alcohol problems after coming home. The biggest and most far-reaching investigation ever conducted on Vietnam veterans, the National Vietnam Veterans Readjustment Study, revealed that 75 percent of veterans with combat trauma had also developed substance abuse problems. Alcohol and drugs are effective, if maladaptive, methods to numb the psychological pain and flashbacks of trauma, but some drugs, particularly amphetamines, can also help re-create the spectacularly addictive intensity of war. In his book *War Is a Force That Gives Us Meaning*, war correspondent Chris Hedges writes, "[W]ar was the ultimate drug experience. But drugs, in the end, cannot compare with the awful power and rush of battle."[114] Vietnam veteran Karl Marlantes echoes that when he writes, "Combat is the crack cocaine of all excitement highs—with crack cocaine costs."[115]

"The crack cocaine of combat is what killed my son," said the father of a Vietnam veteran who committed suicide. "I have memories of walking the sidewalks of Grand Rapids with Tom and sailing with him on Elk Lake when I totally failed to relate to his recovery from his bout with 'crack cocaine.' There is so little understanding. We know that among veterans in Portland, the wives and the mothers of veterans' children are the heroines of the time. Yet we

---

114. Hedges, *War Is a Force That Gives Us Meaning*.
115. Marlantes, *What It Is Like to Go to War*.

are unable to help them to get relief from living with desperate husbands and fathers they dare not leave alone with their children."

For some of those desperate veterans, crystal meth most closely replicates the charged intensity of being in a war zone and the rush of being hyper alert for hours, sometimes days, on end.

"I miss the adrenalin," said Iraq war veteran Matt Hallman, who crashed into a guardrail while driving high. Writing for *Metro Philadelphia*, Tommy Rowan reported on October 21, 2013, that Hallman's jaw was pulverized and had to be wired shut for half a year. He was high when he went to Veterans Court, which sent him to the VA to get treatment for drug addiction. Hallman, an Army infantryman, served two tours in Iraq that were "like being high," he said. "There's just no feeling like that in the world. . . . It's just absolute excitement." The thrill of combat became normal over there, and drugs help re-create that normal over here.

It never once crossed my mind that Lorin was doing drugs. There's a lot of overlap between PTSD symptoms and the early stages of crystal meth addiction: sleeplessness, increased irritability, avoidance, hyper-vigilance, or paranoia. I just figured his war trauma was worsening, and clearly it *had* escalated if using meth seemed like a sensible way to self-medicate. But the potential for drug use didn't occur to me, because who starts using crystal meth at fifty-two? Looking back—and I've been doing a lot of that lately—I see that nearly all of the signs of meth use were there: increased energy, weight loss, dishonesty, money problems, an insatiable appetite for pornography, manic bursts of activity where he'd start a project and then leave it undone, and pronounced aggressiveness. Lorin had also been picking at his hands constantly, until they bled. The only symptom he didn't have was the missing teeth and deeply discolored enamel of "meth mouth."

I DON'T KNOW IF I was incredibly ignorant and in denial, or too supportive or a pathological enabler, although I'm not sure it's enabling if you don't know they're using. What I did know was that I wasn't going to keep making excuses for inexcusable behavior anymore. I cannot imagine what it must have been like for Lorin to feel so lost meth seemed like a good idea. But I know how bad living with him had become while he was secretly using drugs. Because it's one thing to engage in self-destructive behaviors you admit to and that cause no overt harm to others, but self-destructive illegal activities that jeopardize employment status and financial standing and require dishonesty while imperiling the lives, safety, and security of the people closest to you are another proposition altogether. Now that Lorin was in treatment, I could tell him about the terrible hurt he caused me without fear of reprisal.

The doctors at Walla Walla had worked up a new drug regimen for him, and taking meds is mandatory when you're an inpatient. His voice sounded brighter every time he called, and there was more of him "there." After each of those calls, I sat staring at the phone in wonderment for a few seconds after he'd hung up. Not quite halfway through treatment, Lorin called during a break to ask if I would transfer funds to his account and the conversation went south pretty fast. Lorin said he needed to hang up, and I appreciated his newfound ability to interrupt his own escalation. However, he didn't get to use that as an excuse to avoid hearing some of the ways his behavior had affected me. The damage to my credit and the financial losses that had nearly cost me my home was bad, and the porn was worse, particularly after years of his sexual rejection of me. But it was the endless betrayals and aggressive attacks when I tried to help or had unknowingly caught him in a lie that had destroyed my trust and so badly damaged my heart. I emailed him the next morning:

Lorin,

What might have seemed like an effort on my part to control you over these past four years was, from my perspective, an effort to help you. And us. I kept identifying support and services, only to be told that you weren't ready. That I needed to back off. I did, eventually, but not without grave concerns and misgivings. Not the least of which was that by the time you were ready, I would be done. That by adhering exclusively to a timeline of what was comfortable for you meant abdicating a timeframe that was comfortable for me. That the longer the shit dragged on, the worse it would get, and that eventually, too much damage would be done. That rather than being able to save the limb, we would have to amputate. And now here we are.

I cannot fix what I allowed to happen; all I can do is refuse to allow it to happen ever, ever, ever, again. For far too long, I backed down. I swallowed my words, and my fear, and my anger, and my needs. Too often, and to my detriment. So when I express my reality, and I hear you on the phone laughing sardonically (def.: characterized by bitter or scornful derision; mocking; cynical; sneering) I am painfully reminded of just exactly how fucking bad these last years have been. And how fucking bad I need the hurt to stop. And how fucking much I will sacrifice in order for that to happen.

I had begun to see that the emotional abuse and mental torture typical of disabled veterans who didn't deal with their PTSD could

217

create its own kind of battered woman syndrome in the spouses. Women who are physically and mentally abused over an extended period by a husband or significant other develop a cluster of symptoms, including fear, low self-esteem, depression, and loss of the internal will to leave, which is frequently coupled with a perceived inability to escape. Often, they are financially tied to, or dependent on, the aggressor. My caregiver stipend would stop as soon as I left Lorin, and since it wasn't considered a job—even though the compensation scale was set by caregiver pay rates in the region— I wouldn't be able to claim unemployment. Without work, I had no money and nowhere to go, not for long, anyway. I could go to a women's shelter for thirty days max, but would eventually wind up on the street if I couldn't find a job. There are very few threads in the social safety net to support divorced, unemployed, childless, middle-aged women in crisis, veteran's caregiver or not.

I was terrified of losing my animals and becoming homeless, so when Lorin said he'd be going to an inpatient PTSD program after he finished drug treatment, I was cautiously optimistic. He had wanted to remain at Walla Walla for that, but was told that his issues and irritability were significant enough that the VA doctors felt he needed a more intensive program. Lorin did some scouting around and liked what he learned about the American Lake VA's PTSD program, which had a moral injury component. But it might be a month or two before he could get in. In the interim, he would come home. I was skittish about seeing him again, much as I wanted to. I was afraid that maybe nothing had changed while desperately hoping that everything had. Just before he'd left for treatment, Lorin asked what it would take for me to stay in our marriage.

"Stop the lies," I said. "Even if it's uncomfortable, tell me the truth. Get treatment for PTSD. Go to couples counseling. Be nice to me, spend time with me, hold my hand. Act like you love me."

A husband's abstaining from crystal meth does not a marriage make. He needed to show up for me, and for us. And when he got back from Walla Walla, he did. He walked through the door in early May of 2014, and for the first time in years, my husband was home. We went out for dinner a few nights later, which we hadn't done in ages. *You*, I thought, *I remember you.* I hadn't forgotten any of what had happened; I was no less hurt or angry. But if he'd do the work, I would, too.

Lorin came back with a cardboard box full of the medications prescribed at Walla Walla. But he refused to take them, and over the next three weeks, as the prescription drug levels in his bloodstream gradually disappeared, so did Lorin.

"He reverted to what he had been. It was a heartbreaker," states Daniel Keyes, the author of *Flowers for Algernon.* In that book, Keyes is speaking about the remarkable improvement of a learning-disabled student who then regressed when he was withdrawn from instruction. He may as well have been referring to Lorin. By the beginning of June, Lorin had gone back to many of his old behaviors, and I resumed the self-medication, drinking a bottle of wine a couple of times a month. After he postponed his admission to the American Lake PTSD program in early July, I went back to drinking almost every week.

"They're understaffed in my section, and I was already gone for six weeks," Lorin complained. "I have to work with these people, and I don't want them mad at me."

"What about me, Lorin?" I asked. "Don't you ever worry about making me mad with your lies?" There were new ones that I was worried about.

A few weeks earlier, I'd accompanied him to a primary care appointment at the VA, and while we waited for the doctor, a nurse came in and got Lorin's vitals. He rolled up his sleeve for the blood pressure cuff and there were bruised, grayish-purple knots and scabbed-over sores in the crook of his elbow. Lorin quickly pulled his sleeve back down and refused to answer the question in my eyes. We'd driven separate vehicles, but when we got home I asked, "What's wrong with your arms?"

"It's just from carrying wood," he said.

"Wood? It's June, we haven't used the wood stove for months. How much wood are you carrying? I carry wood and my arms don't look like that."

"I carry more, and I do a lot of other stuff too. Maybe they got torn up when I was working on the fence."

He kept looking away, so I knew he was lying, but I didn't know why and I let it go. Until it dawned on me that maybe they were track marks. So I Googled "track marks." And I saw that the tiny needles I found in his pants pockets months ago weren't from his job, like he'd said, they were from him shooting up. After I settled down, I approached him in the kitchen.

"Lorin, I know you told me that you got those marks on your arms from carrying wood, but that's not what they're from, is it?"

"No," he mumbled.

"What's that? Speak up, soldier."

"No, they're not."

"So you weren't just smoking meth, like you said, you were shooting it," I said. "And you lied to me about that. And if you got to the point where you were shooting it, you were probably using for a lot longer than a year. So you lied to me about that, too."

"Yeah."

"Oh, Jesus, Lorin, what have you done?" I begged, and I slowly slid down with my back against the wall until I was seated on the floor, elbows on my knees, holding my head in my hands.

Track marks. On my husband. God, now. *Where are you* now?

I sat, weeping, on the kitchen floor for a very, very long time. And yet I would not give up. I clung to the memory of the marriage we'd had and the promise, however faint, of being married like that again, and I tried to breathe the life back into us. I found another marriage counselor who had retired after more than twenty years with the Air National Guard. I liked him for his no-nonsense, results-oriented manner, and I thought that, with his Guard service, he'd be perfect. But Lorin despised the man and walked out during the third session. The counselor had been gently, but persistently, pressing Lorin to get specific about what he wanted for our marriage, and to explain why he wasn't willing to have sex. Lorin refused to have that conversation, but he did say that he'd find a different marriage therapist. I waited for Lorin to make that appointment, and while I waited, I stumbled across a pipe and other drug paraphernalia.

Each time, Lorin assured me that they were old, and he just hadn't gotten around to throwing them out. I didn't think he was using, but I didn't know what to believe anymore. He kept saying that he would go to PTSD treatment as soon as he got a break at work. I wanted to believe that, too, but there's a lot of space between believe and know, and I could not hang there forever. I wanted to give him the benefit of doubt, but I had to give myself the benefit of hope. I marked the calendar sixty days out, and began to toss a coin every morning, writing heads (I stay) or tails (I go) in a new square every day. Whichever one there were more of in two months would be the decider. When there are no good decisions to be made, it's difficult to make any at all.

I told Lorin what I was doing and why, and he huffed and stalked off. He didn't want to talk about it, but I did. I phoned a friend from Spokane who had attended our wedding. She hadn't seen Lorin since we left Spokane in 2003, but I stayed with her last time I was back there, and we kept in touch. She'd heard the highlight reel of what had been happening, but when I said I didn't think I could stay married if Lorin refused to deal with his PTSD, she accused me of being selfish and unsupportive. I was a little put off. She had two children and was divorced herself, from a man who wasn't a veteran with severe PTSD. "Poor Lorin, look at everything he's been through. He needs you to help him. The Lorin I saw at your wedding was a good, kind man. Look how much he's sacrificed."

I resented feeling like it was okay for everyone else to get divorced because they *hadn't* been married to an injured veteran. I also resented the seeming irrelevancy of the fact that my injured veteran had treatment options and services available to him that he refused to take advantage of. I was a little pissed off that my friend seemed to be supporting Lorin for making bad choices, and chastising me for not being willing to eternally bear the brunt of them. But mostly I was at the end of my rope and was unable to monitor myself and respond appropriately when friends or family said anything that rubbed me the wrong way.

"He *has* sacrificed," I snapped, "and so have I. What have *you* sacrificed?"

She accused me of being a narcissist and disconnected. Probably she was right to cut me loose. I had already suspended contact with my dad and sister after I realized that they were too often on the receiving end of my fury and fear. I had sent them an email stating I would be going "dark" until I was able to conduct myself decently. I hadn't been very decent with my friend, either, and I received an email from her the following night telling me she had unfriended me on Facebook. I shouldn't bother calling again, ever, because if that's how I was going to treat my poor husband, I was on my own.

I'd been on my own for years, trying to help Lorin and being bullied by him when I did. I continued to find resources and referrals for yoga, acupuncture, and other services he said he wanted. I kept hoping he'd go to treatment, and wishing he'd take marriage counseling seriously, but he kept lashing out at me because he didn't want to hear that anything was wrong. The damned if you do/damned if you don't dynamic is common to partners of combat veterans. Jackie Grimesey reported that many veterans' caregivers said that "their efforts to help their partner are met with his anger and resentment."[116]

In an effort to advance understanding and support for combat vets with PTSD and their intimate partners, Dr. April Gerlock teamed up with two other researchers to study a "developing dyadic relationship model."[117] The research showed that the ability of couples "to mitigate the negative impact of PTSD" depends on three components. The first element is mutuality, which is expressed by sharing thoughts, tending to and being receptive of the feelings of the other, and participating in mutually enjoyable activities. The couples who were able to achieve a higher degree of mutuality had

---

116. Grimesey, "The Impact of Combat Trauma."

117. Gerlock, Grimesey, and Sayre, "Military-Related Post-Traumatic Stress Disorder," *Journal of Marital and Family Therapy.*

markedly more functional relationships. The second factor hinges on having a balanced locus of control, which refers to the degree to which a person perceives themselves as having at least some level of control over what's happening in their lives. If both partners viewed themselves as having a measure of agency over the events in their lives, the relationship was enhanced. The third aspect Gerlock's team discovered is that the capacity to tolerate weakness is "paradoxically powerful depending on the degree to which it is accepted and integrated or used to exploit or demean."

Once the veteran was able to tolerate his own weakness and recognized the need for help and accepted assistance from his partner, it was beneficial for both. When the veteran expressed intolerance for weakness by refusing to get help, and responded with anger and annoyance to the partner's efforts to help, the couple was typically distressed. According to the study, in the distressed couples the "partners contend not only with PTSD symptoms (e.g., nightmares, social isolation, and anger and aggression), but find themselves protecting the veteran from PTSD symptom triggers as part of their caregiving role. In doing so, they themselves become an identified trigger and are resented for it as the veteran describes this behavior as controlling." The veteran's overwhelming need to control is frequently manifested in heightened verbal and physical aggression, including IPV. Gerlock found that "veterans experienced the partner's caregiving as much needed support, but also as a threatening reminder of their own diminished capacity."[118] I just thought I was helping.

---

118. Ibid.

Two days before his July 4th admit date for the American Lake PTSD program, I called to ensure that the VA would reimburse his travel costs. That's standard operating procedure, but I didn't want to encounter the same confusion and delays we'd had to navigate to get the travel funds released for Lorin's mileage to Walla Walla. The drive from our house to American Lake was at least eight hours, depending on traffic, and Lorin wouldn't make it there before 5 p.m. When a veteran arrives after regular business hours, the VA puts him or her up at a nearby hotel, and the vet is supposed to check in first thing the next morning. After I got confirmation that everything was a go, I went upstairs. Lorin was in his office, throwing things into the backpack he takes to work.

"Hey, Lorin, you're all set with the travel office, and I also had them make a reservation for a hotel room close to American Lake," I said. I was feeling pretty good about handling the logistics. Now all he needed to do was show up.

"I resent you being my caregiver," said Lorin.

"Fine. I'll quit the program, and we can go back to being husband and wife, without me doing any of the caregiver stuff."

"If you lose that caregiver money, I'm not paying your half of expenses," he snapped. Finances were a trigger for him, so I let it go. A short time later, he came pounding down the steps and hustled out the door, late for work.

I approached Lorin the next morning, after he'd had time to cool off. I poured myself a cup of coffee and went outside to join him. I pulled up a chair at the patio table where Lorin was fingering his smartphone. From the number of cigarette butts in the can, it was evident that he'd been up for a while. Or maybe he'd never gone to bed.

"Hey, I know you resent when I try to help you, so what can I do differently?" I asked. "I need you to help me help you."

"I was just trying to be honest with you, and now I am getting beaten up for it."

"Lorin, I am not beating you up for it. I heard what you said, I appreciate your honesty. Since you complain that I never listen to you, I am reflecting back to you what you said in the hopes that you will see that I *do* listen. I'm not beating you up."

"Why the fuck didn't you tell me you were going to take the mortgage payment out of my account?" he demanded.

"I did, yesterday morning. Remember?"

"Well, now my account's overdrawn, and I don't have any money."

How could he possibly have blown through the $500 remaining in the account after I had transferred his portion of the mortgage payment less than twenty-four hours ago?

"Are you blaming me?" I asked. "I told you yesterday that I was going to transfer the money. By the way, good morning. Is this really how you want to start the day?"

"I didn't know you were going to take the money out *that day*. Now my account's overdrawn again, and I don't get paid until Thursday."

"So is it my fault that your account's overdrawn?" I asked.

"Oh. So, what? You're saying it's my fault?" asked Lorin. "I'm just trying to get my feet on the ground. And every time I think I'm getting ahead, something like this happens. Nice fucking support network."

"What do you mean?"

"You won't learn how to support me," he said. "You're supposed to know what my triggers are and don't do them so I don't relapse.

But you won't even go to Al-Anon meetings unless I go to some kind of support group or recovery group. It doesn't work that way."

"Yes, actually, it does. I am happy to go to Al-Anon meetings when you go to NA meetings or the support group for vets in recovery at the VA. I can't do this for you, Lorin. That's not my job. You're supposed to know what your triggers are, not me. Treatment was supposed to have given you some tools to either avoid or deal with those triggers in a better way. Quit blaming me for your behavior. And who else is in your support network? Because I can't be the only one you've got. I've been carrying you for years, and I am worn out."

"Oh, why is it always about you?"

I wanted to hit him. I didn't, and I never have, but I wanted to start then.

"It is not about me," I said, "and for years and years and years, it hasn't been about me at *all*. Not one iota. But I get to matter, too. I *need* to matter."

"You need to lower your standards. Your expectations are way up here, and you need to lower them to down here," he proclaimed, gesturing with his hand, dropping it so that it hovered about a foot above the pavement.

"Lorin, no, I've already done that. I lowered my standards so much that they were non-existent. And look where that got us. For way too long, I didn't expect anything, because oh, poor Lorin . . ."

"I should just go kill myself, that'd make it easier for everybody," he spat.

I froze.

"I'll just run my car into a fucking bridge. The best thing I can do right now is just kill myself."

The look in his eyes and the way he said it told me that he meant it. I went on high alert and suddenly everything got slow and calm and the conversation that we'd just been having totally disappeared.

"Lorin, are you seriously thinking about hurting yourself?" I asked.

"Yes."

I desperately tried to recall what they'd said to do in this situation at the Applied Suicide Intervention Skills Training (ASIST) I'd gone to when I was working as the veterans program manager at ColumbiaCare Services. Twenty-two veterans kill themselves every day, and although historically the suicide rate is typically lower for the Armed Services than the general population, that had changed dramatically since the onset of the wars. Between 2001 and 2007, veterans of the wars in Afghanistan and Iraq had a 41 to 61 percent higher risk of suicide than the general population, according to a study published in the *Annals of Epidemiology*. I had never gotten any training from the VA Caregiver program around suicidal ideation or how to conduct a suicide intervention. I thought that I was supposed to keep him talking and try to get him to focus on something worth living for.

"Why are you thinking about hurting yourself?" I asked.

"Why not? It wouldn't matter. Everybody would be a lot better off if I was gone."

"Lorin, I love you and that's not true. No one would be better off. I am really concerned about you right now. Are you willing to talk to someone about this?"

"Sure."

"Okay, thank you. I am going to call the Veterans Crisis Line, and get someone for you to talk to, okay? You just stay with me here, Lorin, stay with me."

I went inside, grabbed the phone near the door, and walked into the kitchen. I dialed the number printed on the Veterans Crisis Line magnet I'd stuck on the fridge several years ago. I followed the voice prompt and punched the extension to get transferred to the veterans line. I was put on hold. I walked back outside where Lorin was getting more and more agitated and I tried to calm him down and keep him talking. He was throwing things into his Sorento, threatening to drive off Dodge Bridge and into an abutment.

I was still on hold.

"Lorin, where are you going?" I asked. I'd grabbed his car keys when I'd gone inside to call the crisis line, and I showed them to him.

"Really?"

"Yes, really, Lorin. I can't let you drive like this. Not alone."

"Think about what you just said. You are not getting into the car with me. No way."

"How about I drive my car and you go to the VA with me and talk to someone there? I know you said that you liked Matt Blakeley, how about I go with you and you can talk to him?"

"Nope. I am driving alone. So give me the keys. Now."

"If I call Blakeley and tell him what's happening, will you go in to see him when you get there?" *If you get there. This can't happen.*

"I don't know. Maybe. Give me the keys. You do *not* want to get in the middle of this," warned Lorin.

Where are those asshat shitbag Veterans Crisis Line fucknuts? I could not believe I had been on hold for more than five minutes. Five minutes is forever when you're trying to distract someone enough to keep them alive. Five minutes can be, often is, the differ-ence between saving a life and burying a suicide. *Where* are *they?*

Lorin was growing extremely agitated, making repeated threats to drive into a cement block underneath the bridge. Short of throw-ing myself onto the hood of his SUV, I had run out of options.

I heard a small, distant voice on the phone.

"Lorin, will you talk to the Veterans Crisis Line?" I asked.

"Sure."

He tells them exactly what he told me about his plan. Then he hung up, got in his car, and left. I called the VA and sounded the alarm, leaving voice mails with Lorin's case manager, at the Care-giver Program, and with Dr. Matt Blakeley in the Psychology Depart-ment. Not one answered, so all I could do was pray. About an hour later, Wanda called back from the Caregiver Program to give me an update. Lorin had made it in, she said, and his boss had been alerted and was with him.

Once I knew that at least Lorin was still alive and heard Wan-da's pleasant, professional voice, the adrenalized fear began rolling off of me. I cried, heavily, steadily, shaking off the trauma.

"Stacy, it's okay," Wanda reassured. "You can let it go now. It's okay. We've got him, and you did the right thing."

What if I had screwed up? What if I had said or done the wrong thing and Lorin killed himself right then?

Lorin spent several hours with VA staff talking with Dr. Blake-ley, but ultimately they decided Lorin no longer represented a threat to himself and they turned him loose. The protocol for the VA and the Veterans Crisis Line is to follow up with the vet a few weeks after the intervention. We never heard from either entity about Lorin's suicide threat again.

SERGEANT FIRST CLASS Daniel Wimmer started acting on his threats of suicide while he was still wearing the Army uniform, according to a *McClatchy Newspapers* report by Halimah Abdullah.[119] SFC Wimmer was a Persian Gulf veteran and father of four stationed at Fort Benning, Georgia, working as a drill sergeant. He met his wife, Jennifer, in 2007 and they married seven months later. She got Wimmer admitted into the psychiatric ward at Martin Army Community Hospital after his third attempt to overdose, which was called a "suicide gesture." A suicide gesture is an act that indicates an individual's desire to commit suicide, and one that would achieve that result if successfully completed. Some mental health professionals consider gestures to be a more serious warning of intent to self-harm than a suicide threat. But in the military, suicide gestures are often used to describe the self-harming behavior of a service member who's thought to be trying to avoid duty or deployment.

Wimmer was released from the hospital, and he slashed his wrists a few months later. An intervention of sorts was conducted by Jennifer, a chaplain, and Wimmer's commanding officers, who advised him to take a month off and get more counseling. Jennifer told Abdullah, "[during this time] our relationship was tense because I didn't know what to do to help him." She asked herself daily, "Do I leave or do I stay?"

Jennifer stayed, and it wasn't too many more months before Wimmer killed himself. His wife received a text message from an unknown "Bob" stating that she could find her husband's "body hanging like a Christmas ornament from a tree across from the

---

119. Abdullah, "Military Suicides," McClatchy Newspapers.

range on base. If he knew I was sending this he would be pissed." The military conducted an investigation into Wimmer's suicide and was never able to determine who "Bob" was. During the search, military personnel also had questions for Jennifer.

"[W]hen something like this happens the family is chastised, too, and it's like, 'Well, what did she do? How could she have prevented this?' Spouses are looked at very harshly," Jennifer said.

Colonel Elspeth Ritchie, who served as an Army psychiatrist and spokesperson during the height of the wars in Iraq and Afghanistan, remarked, "People don't tend to suicide as a direct result of combat . . . failed personal relationships are the primary cause." Ritchie put the onus of responsibility for the skyrocketing rates of soldier suicides squarely on the backs of military families when she said, "Families are getting tired. Therefore, they're more irritable, sometimes they don't take care of each other the way they should, are not as nurturing as they should be."

An Army study showed that by 2006 the rate of soldier suicides had hit its highest level since 1980, and the number of soldiers taking their own lives continued to spike for the next several years. The Army's answer was to implement the Strong Bonds program in order to reinforce and strengthen military marriages and other intimate relationships. According to the Strong Bonds website, the weekend retreats can "even start the journey of healing for relationships under fire."

By 2011, the VA had begun offering marriage retreats to veterans and their wives on a very limited basis and is in the process of expanding the program. VA Chaplain Ron Craddock launched the retreat program several years ago, because according to the VA website, "Research shows that 70 percent of our combat Veterans are experiencing marital problems. Twenty percent of them decide to divorce before they even return from theatre. This is staggering. The toll on the individual Veteran is staggering. The toll on his family is staggering."[120]

The toll on marriage is so staggering that combat veterans are 62 percent more likely than noncombat vets to be divorced or separated, reported Janie Blankenship in the March 2003 edition of *VFW* magazine. By early 2015, the majority of my military spouse friends who had been married to an 11 Bravo soldier before the wars began were divorced or living separately from their combat vet. The postwar returns on OIF/OEF veterans' rates of divorce are still in their infancy, but nearly 40 percent of "Vietnam veteran marriages failed within six months of the veteran's return from Southeast Asia."[121] Factor in PTSD, and rates of divorce are double that of vets without the diagnosis. The National Center for PTSD reported that the likelihood a vet with PTSD will have multiple divorces is triple that of veterans without PTSD. But the majority of veterans never see combat, and most of the troops that are deployed never develop PTSD. According to the combat stress hypothesis, what will kill a marriage most effectively are the emotional and psychological problems that come after combat. But they don't have to be fatal wounds. Blogging a response to a caregiver in a situation similar to mine, one vet wrote:

> PTSD . . . I have it . . . I'm in treatment for it and have been since 1992 but you know something? Life is choices, and PTSD

---

120. Veterans Health Administration website, "VA Offers Marriage Retreats for Returning Vets."

121. President's Commission on Mental Health, "Mental Health Problems of Vietnam Era Veterans."

isn't an excuse nor is it a "Free Ride" to misbehave. If your husband isn't in treatment for his PTSD in addition to marriage counseling, present the option to him in such a way that he understands how his PTSD is impacting both you and your children and that if he isn't going to show his family the same "Loyalty" that he showed the people he served with in Combat then it's time that he take a hard look at his priorities and get himself into "Treatment." . . . PTSD may not be "curable" but it sure is "manageable." It seems like you're doing all the work, you're taking on all the responsibility and he's saying "I'm entitled to act this way because I have PTSD."

Wake up, My Brother. "You're going to lose that girl" if you don't show her the same respect and loyalty you showed "Your Brothers in Arms." —Citizens for Veteran's Rights

I showed the post to Lorin in early August 2014, hoping it would help motivate him to follow through this time and get PTSD treatment at American Lake. His new admission date was just a few weeks away and represented the Hail Mary pass that might save our marriage. But when the time came, Lorin canceled. He assured me that he really, really wanted to go, and he would. "Just not right now," he said.

The next day, Lorin gave me a belated birthday card with a sketch of two dinosaurs standing on a rock in the rain, watching an ark filled with animals sailing away. The caption above the boy dinosaur read: "Oh, crap! Was that TODAY?" as the girl dinosaur stared at the boat in despair. The inside of the card read "A bad day is all about perspective."

Lorin stood there, grinning, while I read the card.

"Dude, you know how that ended, right?" I asked.

Not too many days later, I stumbled across another drug stash, a little brown bottle containing a clear fluid. I asked Lorin about it, and he said he'd forgotten he even had it and I could go ahead and throw it away. Later that night I called Lorin's mom, Helen. In the last, worst months before Lorin's meth use came to light, his folks had asked me to let them know if something had changed. Lorin rarely answered their calls or returned messages from them. I hated being the go-between, but they had asked, and I was tired of carrying everything alone. But often the only way I could work up the courage to call was after a few drinks. So when I was half in the bag, I picked up the phone and called Helen, determined that, one way or another, this would be the last call to her I ever made.

I'd been stockpiling Xanax for more than two years. I had a prescription for thirty pills every ninety days, although I rarely took the .25 mg tablets. I had alcohol to help me adapt to the crazy, and now I knew that the crazy hadn't been all in my head. I'd picked up the disordered drinking shortly after Lorin had picked up the meth. I almost never had the urge to binge drink when he wasn't around, but I battled with it almost weekly when he was. So I'd get the prescriptions filled and tuck them in a drawer, just in case. In case things got so bad with Lorin I would have to leave, and divorce him, and lose my home and my animals. When everything had broken loose with his meth use and the truth had finally come out, and my worst-case scenario was becoming the most obvious one, I told Lorin, "I will deny that I ever said this, but I swear to you, if you end up costing me every single thing I love in this world, you will find my cold, dead body in the barn."

I hadn't said another word about it to him or anyone else. I had looked into the milligrams of Xanax required for a lethal dosage. I counted out the pills I'd hoarded and stopped when I reached the magic number. I put the plastic pill bottle back in the drawer.

I retrieved that bottle from the bottom drawer of my bathroom vanity and took it downstairs. I set it on my desktop in the same general location that Lorin had left his meth. Then I picked up the phone, dialed Lorin's mom, Helen, and went outside. I sloppily relayed that I'd discovered more of Lorin's drugs, and that I just couldn't keep doing this. I thanked her for my birthday gift and her support over the past months. Then I said good-bye and went back inside. I poured a fourth glass of wine and sat down at my desk.

I smoothly unscrewed the cap from the orange plastic bottle and shook out a dozen or so pills—the first portion of the lethal dosage—into my cupped hand. I raised my palm to my mouth and licked the Xanax, which stuck to my tongue. I had a plastic bag and duct tape ready to cover my head with the bag and create an air seal by taping it tightly around my neck. A friend of mine had killed himself that way fifteen years earlier, so I knew it would work. He had opened the door to his death with a combination of sedatives and alcohol, but when I was on the threshold, I walked to the kitchen and spat the softening pills in the sink. I poured out the rest of the wine, rinsed my mouth with water, and went to bed. I called a divorce attorney the next morning and told him to get divorce papers ready to file. I would lose my life to keep it.

CHAPTER NINE

The End of Acceptable Losses

I QUIT THE COIN toss for my marriage once I understood that I was betting with my life. I couldn't continue to gamble on becoming another homefront casualty: another Cassy Walton, the next Kristy Huddleston. They, and the hundreds of thousands of others who have been wounded or killed or who have killed themselves when the war came home, should be included in the casualty count. We all loved someone who deployed, and we have sustained service-connected injuries and combat-related losses of our own as a result. The wars in Iraq and Afghanistan, like all wars, will create reverberations of pain, suffering, and death in the families of the veterans who fought in them for generations. Because the number of post-9/11 military families has been a disproportionately small segment of Americans, just as the number of troops has been a tiny percentage of the country's population, the damage incurred in the war at home has been highly and lethally concentrated.

A democratic solution would mandate that the suffering be distributed across the nation by way of war taxation and some required sacrifice or engagement of civilian resources, as happened in earlier wars. A more equitable solution might entail enlisting more troops, and limiting the number and length of deployments for ground combat forces, particularly those with dependents, as happened in earlier wars. A spiritually and morally courageous response would require deciding differently about the next war of choice, so that what happened in earlier wars never happens again.

The lie this country has advanced in order to absolve itself of knowledge and accountability for the injuries inflicted on the families left behind is that collateral damage can be contained. Collateral damage cannot be contained, and I will bear witness to that for the rest of my days. Lorin received the divorce papers the day before September 11, 2014, but I would take back the man he was before he went to war in a heartbeat. My husband was never an acceptable loss to me. An acceptable loss is the phrase used by the military to refer to the allowable level of death and destruction that occurs during combat. It's the cost-benefit analysis conducted prior to engaging with the enemy that weighs the available options and, knowing that some loss is inevitable, determines a tolerable number of troop casualties. The only number that mattered to me—and to most military families—was one.

Just as soldiers fight for those nearest to them in the foxhole, so do their families. Lorin was my one husband, my only love, and his loss wasn't reasonable at all. It wasn't even fathomable. So when he emailed a picture of himself sitting in his HMMV that was taken in the spring of 2005, a few weeks after those children were killed by mortar rounds while running across the field in Iraq, I printed his photo on a poster with the caption: "My husband is NOT an acceptable loss." Not knowing he was already gone.

I carried that sign when I lobbied for better body armor and safer HMMVs for the citizen soldiers serving overseas. I carried that poster when I testified before Congress, and when I met with then senator Obama about the terrible toll of the war at home. I spoke and the senator listened for the better part of an hour, and after that, whenever he saw me in one of the Senate office buildings, or at a hearing or press conference on the Hill, he'd come over to talk for a few minutes, and give me a quick hug. I never met his wife, Michelle Obama, but I like to think that my voice was one of the many that spurred her to partner with Dr. Jill Biden to support the families of service members. Mrs. Obama made improving assistance for military families a central part of her platform while her husband was on the campaign trail in 2008. After President Obama took office, the First Lady made her pledge official.

Recognizing the strain on military families after nearly a decade of war with an unparalleled churn cycle, in April of 2011 the White House launched Joining Forces, "a comprehensive national initiative to mobilize all sectors of society to give our service members and their families the opportunities and support they have earned."[122] Joining Forces was "a challenge to every segment of American society not to simply say thank you but to mobilize, take action and make a real commitment to supporting our military families."[123]

---

122. www.whitehouse.gov.
123. Ibid.

The initiative marked the first occasion an administration had created a strategy specific to supporting the service and sacrifice of military families during wartime. But Joining Forces was an invitation to volunteer, rather than an obligation to sacrifice. Corporations answered the call, as did a variety of charitable groups and religious organizations. But by then, the average American was too far removed from any sense of obligation to sacrifice, in part because they were so far removed from anyone in the service. I remember when people were saying we were all in this together. I heard President George W. Bush say that we were the *United* States, and the War on Terror would require a "great sacrifice" from everyone. Nearly nine years later, I read an article by Colleen Getz in the May 28, 2010, edition of the *Washington Times* about a family whose son made the ultimate sacrifice and what happened one day in sight of this nation's Capitol.

Lance Corporal Justin J. Wilson was coming home. A newly minted Marine, he got married the day before he deployed. At the age of twenty-four, he was killed in Afghanistan by a roadside bomb. When he left, his family was with him, smothering him with hugs and kisses and camera flashes, waving as he boarded the bus. When his casket came back from Afghanistan, they met him at Dover Air Force Base on March 24, 2010. A Marine carry team handled the transfer case containing the Corporal's remains upon his arrival. The Dover landing was the first leg of his final journey on American soil that would end at the Holy Redeemer Catholic Church in Palm City, Florida.

After a long wait in a crowded terminal, the Wilson family got on a commercial flight, with the body of their son down below. They had a layover in DC and stood, silent with grief, at the gate while the announcement was made that the flight was overbooked and they needed six volunteers to give up their seats. The people with boarding passes were told that the seats were for the family members who had met their son's body when it returned from Afghanistan, and were now taking his remains home for his funeral. Three people volunteered.

The airline representative asked again . . . and again . . . and again for three more volunteers from the hundred or so people standing there, with the dead Marine's family in their midst. No one stepped forward. Again the call for people to sacrifice their seats. Silence.

On the verge of tears, the airline representative begged:

"This young man gave his life for our country; can't any of you give your seats so his family can get home?"

Those words lingered in the air for what must have felt like a lifetime to the family of the fallen Marine. Finally, three more people surrendered their seats.

I've never forgotten that article, and I used to bring it up in conversations to illustrate the gap between civilian and military families. I quit referencing the account about the airport because the military families always knew what story I was talking about; civilians never did.

America wasn't at war, *we* were. And it felt like the social contract had been betrayed. This nation was founded on a covenant that individuals would sacrifice some privileges in order to advance the common will and secure mutual protection. In the immediate aftermath of the September 11 attacks, the common will was clearly in favor of war and establishing homeland security, but the majority of individuals shrugged at the suggestion of sacrifice. That left a miniscule segment of the population to pay this country's war check in the midst of the democratic equivalent of a dine-and-dash. Those few who dared to suggest that perhaps everyone should pay a portion of the cost of war by way of a draft, taxes, or some other mandatory contribution, were mocked, attacked, or ignored.

As multiple deployments became the norm, and the toll on the troops and their families became increasingly severe, some military families began speaking out in the hopes that politicians and the general public would pay attention. When the war in Afghanistan was in its thirteenth year, Michael Daly remarked about the lack of focus on the fighting overseas, stating that "most of the country has gone AWOL, walking away from our responsibility to keep those who risk all in our hearts and minds." In an article for the *Daily Beast* Daly claimed that "You can go around all day and not hear anybody even mention Afghanistan. At least people talked about Vietnam."[124]

Feeling betrayed is a less disastrous emotional state than feeling abandoned. "The thought 'so-and-so has betrayed me' protects us from the more painful thought 'no one thinks about me.' And this is one reason why soldiers commonly suffer paranoia," writes psychoanalyst Stephen Grosz in his book, *The Examined Life*.[125] Cultural amnesia eradicates existence, and without existence there can be no meaningful purpose to validate sacrifice. If the cause for which one is fighting, and the people who are fighting it, are abandoned and not remembered, then what's the fighting for? Grosz called the feeling of being alone and forgotten "the catastrophe of

---

124. Daly, "It Wasn't Just Bergdahl," *Daily Beast*.
125. Grosz, *The Examined Life*.

indifference." Journalist Bob Woodward called it the "epidemic of disconnection."

That disconnect was initiated by the Bush administration's abject failure to call upon the country to invest itself in these wars. America used to have a moral code that reinforced the social fabric of the nation when it was at war and dictated the norms of civilian behavior. That code—let's call it a sacred contract—was the promise that the men and women in the Armed Forces would not be on the battlefield by themselves; the country would be there, too. This country honored that promise via scrap drives, rationing, Victory gardens, and war bonds. Elected officials upheld that oath by limiting the number of tours of a service member and implementing the draft, which entailed shielding dependent family members from the deployment of the spouse or parent. Civilian America made good on its word by paying taxes and keeping the war effort in the media, in conversations, and in its conscious awareness. But that promise was broken with these wars.

By 2014 the pledge had been shattered, and the contract itself had been grotesquely inverted by this nation's political leaders. Among them, consider South Carolina's senior senator Lindsay Graham, who asked on January 28, 2014:

> Isn't there a social contract, even though it's not in writing; your kids, your sons, your daughters, individuals will not have to be drafted because others will come forward and do the job voluntarily? What would you pay, if you had to, to prevent your family from being drafted?

The tendency of elected officials to publicly sanction the avoidance of civilian service and sacrifice has widened the gulf between the military and civilian populations. The volunteer military and their families had become "the new American segregation. They know it and we know it," wrote Richard Reeves for *Truthdig*.[126] Prior to his retirement as the chairman of the Joint Chiefs of Staff, Admiral Mike Mullen delivered the commencement speech at Florida State University in 2011. In his remarks he said, "With less than 1 percent of our population serving, I do worry that one day, the American people and our troops may no longer know each other the way we should."

The divide between the defenders and the defended has made the mental health problems facing them and their families worse. Each tour ups the ante that both the troops and their families will develop psychological issues, and the rising rates of mental health problems are tied to the rising rates of service members and veterans and their families who are killing themselves. But the distance between the 1 percent and the 99 percent may also be driving the escalation in suicides. According to a pair of researchers at the US Air Force Academy:

> We have chosen to ask and allow a few to shoulder voluntarily the burden once shared by all. We have chosen to permit our leaders to involve us in wars the majority of citizens do not support. These choices have consequences that may include the creation of a constellation of social, cultural, and political conditions which conspire to elevate the rate of suicide in the Army and Marine Corps.[127]

Multiple deployments to war zones, coupled with ephemeral, insufficient support when troops come back, are leaving thousands of

---

126. Reeves, "The New American Segregation," *Truthdig*.

127. Mastroianni and Scott, "Reframing Suicide," *Parameters*.

veterans adrift. It appears that post-war social isolation is a strong predictor of permanent psychological damage from soldiering. As reported by David Dobbs in the *New York Times*, "PTSD runs higher among veterans who cannot reconnect with supportive people and new opportunities."[128] Social support offers the strongest protection against the development of psychiatric problems. For most returning veterans, the major source of social support is the family. But some of those family members are suffering themselves, and it's hard to lend a hand when yours is broken.

I contend that the social isolation of today's military families has exacerbated the extraordinary rates of mental health problems on the homefront. Family, community, connection, and attachment are protective factors that can shield people from psychological harm, but many of us have fought the war at home alone. Recovery from the wars on either front cannot occur in isolation. According to Dr. Judith Herman, an expert in traumatology, "The fundamental stages of recovery are establishing safety, reconstructing the trauma story, and restoring the connection between survivors and their community."[129] Trauma is best healed when shared, but the great gap between military and civilian sectors has meant that many in the helping professions cannot comprehend the cultural norms and combat-related realities of the post-9/11 military population. As a result, the vast majority of community-based mental health providers are poorly equipped to treat them and their families. A mere 13 percent of civilian psychiatrists, psychologists, and licensed clinical social workers scored well for military cultural

---

128. Dobbs, "A New Focus," *New York Times*.
129. Herman, *Trauma and Recovery*.

competency in a survey conducted by the Rand Corporation, according to Patricia Kime.[130]

"Military cultural competency" refers to the understanding of the language, background, and mores of the Armed Services and the ability to deliver suitable care for service-connected issues and illnesses, including military sexual trauma, combat-related PTSD, depression, and veteran intimate partner violence. The DoD providers who were registered with TRICARE didn't do much better: just 25 percent of them passed muster on cultural competency.

The DoD is taking steps to improve training, and Edmonds Community College, Purdue University, Syracuse University, and the University of Southern California's School of Social Work are among a growing number of schools across the country developing research institutes, training programs, and certificates that will provide the cultural competency to better understand and assist our wounded warriors and their families. But many of those injured troops won't be seeing those providers, and many other veterans don't have war wounds that require care. They all, however, will have to transition from war to peace and from being in uniform to being a civilian, and would be well served by connecting with their communities.

"Society and community are, of course, necessary to modern life; they are also essential to psychological wellness, physical health, and post-war readjustment and reintegration," said Dr. April Gerlock. The reintegration process can be facilitated by the Welcome Johnny and Jane Home listening sessions. Devised by Dr. Paula Caplan, a clinical and research psychologist currently serving as

---

130. Kime, "Rand: Civilian Mental Health Providers," *Army Times*.

an associate at Harvard University's Dubois Institute, the listening sessions are a simple exercise in the potency of human connection. The sessions provide a powerful vehicle for the 99 percent to get to know veterans, help alleviate the strain on their families, and begin to assume a degree of ownership of these wars. In the words of Dr. Caplan, "Listeners are not therapists, and—except for speaking two very specific sentences during the session—they truly do nothing but listen. However, they do so with 100 percent of their attention and their whole hearts."

The full engagement of the nonveteran listener provides a safe space for veterans and their families to speak without fear of harming the close familial relationships, particularly with their spouse and children that they are trying to protect. The main purpose of the session is to reduce veterans' isolation from their wider community. But the project also provides much-needed listening sessions for veterans' loved ones. We, too, are desperately in need of a conversational shelter, where we are seen and heard. The impact of war zone deployments on the people left behind has been overlooked, if not intentionally avoided. The end result has been a silencing of military families, and veterans' caregivers in particular, who are often marginalized in their own lives and invisible in their communities.

Society is involved in the grooming of veterans' spouses and caregivers to endure abusive situations, as is the military, the VA, and veterans themselves. Grooming is the process of manipulating an individual into a situation that makes them more isolated, dependent, willing to trust, and more vulnerable to abusive behavior. That's precisely what had happened with me, and I was struggling to figure out why. So I called my friend Tammara, who had twenty years of experience in the trenches of mental health case management. Because of that background, she had become my go-to resource on all things related to behavioral disorders, drugs, and dysfunction.

"Any kind of grooming is totally focused on or dedicated to the normalization of an abnormal situation," said Tammara, who had recently taken a job as a probation and parole officer for the state of Montana. "It's done to switch the blame for the activity from the perpetrator to the victim. It becomes the fault of the child for being so sexy, or the fault of the veteran's spouse when he is triggered."

From the moment our loved one joins the military, the spouse is inculcated in a hierarchical culture of silence, violence, loyalty, and acceptance. The insular nature of the military culture, wherein secrecy is often required and sometimes essential for survival, coupled with the deepening divide between civilian and military cultures, helped to ensure that there would be no dissent within the invisible ranks at home. There is a strong, unifying distinction between the military and nonmilitary that translates to a general us/them mentality, ultimately fostering a sense that civilians cannot understand. This belief system effectively isolates the soldier and the spouse from social contacts or outside sources of support. So, when the four wives at Fort Bragg were murdered by their soldier-husbands in 2002, rather than question how the war was coming home, those first cracks in the homefront were paved over with proclamations of patriotism. They were filled with flags and yellow ribbons and bumper stickers boasting that we support the troops. And support was equated with silence.

"We become complicit in the abuse the first time we excuse it," said Tammara when we were talking on the phone in early 2015 about another spate of veteran violence that had ended the lives of at least half a dozen military family members between September and December of the previous year. Casualties included Jessica Arrendale, who was shot in the head by her boyfriend, Antoine Davis, a Marine who served in Iraq. Nicole Stone, the ex-wife of Iraq War veteran Bradley William Stone, and five of her relatives all died during Bradley Stone's killing rampage in December of 2014. Less than a week earlier, a VA psychiatrist had assessed Bradley as having no suicidal or homicidal tendencies. After Stone committed suicide, various media reported that Evan Weron, a neighbor of Nicole's, said that she "would tell anybody who would listen that he was going to kill her and that she was really afraid for her life."

But many of us who experienced it typically excused our veteran's violence because they'd been to war and we hadn't. Some who clamored for swift, severe justice for the veteran convicted of killing *American Sniper* author Chris Kyle seemed willing to grant exemptions for the service-connected murders of spouses because the military was going to war so that civilian America didn't have to. Once established, the abuse is maintained by a shroud of secrecy that's often reinforced with threats, shaming, and guilt, and the victim helps to maintain the silence.

Military spouse silence about domestic violence is incentivized by the fact that speaking out could result in a loss of their husband's rank, or an other-than-honorable discharge, which would strip service members and their families of benefits. There is an undercurrent of thought in the military and veterans' community that to speak out is to betray the soldier and the warrior culture, especially during war time. Speaking out about service-connected domestic violence means that you are not Army Strong, you are not a good soldier's wife. Speaking out means that you don't "Support the troops."

"In fact, the 'support' in that slogan generally means acquiescence when it comes to American-style war," wrote William Astore, a retired US Air Force lieutenant colonel and former professor at the Air Force Academy and the Naval Postgraduate School. "The truth is that we've turned the all-volunteer military into something like a foreign legion, deploying it again and again to our distant battle zones and driving it into the ground in wars that amount to strategic folly. Instead of admitting their mistakes, America's leaders have worked to obscure them by endlessly overpraising our 'warriors' as so many universal heroes. This may salve our collective national conscience, but it's a form of cheap grace that saves no lives—and wins no wars."[131]

Seeing the hero as a trauma victim becomes an exoneration for aggression. Verbal abuse and intimate partner violence are rationalized and tacitly excused because the vet was triggered, but he served his country, so he's a hero and it's not his fault. It's his wife's fault. Spouses became the cannon fodder in the war at home. It has become culturally acceptable and politically expedient to sacrifice the spouses of service members to the gods of war because "you knew what you were getting in to."

"It's not just veterans' spouses being groomed, it's the entire fucking nation," said Tammara. We were talking about the public discourse around post-9/11 troops that branded all returning veterans as heroes of war or victims of trauma. It's the social swing of the pendulum from when the nation vilified Vietnam vets and called

---

131. Astore, "Groundhog Day," *TomDispatch.*

them baby killers when they came home. That wasn't true of the Vietnam vets, but it's the cultural story that sprang from the country's collective guilt and deep-seated shame about Vietnam. Likewise, it's not true today that all post-9/11 vets are heroes or victims, but that's the cultural story we've created to compensate for the past. That's the story that many of the wives, girlfriends, and moms of veterans hear, and they think, "Oh my God, this poor guy. I will do whatever it takes to support him and take care of him."

The expectation of care regardless of cost to the caregiver is reinforced implicitly and explicitly by the Departments of Defense and Veterans Affairs. We are turned away from mental health services and constantly reminded that the service member and veteran matters more than us. The DoD's mental health professionals preach to the wives about resilience, but they aren't the ones who've been woken up at three in the morning because their husband has shot the dog, or was holding a gun to their head or a knife at their throat.

A VA program officer who was also a Vietnam veteran told me that "It's the wife's responsibility to set the tone for the whole household." Another veteran's advocate asked me, "Why don't you take care of him?" If our veteran does not endorse treatment for behavioral issues that are creating havoc in our homes, we are instructed to adapt and to change *our* behavior, and coached on how to prevent, minimize, and repair the consequences of our veteran's conduct. The primary responsibility is shifted from the veteran who committed the violence to the spouse. Even before our soldier comes back, we are prepped to accept negative changes in behavior because we can't expect him to be the person he was before. We are instructed to "be patient and give it time."

We are rewarded with a National Guard Freedom Salute clock to help us keep track of that time. We are rewarded by being told that we are "super spouses," that we are the "heart of the Army." We are rewarded with free tickets to movies and concerts and ball games, preferential seating on airplanes, and a 10 percent discount at most stores and restaurants. If our veteran is sufficiently wounded, we are rewarded with membership in the VA Caregiver Program.

Most veterans' caregivers want to help their husbands, and it feels good to be able to when he's willing to help himself. Too often, though, after the initial attention and positive reinforcement, the caregiving spouse is largely left to fend for herself. This de facto isolation may not be intentional, but the traumatized veteran's refusal or inability to socialize effectively ostracizes them both. The gap between soldiers and citizens cements it. Most of society no longer knows the people who serve, and much of the country has largely ignored—if not forgotten—that we are still at war. It's extremely difficult to have a conversation when you are no longer sharing the same reality.

So we retreat, and remain in place as our lives get smaller, and smaller, and smaller. We become participants in our own oppression and are obligated to accept it. The VA caregiver training manual includes a section that educates the caregiver on how to serve as an advocate for the veteran, which requires the caregiver who is being abused to act as a proxy for her aggressor and to fight the veteran's battles with the VA and elsewhere. In the process, the caregiver assumes more and more responsibility in order to avoid potentially dangerous conflicts. And in the midst of a powerful, overwhelming fear of losing the emotional bond, even if it is one-sided, the survival instinct of the traumatized veteran's traumatized spouse is subdued. She becomes acclimated to a relationship with physical or psychological aggression, and "without physical intimacy, without emotional intimacy, without predictability, without trust," said Tammara, speaking of her own experience and that of so many others. "That's where it ends up. Best you can hope for is some kind of benign coexistence."

But whatever you do, you'd better not abandon him like the Vietnam vets were abandoned when they got back. That message has been internalized by too many wives of combat vets with invisible injuries, and then we do things we wouldn't normally do. We agree to things we never would have before, and we accept abuse that was unacceptable, even to us, just a few years earlier. I am responsible for allowing the erosion, but the responsibility is not mine alone.

According to Peter Bernstein, who treats trauma victims at his eponymous institute, "Partners of trauma-affected individuals often feel alone and rejected on some level. They may feel they must always tread lightly in their relationships. They may end up feeling helpless and powerless. . . . Trauma-affected individuals often promote these feelings of powerlessness, because they are committed at all costs to maintaining control and protecting themselves from feeling their pain."[132]

The VA is also complicit in the cover-up of veteran violence in the home. According to Oregon state law, and most other states, workers in certain professions must make reports if they have reasonable cause to suspect physical injury, sexual or emotional abuse, neglect, or financial exploitation. People in the helping professions, such as doctors, psychologists, social workers, licensed

---

132. Bernstein, *Trauma: Healing the Hidden Epidemic.*

professional counselors, nurses, and case managers, are called mandatory reporters because they have regular contact with vulnerable and at-risk populations. Oregon's at-risk populations include: infants and children, people who are elderly or dependent, individuals with mental illness or developmental disabilities, and residents of nursing homes and other health-care facilities. Oregon is one of fewer than a dozen states where the commission of domestic violence in the presence of one of the parties' minor children is classified as a felony. Veterans' wives are also identified as a high-risk population in Oregon, per the language I wrote for the Oregon Department of Justice 2014–2016 STOP VAWA Implementation Plan.

Caregiver Program staff at the VA in White City said that well over half of the program participants have suffered at least one known incident of veteran intimate partner violence. On occasion, their children have witnessed the assault. When care-givers disclose the abuse to VA personnel, we are typically asked if we are safe now, and told to pack a "bug out bag" and keep it handy in case we have to run. Conversations with dozens of VA service providers, who are all mandatory reporters, revealed that they seldom report an incident of veteran violence toward the caregiver even when there are children in the home. One local caregiver who did report it told me that, after her veteran was charged with domestic violence, they'd have appointments at the VA, and "everybody was mad at me. We are not supposed to talk about it. *I* got in trouble."

Domestic violence is one of the conditions that can terminate the veteran's eligibility for the Caregiver Program. However, if the vet is kicked out, he will continue to receive disability payments,

VA health care, and counseling, but the caregiver will lose their monthly stipend and support. The financial security of many of the wives of service members and veterans is disproportionately tied to the spouse. Most caregivers cut their hours or quit their jobs to take care of their vet, and the DoD reports that the unemployment rate for military spouses is a ridiculously high 26 percent, more than four times the national average. With a stagnant economy and a country struggling to work its way out of a recession, the economic reality of leaving can be as frightening as the danger at home. But my biggest barrier to leaving was accepting the loss of love and the life I once had.

Shortly after I had filed for divorce, I received an email from a veteran's wife seeking advice and resources. Her husband had been abusive and aggressive, and he abandoned her and their children. He refused to get help for his PTSD, and she wanted to know what she could do to get her husband back. I replied:

> I am going to tell you what you already know, but I do so with the same love I had to find in order to walk through this myself. It is not possible to get your husband back. Haven't you already done every single thing you could to save him? Haven't you loved him so hard that you bled, figuratively, if not literally? And still your willingness to take on his wounds wasn't enough to heal him. There is nothing that can prepare anyone for marriage with a PTSD spouse. Nothing. There's no amount of smart that will fix it. And no matter how wide, deep, or forever your love for him, that love CANNOT save your veteran. Your veteran can save your veteran. You can love him while he saves himself. If he is not willing to save himself, you can still love him, but if you stay, you will be fragged for the Rest. Of. Your. Life. You choose.

Get a good attorney. Get a great counselor/therapist. Get to
work. Breathe. Grieve. Move. Resurrect.

That's what worked for me. Only as I began to detach from Lorin
did I start to see that I had all of the classic indicators of secondary
PTSD: irritability, social withdrawal, substance abuse, avoidance,
hyperawareness, and suicidal ideation. Every one of the symptoms
abated as I gradually severed the emotional cord that had tied me
to him for so long, and been the conduit for the insidious traumatic
infection. But I did not do it alone.

Finding a counselor took weeks, and when at last I located one
that understood some of the dynamics of living with a combat vet
with untreated PTSD, the sessions weren't covered by insurance.
Her two-plus decades of working at the VA, and her knowledge
about the perniciousness of PTSD in the home, far outweighed the
cost. I tried three different prescriptions for depression, including
Pristiq and Lexapro, but discontinued them after the immediate
onset of severe headaches, nausea, or sleeplessness. Something had
changed in my physiology that made those pharmaceuticals intolerable, so I looked into alternative medicine and began taking Saint
John's Wort, a natural supplement to treat depression, as well as
some flower essences and remedies.

I got outside more, and made solitary kayak trips down the Rogue
River, benefiting from Jeep therapy on the fifteen-mile drive to Shady
Cove and back. Driving the Wrangler with the soft top off, savor-
ing the smell of sun-warmed hayfields and seeing pastures peopled
with cows and horses inevitably whisked away whatever had been
bothering me. I'd hike a few miles on Table Rock every week for the
serenity I found on the trail. The "rhythm and repetition of walking

has a tranquilizing effect on your brain, and it decreases anxiety and improves sleep," according to nutrition-and-wellness expert Ann Kulze, MD. Hiking, swimming, rowing, bicycling, drumming, horseback riding, and other types of bilateral movement encourage the release of chemicals that create new neural pathways. I didn't know the science behind it, but I began going to drumming circles. I felt a little awkward and a lot skeptical at first, but I felt better afterward, so I kept going back. Drumming has been shown to jump-start "the natural information processing system that shuts down during trauma," according to the Virginia Center for Neurofeedback.

"When drumming, we experience something called hemispheric synchronization, where both sides [of the brain] work at the same time," said psychotherapist Robert Lawrence Friedman, author of *The Healing Power of the Drum.* The physiological shift has a profound genetic counterpart. According to a 2005 study, drumming, or any kind of recreational music-making, changes the way an individual reacts to stress on a molecular level.[133] Muhammad A. Sharaf, PhD, one of the scientists who conducted the study said, "We showed for the very first time, that we could turn off the DNA-based switches that literally turn on components of human stress responses." Drumming helped me feel calmer and more present, more engaged in the moment, and I also started going to a women's support group. In talking to other wives of combat vets with PTSD, I discovered I wasn't alone in self-medicating with alcohol.

Adapting to dysfunction is not the highest expression of love. "You don't have to set yourself on fire to keep someone else warm," said veteran caregiver Kathleen Harris Causey in a note to me

---

133. Bittman et al., "Recreational Music-Making," *Medical Science Monitor.*

after I told her why I had gotten divorced. The ultimate evidence of love is releasing someone to be who they are. Lorin had been showing me who he was after war, and I refused to accept it. A friend of mine, whose son is also an Iraq war vet, once said, "When someone shows you who they are, believe them." Believing meant grieving who he had been, and who we might have become together. Grief sneaks up on you, and there were days that fall spent sitting in a dark theater during an afternoon matinee with tears coursing down my cheeks. I tried to do my mourning alone or in the shadows, but the thing about grief is that sometimes it cannot be controlled. You'll think you've got it together, and then you find you don't.

My attorney informed me that Lorin had not responded to the divorce papers, and the timeline for doing so had expired. The next step was to have the court file a judgment in my favor granting the divorce. That would come in early November, just a few weeks away. I cried after I got off the phone with my lawyer, but I had to focus on looking forward now, not back. I was very much looking forward to going back to church; I hadn't attended since 2003. In the run-up to the war in Iraq, Pope John Paul II had consistently said, "If you invade Iraq, God is not with you." When Lorin deployed to Iraq in 2004, it was evident that God had gone away. Over the past year, I had begun to wonder where, and two days after the phone call, I went to the Center for Spiritual Living in Medford. The morning service had already started, so I snuck in and took a seat. The center didn't have an actual church; they just rented out a large meeting space at a local strip mall. Of the one hundred or so chairs lined up in rows, maybe half of them were occupied, mostly by middle-aged or elderly folks, with a smattering of children under the age of ten. Neale Donald Walsch, author of the Conversations with God book series, was serving as the interim spiritual director. Shortly after I sat down, he asked if anyone in the congregation had an announcement.

I listened with half an ear as a gal reminded the group that they were raffling tickets and had coffee mugs for sale. The next speaker made a quick pitch for an upcoming study group, and then the microphone was passed to a middle-aged lady.

"We're still short of our fundraising goal for the Peace Pole that we want to put up outside the church. Please make a donation if you haven't already," she said. "For those of you who don't know, the Peace Pole has 'May Peace Prevail on Earth' written on every side in different languages. There are Peace Poles in 180 countries, and we want to have one here as a reminder to pray for peace."

I hung my head and raised my hand, tears streaming down my face, falling onto the carpet. I was handed the microphone but was too shaky to stand, and just sat there for a minute or two (or three), struggling to rein in the tears as the congregation quietly waited.

"You get that Peace Pole and you pray for peace. I am . . . I am . . ." I cleared my throat and shook my head to try to stop the tears, and then continued. "I am losing my husband to war and he hasn't been at peace since he got home."

Then I dropped my head again, weeping in the stillness of the sanctuary, while someone came over to get the mike. After Mr. Walsch had the microphone again, he thanked me and my husband for the service that we provided.

"I know that it's hard to believe, but even in your darkest moments, God is with you," he said. "And remember that to the best students go the most difficult lessons."

I resisted learning for so long that the education very nearly killed me. But as the Greek poet Aeschylus once wrote, "Even in our sleep, pain that cannot forget falls drop by drop upon the heart, until, in our own despair, against our will, comes wisdom through the awful grace of God."

*   *   *

I wish that the Guard family programs and services had been fully functional when these wars began, and tailored to the unique circumstances of the families of reservists. I wish there had been culturally competent mental health providers readily available to serve military family members. And I wish that, in addition to getting literature about what might happen when my soldier came home, I'd gotten some information about what might happen with me when he left. I also wish the DoD had provided returning Guard and Reservist troops with mental health care that was at least comparable to that available for active-duty veterans. Mental health issues are 44 percent higher in Guard and Reservists than their active-duty counterparts, according to the Veterans for America, yet they receive inferior services, leaving their families to suffer the consequences. Those consequences appear to be especially intense for kids, many of whom experience prolonged psychological distress even after the deployed parent returns. I wish that vet centers would offer age-appropriate therapy for the children of veterans, and that providers would begin screening those kids for PTSD. I asked Tracey Haeckler, an Oregon National Guard family assistance specialist, how support for Guard kids could be improved while the soldier is away.

"My wish is to see a military child mentorship program implemented in every school district (if not every school), and schools should be notified of upcoming deployments," she said. "I would like to see a self-identifying option for military families when they register children for school that matches them with a counselor, teacher, or even a teenage student that has experienced a deployment. A person that every military child knows that they can go to when needed to talk and express their feelings in a safe environment."

I wish the VA would create a safer environment for caregivers by making domestic violence and suicide ideation screenings mandatory for all personnel and Caregiver Program providers who interact with partners of veterans with combat-related PTSD. Many of those partners have been abused by their veteran, and suffer severe psychological distress. Depression and suicidal ideation are rampant in that segment of the caregiver population.[134] Not only do veterans' caregivers need to be screened for suicidal ideation, the caregivers also need to be trained in how to conduct a suicide intervention. I called Ben Bryan at the White City VA Suicide Prevention office in February 2015, seven months after I did Lorin's intervention. I suggested they might want to start screening caregivers for thoughts of suicide, and then I learned that they still had not conducted a suicide intervention training for the caregivers.

"Ben," I sighed, "veterans' caregivers need that training because they are the ones most likely to have to use it. Vets don't generally make suicide threats while at work or during VA office hours."

---

134. Manguno-Mire et al., "Psychological Distress," *Journal of Nervous and Mental Disease*.

"Yeah, you're right. I'm emailing the caregiver program right now to set that up," replied Ben.

"That's great, thank you, but it's asinine that it hasn't happened already. It's asinine that it took a phone call from me for that to happen." I wish I had more tolerance, but tolerating certain things has proven to be fatal.

I wish more of the trauma-informed programs serving veterans would be expanded in light of the fact that traumatized people who don't deal with their own trauma will inevitably traumatize others. When I was living with Lorin's war trauma, it tapped my latent traumatic experience of growing up with a parent who was reenacting *their* experience of *their* parent's war trauma. In his book, *Trauma*, Dr. Peter Bernstein writes, "The unresolved energy and emotions from those experiences often intensify the emotions associated with our current circumstances. When we experience this, responding to our situation appropriately becomes even more difficult than usual. This is known as co-occurring trauma."[135]

I wish I had been aware of that when I was in the midst of it, and I hope there comes a day on this planet where the transgenerational transmission of combat trauma is something we used to do. Until then, I hope we come to understand that just as PTSD vets are a unique population presenting a cluster of symptoms and challenges specific to combat, deserving of their own treatment program provided by a federal government department, so too are the people who bear the burden of the war at home. Achieving optimal wellness in a sick environment is impossible, but getting better is doable. The VA has all manner of employee wellness programs in

---

135. Bernstein, *Trauma: Healing the Hidden Epidemic.*

place to support the staff who clock out at the end of the day, and usually don't have an injured vet waiting at home. I wish the VA would consider making those same programs and resources available to veterans' caregivers, who are on-call around the clock, and have no sanctuary called home to go to. If, as a military mom once told me, having your soldier deployed is like being in the waiting room of the ER for a year, being a caregiver for a combat vet with untreated post-traumatic stress is like being the ball boy at a shooting range.

I wish the VA would help reduce the wear and tear on those caregivers and the families of veterans by working with all of them to develop an Individual Support Plan. When I spoke with Chris Smith about his son, Cody, who was back in drug treatment at the VA in the fall of 2014, Chris suggested that the Individual Support Plan they used at his nonprofit to help the assisted living residents and their families could easily be adapted for use with veterans and their families. By taking a team approach, the vet and his caregiving family members are all involved in setting and meeting goals, and are accountable for their respective roles in meeting them. Given that the families of PTSD-diagnosed veterans are always affected by the trauma, I wish the VA would measure the family members' mental and physical well-being in studies on PTSD. Because the families cannot carry this alone, I wish more communities would implement the listening sessions of the When Johnny and Jane Come Marching Home project, perhaps making town halls and other safe public spaces available after the parades on the Fourth of July and Veterans Day.

I hope Military Spouse Appreciation Day (May) and Gold Star Mothers Day (September) become more significant opportunities for us to honor the service and sacrifice of military families. I hope we will also learn more about how to embrace the families of the more than nineteen thousand service members who have died on active duty since September 11, 2001, from combat, accident, illness, suicide, or other causes. The Associated Press reported on January 4, 2015, that thousands of military widows, widowers, parents, siblings, and children are describing their grief in the largest study ever conducted of bereaved military families.[136] I am optimistic that the results of the federally funded project being performed by the Center for the Study of Traumatic Stress will help the nation better help the survivors. Particularly those who struggle with complicated grief, an intense, long-lasting form of grief that keeps the loss ever-present and interrupts the natural healing trajectory, increasing the likelihood of suicide.

I hope we prioritize the safety of military children and the families of veterans. The Talia Williams Child Abuse Notification Act, requiring that the military immediately report any child abuse or suspicion of child abuse to state child protective services, should be passed immediately and unanimously. I hope that the Kristy Huddleston Act is sponsored, introduced, passed, and implemented before too many more veterans' wives and children lose their lives. I wrote the legislation in October of 2013 and submitted it to my Oregon Senators Ron Wyden and Jeff Merkley. My proposed bill would amend Title 38 of the United States Code to provide transitional compensation, assistance, and support services to family caregivers and dependent children who are victims of veteran intimate partner violence and dependent abuse. The bill would

---

136. "How Do Military Families Handle Grief?" Associated Press.

also provide medical care and counseling for those caregivers and dependent children, and improve their access to, and the availability of, trauma-informed, culturally competent crisis shelters and transitional supported housing projects. The draft languished on the desks of the Oregon senators for a year and a half, while dozens of family members were killed by their veteran.

The Violence Against Women Act (VAWA) implemented by the Department of Justice includes provisions to protect Native American women and the lesbian, gay, bisexual, transgender, and queer community. The federal VAWA offers no protection whatsoever for the partners and caregivers of combat veterans with PTSD and/or traumatic brain injury. I hope that changes soon. I also hope Congress will reintroduce—and this time pass—the Veteran and Military Caregiver Services Improvement Act of 2014. The bill would allow veterans to transfer post-9/11 GI Bill benefits to their dependents, permit caregivers to be eligible for child-care programs, provide crucial financial advice and legal counseling, and allocate for essential respite time. Lawmakers at both the state and federal levels could support a Post-Combat Family Care tax to help pay for the programs and services to support the veterans and family members who will be living with the consequences of combat for the rest of their lives. The tax revenue could also underwrite the expense of empanelling House and Senate Veterans Affairs Subcommittees on Families of Veterans. Such a tax would provide a long-denied chance for all Americans to invest in these wars, and would be a powerful opportunity to monetize vital democratic values.

But new laws are not enough. We cannot legislate conscience, but we can construct public platforms upon which our better selves can stand, and I pray that we do. We could start with an American Truth & Reconciliation Commission (TRC) on the war in Iraq.

By 2015, several polls indicated that nearly 76 percent of the country regarded the Iraq war as a mistake, precisely the percentage that supported the war in 2003. For the second time in American history (the first was Vietnam), the cultural bandwidth evolved rapidly enough within a single generation to transform public opinion on a war. The TRC affords an historic opportunity to formalize and sanctify that shift by engaging the veterans and families who have been harmed by the war, the politicians and pundits who championed the war, grassroots and spiritual leaders, experts on forgiveness, leading practitioners in grief and trauma recovery, and the affected communities in creating solutions that promote repair, reconciliation, and the restoration of relationships. That would be a potent antidote for the epidemic of disconnection between civilians and the post-9/11 military community. A commission could create a container for bearing witness, facilitating forgiveness, and advancing atonement so that this generation of warriors and their families would be less likely to carry the hurt and anger forward for decades, seeding future generations—children yet unborn—with the traumatic legacy of war. An American Truth & Reconciliation Commission would be a powerful demonstration of moral courage and an opportunity to become wiser about the costs of war. And we could apply that wisdom like a balm to the moral injuries of war, a salve for the soul of this nation.

I pray we will move toward a better understanding of the war at home and more compassion and support for those who are fighting it. I pray that, even as we expand our definition of service-connected injuries and collateral damage, we take steps to help the victims heal, and to prevent the damage in future generations. And when *We the People of the United States* know these things, I pray we will demonstrate what we have learned with the understanding that truly, there is no such thing as an acceptable loss.

Now that I am divorced, people often say, "Congratulations!" My divorce is no reason to celebrate. So when someone asks how they should respond, I tell them, "Say the same thing that you would to any other military family member who suffered some loss as the result of these wars." Whether the wound was evident or unseen, or whether they lost their life over there or took their life over here.

Because I've been in that place. That place where there's not a single shred of light. And not one angel knows my name. How many military family suicides are there? No one's keeping track. But I almost became one of them. I've read, and heard, about hundreds of others. Families of veterans are a strong group. We are proud and tough. And we are tired and sad and alone. And so are our kids. But it's hard to help the kids if we can't help ourselves.

Until we reach out, until we overcome the need to always be strong, and allow ourselves to ask for help, until we find that help is there, it won't get better.

Until our families, and neighbors, and friends who aren't touched by war learn to ask, "How can I help?" It won't get better.

We'll never know if we could have saved the little boy who hung himself, or the Gold Star moms who killed themselves, or the Blue Star wives who lost their lives when their vets came back from the front. But what about the next one? What about the next colonel's boy, the next Army spouse, the next veteran's wife? Will we save the next one?

ACKNOWLEDGMENTS

I am deeply grateful to General George Casey (Ret.) and his wife, Sheila Casey, and Admiral Mike Mullen, Joint Chiefs of Staff (Ret.), and his wife, Deborah Mullen. You held the helm during one of the most challenging times in the history of this nation's Armed Forces and their families. You served with dignity, honor, courage, and grace, and you always had our six. I'd like to acknowledge Rosemary Williams for her generosity with pretty much everything, and the stellar SITREPS: Foam the runway! Many thanks to Ariana Del Negro, Chris Smith, Karen Francis, Tim Kahlor, and Scott Russo, PhD, for participating in interviews. Thanks also to Jennifer Daniels, PhD, along with Belle Landau and Margaret Eichler, PhD, of the Returning Veterans Project, for generously sharing their research and critical work to help our veterans and families heal.

My own healing would have been harder without the support of Tiziana DellaRovere, Louie Goldberg, and Diane Werich. That healing might have been impossible were it not for Representative Sal Esquivel and Jan Esquivel, Captain Karl (Ret.) and Tracey Haeckler, and Leslie Hunter and the Flying L Ranch. When I needed a safe place to be, you provided it. I am profoundly grateful. I am indebted to J. R. Westen for guiding me to shore when

Acknowledgments

I was drowning in an endless ocean of grief. And *namaste* to Ren Hurst for reminding me that I already knew how to ride on my own power. Thanks to Russ Hersrud and Shannon Gilbert for being willing to love me when I was at my most unlovable. Thank you to P. J. Trepanier, Raybird, Mike, and Nick. P. J., buddy, you grabbed on and refused to let go, helping to save my life with an unexpected friendship that contained some small sliver of joy every day. The next pedicure's on me. I'd like to give a shout out to Neale Donald Walsch and the crew at the *Conversations with God* New Year's Retreat, where I finally resolved to be happy.

I am indebted to Judy Blunt of the Pacific University MFA in Writing program and Dawn Frederick of Red Sofa Literary for their support during the early days of writing. Maxim Brown and the team at Skyhorse Publishing carried these pages over the finish line, and Maxim's editorial guidance and patience made this a better book than it would have been otherwise. If mistakes were made, it's likely that they were mine.

BIBLIOGRAPHY

Abdullah, Halimah. "Military Suicides Are Causing Civilian Casualties, Too." McClatchy Newspapers, February 28, 2010.

Alvarez, Lizette and Dan Frosch. "A Focus on Violence by Returning G.I.'s." *New York Times*, January 1, 2009.

Alvarez, Lizette and Deborah Sontag. "When Strains on Military Families Turn Deadly." *New York Times*, February 15, 2008.

Army's Mental Health Advisory Team (MHAT) Report, February, 2008.

Astore, William. "Groundhog Day in the War on Terror." *TomDispatch*, February 1, 2015.

Barnes, Greg. "Love and War: 'He Just Wanted to Be Part Of Something Big.'" *Harrison Daily Times*, July 24, 2010.

Beckham, J. C., B. L. Lytle, and M. E. Feldman. "Caregiver Burden in Partners of Vietnam War Veterans with Posttraumatic Stress Disorder." *Journal of Consulting and Clinical Psychology* 64, 5 (October 1996): 1068–72.

Begley, Sharon. "How Stressed Parents Scar Their Kids." *Daily Beast,* September 12, 2011.

Bergland, Christopher. "The Size and Connectivity of the Amygdala Predicts Anxiety." *The Athlete's Way*, November 20, 2013.

Bernstein, Peter. *Trauma: Healing the Hidden Epidemic*. Petaluma, CA: The Bernstein Institute for Integrative Psychotherapy & Trauma Treatment, 2013.

Bill Moyers Journal. "The Conversation Continues. Interview with Andrew Bacevich." *Truthout Progressive Pick of the Week*, June 2, 2011.

Bittman, B., L. Berk, M. Shannon, M. Shara, J. Westengard, K. J. Guegler, and D. W. Ruff. "Recreational Music-Making Modulates the Human Stress Response: a Preliminary Individualized Gene Expression Strategy." *Medical Science Monitor* (February 2005): 31–40.

Booth, Bradford, Mady Wechsler Segal, and D. Bruce Bell with James A. Martin, Morten G. Ender, David E. Rohall, and John Nelson. "What We Know about Army Families: 2007 Update." *Arlington: U.S. Department of the Army, Family and Morale, Welfare and Recreation Command*, 2007.

Boyle, Annette M. "Domestic Abuse Tied to Range of Health Issues." *US Medicine*, May 2014.

Breggin, Peter R. *Medication Madness: The Role of Psychiatric Drugs in Violence, Suicide, and Murder*. New York: St. Martin's Press, 2008.

Brown, Ethan. *Shake the Devil Off*. New York: Henry Holt and Company, 2009.

Calhoun, P. S., J. C. Beckham, and H. B. Bosworth. "Caregiver Burden and Psychological Distress in Partners of Veterans With Chronic Posttraumautic Stress Disorder." *Journal of Traumatic Stress* Vol. 15, No. 3 (2002): 205–212.

CBS News. "Collateral Damage: The Mental Health Issues Facing Children of Veterans." CBS News video, 9:31. March 16, 2014.

http://www.cbsnews.com/news/collateral-damage-the-mental-health-issues-facing-children-of-veterans/

Collins, Elizabeth M. "Army psychiatrist: Military Children Have Increased Mental-Health Risk." Army News Service, October 8, 2009.

Committee on the Initial Assessment of Readjustment Needs of Military Personnel, Veterans, and Their Families; Board on the Health of Select Populations. "Preliminary Assessment of Readjustment Needs of Military Personnel, Veterans, and Their Families." *Institute of Medicine of the National Academies.* March 31, 2010.

Daly, Michael. "It wasn't Just Bergdahl. On Afghanistan, All of America Is AWOL." *Daily Beast*, June 11, 2014.

Daniels, Jennifer. "Burden of Care and Social Support Indicated by Spouses of OIF and OEF Reserve Veterans Diagnosed with PTSD." PhD diss., Capella University, 2013.

Daum, Meghan. "Caregivers: Celebrating the Invisible War Heroes." *Redbook*, November 12, 2012.

Department of Defense. *Plans for the Department of Defense for the Support of Military Family Readiness: Report to the Congressional Defense Committees Pursuant to Section 1781b of Title 10, United States Code.* Washington, DC, 2010.

Department of Defense. "Health Care Survey of DoD Beneficiaries." April 2005.

Department of Veterans Affairs. "VA Offers Marriage Retreats for Returning Vets." February 23, 2012.

Dinola, Gina M. "Stressors Afflicting Military Families During Military Deployment." *Military Medicine* 173(5) (May 2008): v–vii.

"Direct Evidence that Autism Starts During Prenatal Development." *Autism Speaks*, March 26, 2014.

Dobbs, David. "A New Focus on the 'Post' in Post-Traumatic Stress." *New York Times*, December 24, 2012.

Dwyer, Liz, interview with Ron Astor, "A Staggering Percentage of Military Kids Have Mental Health Issues—Will This Simple Fix Help?" *TakePart.com*, March 25, 2014.

Fauntleroy, Glenda. "Parents' Military Deployments Take Emotional Toll on Teens." *Center for Advancing Health Press Release*, July 26, 2011.

Flake, Eric M., B. E. Davis, P. L. Johnson, and L. S. Middleton. "The Psychosocial Effects of Deployment on Military Children." *The Journal of Developmental & Behavioral Pediatrics* Vol. 30 Issue 4 (August 2009): 271–278.

Franklin, T. B., H. Russig, I. C. Weiss, J. Gräff, N. Linder, A. Michalon, S. Vizi, and I. M. Mansuy. "Epigenetic transmission of the impact of early stress across generations." *Biological Psychiatry* (2010): 68:408–415.

Friedman, Robert Lawrence. *The Healing Power of the Drum*. Incline Village, Nevada: White Cliffs Media Co., September 2000.

Gerlock, April A., Jackie Grimesey, and George Sayre. "Military-Related Post-Traumatic Stress Disorder and Intimate Relationship Behaviors: A Developing Dyadic Relationship Model." *Journal of Marital and Family Therapy* Vol. 40 Issue 3 (July 2014): 344–356.

Getz, Colleen M. "Seeing a Fallen Soldier Home." *Washington Times*, May 28, 2010.

Gibbs, Deborah, Sandra L. Martin, Lawrence L. Kupper, and Ruby E. Johnson. "Child Maltreatment in Enlisted Soldiers' Families During Combat-Related Deployments." *Journal of the American Medical Association* Vol. 298 No. 5 (August 2007): 528–535.

Goleman, Daniel. "Stress and Isolation Tied To a Reduced Life Span." *New York Times*, December 7, 1993.

Good HouseKeeping, "Heart-Health Guide." (February 2010): 66.

Goodman, Brenda. "How the 'Love Hormone' Works Its Magic." *HealthDay*, November 25, 2013.

Green, Tavia D. "Clarksville Murder Trial: Toddler's Injuries Blamed on Mudding Accident, Bath Fall." *Leaf-Chronicle*, May 20, 2014.

Grimesey, Jackie. "The Impact of Combat Trauma on the Veteran's Family Members: A Qualitative Study." Retrieved from Electronic Theses and Dissertations database, Gumberg Library Digital Collections, Duquesne University, 2009.

Grosz, Stephen. *The Examined Life*. New York: W.W. Norton & Company, 2013, 83.

Guiden, Mary. "Adolescent Boys among Those Most Affected by Washington State Parental Military Deployment: UW Study." *UW Today*, July 21, 2011.

Harris, Nadine Burke. "Doctor: Childhood Trauma Can Destroy Your Health Decades Later, Yet America Ignores It." *AlterNet*, June 25, 2015.

Health Care Survey of DoD Beneficiaries, April 2005.

Hedges, Chris. *War Is a Force That Gives Us Meaning*. New York: Public Affairs, 2002, 162–3.

Hefling, Kimberly. "More Military Children Seeking Mental Care." Associated Press, July 7, 2009.

Herman, Judith. *Trauma and Recovery*. New York: Basic Books, 1992, 1997, 3.

Hodes, Georgia E. "Sex, Stress, and Epigenetics." *Biology of Sex Differences Journal* (January 21, 2013).

Hoge, Charles W., Carl A. Castro, and Karen M. Eaton. "Impact of Combat Duty in Iraq and Afghanistan on Family Functioning: Findings from the Walter Reed Army Institute of Research Land Combat Study." *Human Dimensions in Military Operations—Military Leaders' Strategies for Addressing Stress and Psychological Support Symposium*. Paper prepared for the RTO Human Factors and Medicine Panel (HFM) Symposium, Brussels, Belgium, April 24–26, 2006.

Houppert, Karen. "Base crimes: The Military Has a Domestic Violence Problem." *Mother Jones*, July/August 2005 Issue.

"How Do Military Families Handle Grief? Federally Funded Study Looks to Find Out." Associated Press, January 4, 2015.

Howard, Michael. "Addicted to On-Line Porn." *Army Times*, March 31, 2010.

Jaffe, Greg. "How Should Military Treat Those with PTSD Who Lose Control?" *Washington Post*, September 29, 2014.

Jegtvig, Shereen. "Stressful Relationships May Raise Risk of Death." Reuters, May 26, 2014.

Jones, Kelly A., B. Smith, N. S. Granado, E. J. Boyko, G. D. Gackstetter, M. A. Ryan, C. J. Phillips, and T. C. Smith. "Newly Reported Lupus and Rheumatoid Arthritis in Relation to Deployment Within Proximity to a Documented Open-Air Burn Pit in Iraq." *Journal of Occupational and Environmental Medicine* Volume 54 Number 6 (June 2012): 698–707.

Jowers, Karen and Andrew Tilghman, "Military Kids Taking More Psychiatric Drugs." *Army Times*, January 2, 2011.

Kellerman, Natan. "Epigenetic Transmission of Holocaust Trauma: Can Nightmares Be Inherited?" *Israel Journal of Psychiatry and Related Sciences* Vol. 50 No 1 (2013): 33–39.

Kime, Patricia. "ED Cases among Troops Double Since 2004." *Military Times*, September 30, 2014.

———"Families: Vets' PTSD 'Like Living in Hell.'" *Army Times*, February 11, 2013.

———"IG thrashes DoD in final burn pit report." *Military Times*, February 27, 2015.

———"Rand: Civilian Mental Health Providers Don't 'Get' the Military." *Army Times*, November 21, 2014.

Lazare, Sarah. "The Military's Hidden Mental Health Crisis." *Al Jazeera*, November 15, 2013.

"Lengthy Military Deployments Increase Divorce Risk for U.S. Enlisted Service Members." Rand Press Release, September 3, 2013.

Lester, Patricia, K. Peterson, J. Reeves, L. Knauss, D. Glover, C. Mogil, N. Duan, W. Saltzman, R. Pynoos, K. Wilt, and W. Beardslee. "The Long War and Parental Combat Deployment: Effects on Military Children and At-Home Spouses." *Journal of American Academy of Child & Adolescent Psychiatry* Vol. 49, 4 (April 2010): 310–320.

Levine, Amir and Rachel Heller. *Attached: The New Science of Adult Attachment and How it Can Help You Find—and Keep—Love.* New York: Jeremy Tarcher/Penguin, 2010, 12.

Litz, Brett T., Nathan Stein, Eileen Delaney, Leslie Lebowitz, William P. Nash, Caroline Silva, and Shira Maguen. "Moral Injury and Moral Repair in War Veterans: A Preliminary Model and Intervention Strategy." *Clinical Psychology Review 29* (2009): 695–706.

Manguno-Mire, Gina, Frederic Sautter, Judith Lyons, Leann Myers, Dana Perry, Michelle Sherman, Shirley Glynn, and Greer

Sullivan. "Psychological Distress and Burden Among Female Partners of Combat Veterans With PTSD." *Journal of Nervous and Mental Disease* Vol. 195 No. 2 (February 2007): 144–151.

Mansfield, Alyssa J., Jay S. Kaufman, Charles C. Engel, and Bradley N. Gaynes. "Deployment and Mental Health Diagnoses Among Children of US Army Personnel." *Archives of Pediatrics and Adolescent Medicine* (2011): 165 (11): 999–1005.

Mansfield, Alyssa J., Jay S. Kaufman, Stephen W. Marshall, Bradley N. Gaynes, Joseph P. Morrisey, and Charles C. Engel. "Deployment and the Use of Mental Health Services Among U.S. Army Wives." *New England Journal of Medicine* 362 (January 14, 2010): 101–109.

Marlantes, Karl. *What It Is Like to Go to War*. New York: Atlantic Monthly Press, 2011, 166.

Marohn, Kirsti. "Veteran's Suicide Devastates Those Left Behind." *USA Today*, November 16, 2014.

Mastroianni, George R., and Wilbur J. Scott. "Reframing Suicide in the Military." *Parameters* (Summer 2011): 6–21.

McCarroll, J. E, R. J. Ursano, X. Liu, L. E. Thayer, J. H. Newby, A. E. Norwood, and C. S. Fullerton. "Deployment and the Probability of Spousal Aggression by U.S. Army Soldiers." *Military Medicine* 165, 1 (2000): 41–44.

McCloskey, Meghan. "Study Reveals Sharp Rise in Diagnoses of Disorders." *Stars & Stripes*, July 18, 2009.

McFarlane, Alexander C. "Military Deployment: The Impact on Children and Family Adjustment and the Need For Care." *Current Opinion in Psychiatry* 22 (2009): 369–373.

Medical News Network. "Social Isolation Alters Immune System at Genetic Level." Posted on September 17, 2007. https://medicalnewsnetwork.wordpress.com/tag/isolation/

Mehta, Divya, Torsten Klengel, Karen N. Conneely, Alicia K. Smith, André Altmann, Thaddeus W. Pace, Monika Rex-Haffner, Anne Loeschner, Mariya Gonik, Kristina B. Mercer, Bekh Bradley, Bertram Müller-Myhsok, Kerry J. Ressler, and Elisabeth B. Binder. "Childhood Maltreatment is Associated with Distinct Genomic and Epigenetic Profiles in Posttraumatic Stress Disorder." *Proceedings of the National Academy of Sciences of the United States of America* Vol. 110 No. 20 (May 14, 2013): 8302–8307.

Michaud, Martin, Laurent Balardy, Guillaume Moulis, Clement Gaudin, Caroline Peyrot, Bruno Vellas, Matteo Cesari, and Fati Nourhashemi. "Proinflammatory Cytokines, Aging, and Age-Related Diseases." *Journal of the American Medical Directors Association* Vol. 14 Issue 12 (December 2013): 877–82.

Miles, Donna. "General Provides Yellow Ribbon Program Perspective." *American Forces Press Service*, November 1, 2010.

Military Times. "The Human Toll of Child Abuse in the Army." July 29, 2013.

National Alliance for Caregiving and United Health Foundation. "Caregivers of Veterans—Serving on the Homefront. Report of Study Findings." November 2010: 17. Updated November 2012.

NPR. "Military Families Learn To Live With 'New Normal.'" *All Things Considered*, March 21, 2009.

Nutt, Amy Ellis. "Wounds of War That Never Heal." *Washington Post*, January 19, 2015.

Office of the Surgeon Multi-National Force-Iraq and Office of the Surgeon General United States Army Medical Command. "Army's Mental Health Advisory Team (MHAT) Report." February 2008.

Olien, Jessica. "Loneliness Is Deadly." Slate.com, August 23, 2013.

Peacock, Virginia. "Military, Veteran Caregivers Need Our Support." *The State*, December 3, 2014.

Pearce, Joseph Chilton. *The Biology of Transcendence*. Vermont: Park Street Press, 2002.

Picard, Carissa S. "The Invisible Injuries of the Invisible Ranks." *TruthOut.org*, January 2, 2009.

President's Commission on Mental Health. *Mental Health Problems of Vietnam Era Veterans*. Washington, DC: US Government Printing Office Vol. 3 (1978): 1321–1328.

Rand Corporation, The. "Lengthy Military Deployments Increase Divorce Risk for U.S. Enlisted Service Members." *Rand Press Release,* September 3, 2013.

Reeves, Richard. "The New American Segregation: The Military." Truthdig.com, May 31, 2011.

Renaud, Edwin. "The Attachment Characteristics of Combat Veterans with PTSD." *Sage Journals. Traumatology* Vol. 14 No. 3 (September 2008): 1–12.

Rentz, Danielle E., Stephen W. Marshall, Dana Loomis, Carri Casteel, Sandra L. Martin, and Deborah A. Gibbs. "Effect of Deployment on the Occurrence of Child Maltreatment in Military and Nonmilitary Families." *American Journal of Epidemiology* Volume 165, Issue 10 (2007): 1199–1206.

Renz, Tabatha. "Military Spouses: Burdened and Alone." *Policy-Matters Journal*, March 19, 2014.

Robson, Seth. "Some Seek Mental Health Checks for Spouses of Multiple-Deployed Soldiers." *Stars & Stripes*, July 5, 2009.

Rosenblatt, Franklin D., Major. "Non-Deployable: The Court-Martial System in Combat from 2001 to 2009." *Army Lawyer*, September 2010.

Rowan, Tommy. "Fighting Back: An Iraq War vet battles substance abuse, personal demons and reality on his road to redemption." *Metro Philadelphia*, October 21, 2013.

Sanderlin, Rebekkah. "At War: Notes From the Front Lines." *New York Times*, May 3, 2011. http://atwar.blogs.nytimes.com/2011/05/03/we-got-him/

Sandza, Richard. "The Army's hidden child abuse epidemic." *Military Times*, July 29, 2013.

——"Pentagon Launches Major Child Abuse Study." *Army Times*, November 16, 2013.

Shane, Leo, III. "Critics: VA Caregiver Programs Need Improvement." *Military Times*, December 3, 2014.

Shannon, Torrey. "Beware of the Wounded Warrior's Wife." *Huffington Post*, February 13, 2012.

Shulevitz, Judith. "The Science of Suffering." *New Republic*, November 16, 2014.

Siegel, Benjamin S., Beth Ellen Davis, and the Committee on Psychosocial Aspects of Child and Family Health and Section on Uniformed Services. "Health and Mental Health Needs of Children in US Military Families." *Pediatrics*, Volume 131, Number 6 (June 2013).

Siddique, Ashik. "Combat Vets' PTSD Symptoms Raise Spouses and Partners' Blood Pressure." *Medical Daily*, March 8, 2013.

Sisk, Richard. "The Toll of War: MilWives and Suicide." *War Report Online*.

Smith, Jodi Jones. "What to Say to 'Thank You for Your Service.'" *Washington Post*, November 23, 2011.

"Social Isolation Alters Immune System at Genetic Level." *Medical News Network*, September 17, 2007.

Sullivan, Julie. "Measures of Sacrifice: Answering the Call to Military Binds Patriotic Oregon Family." *Oregonian*, July 3, 2010.

Szalavitz, Maia. "Abused Children May Get Unique Form of PTSD." TIME.com, April 30, 2013.

Tanielian, Terri, Rajeev Ramchand, Michael P. Fisher, Carra S. Sims, Racine S. Harris, and Margaret C. Harrell. "Military Caregivers: Cornerstones of Support for Our Nation's Wounded, Ill, and Injured Veterans." Rand Corporation Report, March 2013.

Tilghman, Andrew. "Deployments and Child Deaths." *AirForce Times*, September 2, 2011.

Trotter, Benjamin B., Meghan E. Robinson, William P. Milberg, Regina E. McGlinchey, and David H. Salat. "Military Blast Exposure, Ageing and White Matter Integrity." *Brain, A Journal of Neurology*, June 1, 2015.

Tull, Matthew. "Sexual Problems in Veterans with PTSD." About Health.com, April 16, 2014.

US House of Representatives Committee on Appropriations—Democratic staff. "United States Army Military Readiness Report." Washington, DC, (September 13, 2006): 2.

Van Der Kolk, Bessel. *The Body Keeps the Score.* New York: Viking, 2014.

Veterans Administration. "Veteran's Administration Spotlight on Women Cyberseminar Series." *Cambridge Transcriptions,* January 23, 2012.

Wheeler, Angela. "Coping Strategies of National Guard Spouses During Times of Deployment." Paper presented at the annual meeting of the American Sociological Association, Montreal Convention Center, Montreal, Quebec, August 11, 2006.

Whiteman, Honor. "Frequent Arguing 'Dramatically Increases Risk of Middle-Aged Death.'" *Medical News Today*. MediLexicon, Intl., May 9, 2014. Retrieved from website December 22, 2014. http://www.medicalnewstoday.com/articles/276531.php

Williams, C. M. "The 'Veteran System' with a Focus on Women Partners: Theoretical Considerations, Problems, and Treatment Strategies." In T. Williams (Ed.), "Post-Traumatic Stress Disorders of the Vietnam Veteran: Observations and Recommendations for the Psychological Treatment Of The Veteran and His Family." Cincinnati, OH: *Journal of Disabled American Veterans*, (1980): 73–122.

Winch, Guy. *Emotional First Aid*. New York: Hudson Street Press, 2013.

"Women War Veterans Face Higher Risk of Mental Health Problems During Pregnancy." *ScienceDaily*, December 21, 2010.

Wood, David. "Military And Veteran Suicides Rise Despite Aggressive Prevention Efforts." *Huffington Post*, August 29, 2013.

Zarembo, Alan. "Military Children More Likely to Have a History Of Suicide Attempts." *Los Angeles Times*, March 19, 2015.

———"Multiple Military Deployments May Raise Teen Suicide Risk." *Los Angeles Times*, November 18, 2013.

Zoroya, Greg. "Study: Bomb Blasts May Cause Early Aging in Brains of Troops." *USA Today*, June 1, 2015.

Zoroya, Greg and Meghan Hoye. "Veterans' Disability Costs Climb." *USA Today*, January 16, 2013.